Lean Six Sigma
for Law
Second Ed

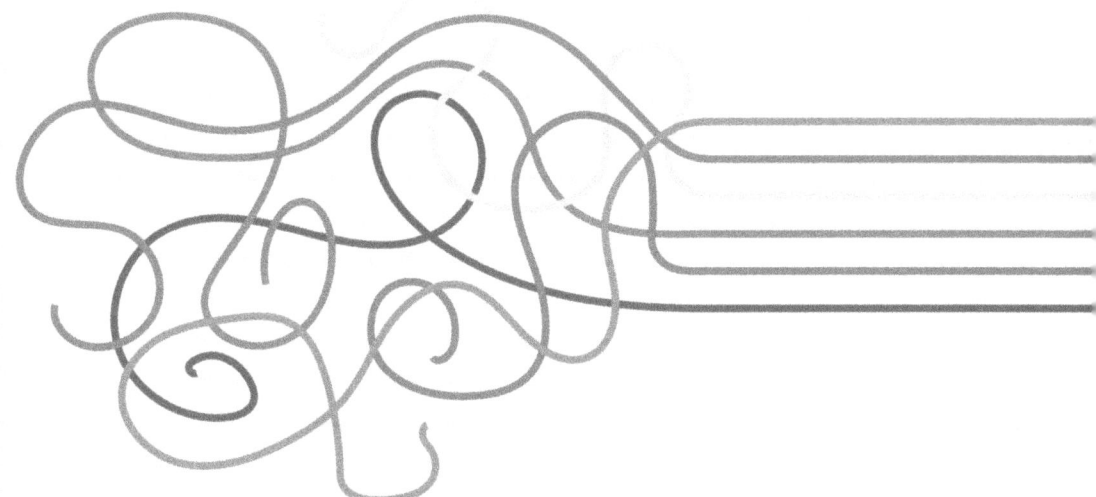

CATHERINE ALMAN MACDONAGH JD

Commissioning editor
Alex Davies

Managing director
Sian O'Neill

Lean Six Sigma for Law, Second Edition
is published by

Globe Law and Business Ltd
3 Mylor Close
Horsell
Woking
Surrey GU21 4DD
United Kingdom
Tel: +44 20 3745 4770
www.globelawandbusiness.com

Lean Six Sigma for Law, Second Edition

ISBN 978-1-83723-079-2
EPUB ISBN 978-1-83723-080-8
Adobe PDF ISBN 978-1-83723-081-5

© 2025 Globe Law and Business Ltd except where otherwise indicated.

The right of the contributors to be identified as authors of this work has been asserted by them in accordance with sections 77 and 78 of the Copyright, Designs and Patents Act 1988.

All rights reserved. No part of this publication may be reproduced in any material form (including photocopying, storing in any medium by electronic means or transmitting) without the written permission of the copyright owner, except in accordance with the provisions of the Copyright, Designs and Patents Act 1988 or under terms of a licence issued by the Copyright Licensing Agency Ltd (www.cla.co.uk). Applications for the copyright owner's written permission to reproduce any part of this publication should be addressed to the publisher.

GPSR Compliance: EU Authorised Representative: Easy Access System Europe - Mustamäe tee 50, 10621 Tallinn, Estonia, gpsr.requests@easproject.com

DISCLAIMER
This publication is intended as a general guide only. The information and opinions which it contains are not intended to be a comprehensive study, or to provide legal advice, and should not be treated as a substitute for legal advice concerning particular situations. Legal advice should always be sought before taking any action based on the information provided. The publisher bears no responsibility for any errors or omissions contained herein.

Contents

Executive summary vii

About the author xiii

Acknowledgments xv

About the Legal Lean Sigma Institute xxi

Foreword xxiii

Introduction xxvii

Chapter 1: An introduction to Lean and Six Sigma
for law (plus some project management) 1
    What is process improvement? 1
    Process basics 2
    Process measurement 5
    What are Lean and Six Sigma? 6
    Lean's eight kinds of waste 8
    Six Sigma – getting to error-free 10
    Mapping process improvement 14
    Project management 15
    The art and science of legal process improvement 18

Chapter 2: The five key principles of Lean Sigma 21
    Maintaining the client's perspective 21
    1. Specify value in the eyes of the client 21
    2. Reduce waste and variation 23
    3. Make value flow at the pull of the client 23
    4. Align and empower employees 25
    5. Continuously improve in pursuit of perfection 25

    The "laws" 27
    Applying the Lean Sigma principles 28

Chapter 3: DMAIC – A data-driven, problem-solving framework ... 31
    Using DMAIC for projects 31
    Why DMAIC is effective 32
    The five steps of DMAIC 33
    The Kaizen approach 49
    In DMAIC we trust 50

Chapter 4: Additional process improvement methodologies ... 53
    DMADV 54
    Legal WorkOut® 55
    Plan, Do, Check, Act 56
    Pure technology 58
    AI and the transformation of law 60
    Business process redesign / reengineering 62
    Theory of Constraints 64
    5S 66
    Gemba Walk 68

Chapter 5: Process improvement projects ... 71
    Process selection 71
    Case studies – intake 72
    PI practitioners 78
    PI project roles and responsibilities 79
    Team success factors 83

Chapter 6: Mastering key PI tools ... 85
    Project charters 86
    Stakeholder analysis 87
    Process mapping 90

Chapter 7: The case for process improvement ... 95
    Most processes fall short of their potential 95
    The profession is a business, and it has changed 96
    The risks are greater than the challenges 99

Gaining buy-in for process improvement 100
Linking quality and performance 102
Understanding changing client expectations 104
People and competitive advantages 107
Clients expect efficient processes 107
The pressure to deliver value 110
Uptake of Lean Six Sigma in law firms 111

**Chapter 8: Assessing organizational readiness and
change management** 117
The P+ Ecosystem, Continuum, and Scorecard 118
Assessing operational excellence 123
What is change management? 125
The five critical questions for addressing change 126
Change management models 127
Integrating change management and Lean Six Sigma 131
Change strategies 131

Chapter 9: Getting started and structuring for success 135
Develop skills and learn a common language 137
Process architecture – a systematic approach 139
Process improvement program steering committee 142
Demonstration projects 144
Align with clients 145
Use precedent – learn from others 147

**Chapter 10: Seizing opportunistic approaches
for improvements** 153
Pain points 154
Don't let a good crisis go to waste 156
People first – talent, DEIA, and generational challenges 157
Mergers and acquisitions 164
Capturing effort – time-keeping 167

Chapter 11: Process improvement, pricing, and procurement ... 175
Pricing 175
Procurement 180

Chapter 12: Strategic, systematic, and structured approaches 193
Learning from other industries 195
Early adopters 197
Law firms 205

Chapter 13: Case studies and success stories 229
Legal departments 230
Legal aid 232
Law firms 233
Government 243
Military 249

Chapter 14: Using process improvement to collaborate with clients 255
Success stories 257
Collaborating to improve processes 266
A collaborative approach to process improvement 272

Chapter 15: Creating a culture of continuous improvement 281
Why being a human in the workplace is hard 283
Approaches to process improvement in law 288
Legal Lean Sigma training for continuous improvement
– methods and qualifications 291
Leadership 296
Knowledge management 299
Looking to the future 300

About Globe Law and Business 307

Executive summary

This book is a thought leadership piece that aspires to relate the foundational concepts and vocabulary of Lean and Six Sigma as well as other process improvement methodologies, including Plan, Do, Check, Act (PDCA), Legal WorkOut®, Business Process Redesign (BPR), Robotic Process Automation (RPA), Theory of Constraints, Gemba, and 5S. It describes how they are combined with project management and other approaches originally developed in other industries and explains how they apply and how to employ them in a legal environment.

To state the obvious, law is different to manufacturing. However, the same thinking, frameworks, and tools can produce the same extraordinary results and experiences. It does take some bridging. All legal departments, law offices, and firms, wherever they may fall on the process improvement continuum, will benefit from learning about the use of Lean and Six Sigma in a legal context.

This second edition includes new content in the areas of process improvement, project selection, structure, roles, responsibilities, and planning as well as deeper dives into how to use key concepts, structures, and tools such as the DMAIC (Define, Measure, Analyze, Improve, Control) framework and the activities involved in each phase. It also explores the more important organizational development and strategy elements of building a continuous improvement culture. A review of readiness and operational excellence assessments, change management, and new information that helps make the case for continuous improvement is also included.

Whether your organization is just beginning to hear about these things and is curious about them, has developed skills and is undertaking projects, or has a fully branded continuous improvement or innovation strategy or program grounded in Lean Six Sigma, this book is intended to serve as a resource.

Since the publication of the first edition a decade ago, more people, teams, practice groups, departments, and legal organizations have embarked and traveled on their continuous improvement journeys. Still, there are many who are new to legal and will benefit from learning how to translate the tried-

and-true methodologies to law, and those that remain at the exploratory end of the spectrum and are just "beginning to think about starting".

Change can take a while, especially in our environment. Law, it is well known, can be slow to change. However, our recent collective global experience in making changes quickly, adapting, and "pivoting" in response to the COVID-19 pandemic and its aftermath have taught us that we're actually very good at finding new ways to do things – and then implementing them rather quickly. We've also discovered that those new ways are not only better than the way we had grown accustomed to operating, but they became "the way we do things here" faster than we could have imagined.

There is a lot of pressure to be efficient, so there is no room for complacency in today's environment. It's competitive. Those legal and business professionals in firms, offices, and departments who have been waiting to find out how this PI/PM stuff works for others will learn plenty from those who have gone before them. We do, after all, respect tradition and precedent. But there's a balance to be found between learning from the past and using that knowledge to prepare and act now to better our current and future state. It takes leadership. It takes teamwork. It takes curiosity. It takes a certain relentless drive to improve every day – and the best always want to be better!

Some ideas will come from other industries and our clients – the challenge for us is how we might apply them in our environment. Case studies and inspiration may come from direct competitors, driving readers from a position of mere interest to acting out of necessity. The competition may already have robust programs in place with cadres of skilled Lean and Six Sigma practitioners, a host of project managers, and dozens of completed projects backed by tens of millions of dollars in improvement benefits. So called "New Law" firms and "alternative service providers" (or, as I like to call them, "service providers") are doing and delivering work like document review and contract life cycle management by harnessing the power of process improvement and technology/AI.

This second edition relates updated success stories and case studies to shine a light on those in law that are already employing process improvement and project management approaches and tools. Every firm and department now understands for real that "culture eats strategy for breakfast" and that the key to unparalleled client and employee experiences is to focus on People, Process, and then Platform. More of law is being run like the best businesses in the world.

For every one example that is featured in this book, there are hundreds of teams – small, medium, and large – that are quietly and seriously developing competitive advantages using process improvement. Understandably, many are sensitive about the type and level of information they wish to share and make available to others – after all, it's their version of a "secret sauce". Many are using their successes as the cornerstone of their strategy, marketing, and sales.

I think about process improvement a little like music – we all have the same notes and theory at our disposal. It's how one arranges and performs them that makes the difference between a song you want to listen to over and over throughout your life, a one-hit wonder, and another that you skip past.

So it is with process improvement – we all have access to the same concepts, framework, and tools. It is the combination and the selection of the right people, approach, and tool that makes the difference. One key point to remember is that there is no single "right way" to do process improvement work. Rather, each organization and every project is different. Creating and building a culture of continuous improvement requires us to acknowledge nuances, organizational readiness and maturity, the positioning and competitive landscape for that organization, the classic TOWS (Threats, Opportunities, Weaknesses, Strengths) elements, their clients, and other business drivers.

Why? Because when we do this work, we not only improve the process on which we are working, we also deliver greater value, efficiency, and predictability, while increasing our quality and likelihood of successful outcomes.

If that is not compelling enough, here's another benefit. When we do this work well, it is always done without tradeoffs. Rather, these are golden opportunities to create the proverbial win–win for everyone – the client, the employee, the department, and the firm or office.

In summary, I hope to accomplish several things in the second edition of this book:

1) Explain what Lean and Six Sigma are;
2) Make the connection between and the case for Lean, Six Sigma, and project management;
3) Demonstrate the different ways in which Lean and Six Sigma may be employed in law;
4) Publish a collection of ideas, case studies, and examples to update what was the very first report of its kind on the topic of legal process improvement a decade ago; and

5) Continue to effect – and even accelerate! – the shift toward the applicability and acceptance of process improvement in the law as significantly closer to the norm.

The innovators and early adopters in this space have much to teach us and we owe them a debt of gratitude at the very least for providing us with what those in the law prize – proof and precedent. Lean Sigma and the other ideas in this book work – they all work in legal, and they will work in your organization.

This book is for those interested in learning (or learning more) about the different approaches to Lean Six Sigma, where to get started (or build), why it works, and what the results have been for those who have already tried it.

It is intended to inspire, to provoke, and serve as a catalyst for change and growth. I hope to fuel curiosity, stimulate interest enough for people to experiment, and introduce new ways of thinking and collaborating so that people work even better together. If this facilitates the adoption of process improvement strategies in the legal space, I will have accomplished my mission. Ideally, this will help readers to engage in deep thinking, collaborative discussions, and decision making, which will be different for each team, group, department, or organization. We will ask ourselves the following:

- What needs to be done more efficiently, where, and why do we need to be more efficient? (Hint: think everything, everywhere, but not all at once.)
- How can we work even better together?
- How can we harness and unleash the power of teams?
- Can we create the right conditions for a cross-functional, diverse team to collaborate in an inclusive, practically fail-safe environment?
- How, when, and where would we start to learn or employ these concepts and tools?
- How might we use the methodologies and toolkits of Lean and Six Sigma?
- What are our drivers for improvement and innovation?
- How does continuous improvement support or become a key element or even the center of our culture or strategy?
- What are the specific applications, obstacles, and lessons learned from others that we can and should try?
- What results have been achieved by others and how do they help us imagine what is possible for us?
- What kinds of improvements have been made? How do they translate into benefits and for whom?

- In what ways do the framework and outcomes of process improvement help us change the conversations and enhance the experiences of our brand, employees, clients, referral sources, prospective clients, and others?
- How do we use process improvement and project management to respond to the pressures we are feeling and deliver greater value to ourselves and our clients?
- What competitive advantages can we develop by using Lean and Six Sigma and the other methodologies in this book?
- How might we assess our readiness and how can we figure out what will work for us?
- Where do we start?
- How do we design, build, test, and structure a process improvement or continuous improvement program? What resources do we need to do it right?
- What's next?

As Jordan Furlong wrote so many years ago:

"Lawyers must accept and act upon a single new reality: we cannot continue to make a living in the law the way we used to... We must create sustainable cost advantages through adoption of technologies and processes."[1]

That thought is evergreen. Change is constant. As a profession and a business, law has progressed, no question, and it must continue to evolve. This book is offered to help and inspire the people who are responsible for ensuring the success of their organizations, both now and in the future. Those who ignore the opportunities that exist or fail to peek around the corner and prepare for what's there do so at their own risk. In contrast, those who seize them will not just survive, but thrive.

If that's not enough, they'll find and fulfill their purpose while operating at their highest and best use. They'll have fun along the way too, because improving processes is some of the best work anyone can do!

Reference

1 Furlong, J. "You say you want a revolution" blog post, 20 December 2013; see www.law21.ca/2013/12/say-want-revolution.

About the author

Catherine Alman MacDonagh is an award-winning lawyer entrepreneur who serves as a catalyst for growth, is driven to help people work even better together, and assists organizations in developing competitive advantages. She is known as a legal pioneer and for leveraging her experiences in law, including as a corporate counsel and law firm executive, to consistently innovate and launch first-to-market offerings to the legal industry.

A Legal Lean Sigma® Black Belt, certified Six Sigma Green Belt, and Accredited Partner of the Smart Collaboration Accelerator, Catherine is the CEO and a founder of the Legal Lean Sigma Institute, which remains the first and only company to provide process improvement and project management certifications, courses, and workshops designed specifically for law.

Catherine created Legal Lean Sigma® to bridge the concepts employed so successfully in manufacturing and other industries to practical and relevant applications to the unique aspects of the legal industry. She also invented both the multi award-winning Legal WorkOut®, a collaborative method of engaging in process improvement that delivers rapid results and harnesses the power of diverse, cross-functional teams, and Legal Lean Sigma Design Thinking™, an amalgamation of methodologies and tools that unleashes creativity and produces innovative products and approaches.

Catherine is an adjunct professor at Suffolk Law School where her PI/LPM course is a requirement of the Legal Innovation and Technology concentration. She is a frequent guest lecturer at other academic institutions and a highly rated keynote and presenter at industry events.

Catherine also offers coaching, training, and strategy consulting services through String of Pearls Companies, including FIRM Guidance Consulting, and Mocktails LLC, where she is the Chief Enthusiasm Officer and conducts business development programs with a completely novel and experiential approach to networking training for lawyers (and everyone else).

Catherine is also a co-founder of the Legal Sales and Service Organization, which has presented the annual RainDance Conference since its launch in 2003 as well as coveted sales and service awards in law

About the author

A serial entrepreneur from her childhood days, she is an idea factory who thinks that curiosity, "trying things", and resiliency are vital for transformation. They are also keys to becoming a learning organization and fostering a culture of continuous improvement. Her early experiences in improv, theater, and working as a summer camp counselor allowed her to develop unique skills that are invaluable in working with professionals, especially in a legal environment.

She is a member of the Association of Legal Administrators; she currently serves on the Professional Development Advisory Committee and, as a member of the Standards Review Committee, contributed to the development of the Uniform Process Based Management System's standard code set. She has a long history of involvement with the Legal Marketing Association, which elected her to the Hall of Fame, serving on the International Board, Northeast Regional Board, LMA New England Chapter President for two terms, co-chair of the Education and Sponsor Relations Committees, Annual Conference Advisory Committee and on many task forces.

Catherine lives in Florida, USA. She enjoys spending time with her family (of two and four legs), friends, and smart, nice people. She is committed to volunteer work and is active in her community, serving as the first president of her community's HOA. She is a volunteer Chef for Lasagna Love, which feeds people, spreads kindness, and strengthens communities. A suicide loss survivor, Catherine has a particular interest in removing the stigma around depression and in preventing suicide. Her work in this area includes more than five years of service on the American Foundation for Suicide Prevention Greater Boston Board.

Catherine is the author of *Lean Six Sigma for Law Firms*, and this, the second edition of that title. She has also co-authored and contributed to numerous other publications.

Acknowledgements

I've explored a variety of roles in the law – lawyer, corporate counsel, law firm executive, consultant, scholar, guide, facilitator, teacher, professor, legal technology marketing and sales director, and legal aid paralegal. I discovered that process improvement work involves some of the most creative, fun, challenging, and rewarding experiences. It's because it harnesses and unleashes the exhilarating power of a cross functional, diverse team; it provides the frameworks and tools that facilitate our ability to collaborate and make things better for everyone, while producing competitive advantages. Also, it changes the conversation from "us/them" to just "us". It's deeply satisfying, and I love it. I think the world needs a whole lot more of this.

I appreciate my good fortune at having discovered "my why" while acknowledging that traveling the entrepreneurial paths to be able to conceive and bring innovation to law and first to market ideas to life are often winding and the terrain uneven. While I often say, "If you want something done, give it to a busy woman", the reality is that work and life successes are things that one realizes alone. I am forever grateful to and for those who journeyed with me.

Thanks to...

My dear family, friends, people, and colleagues for your love and support. You believe in me, encourage me to dream and pursue my big ideas, sustain me in the most challenging moments, and celebrate with me. You are my inner circle (and you know who you are!). You lift me up, create safe spaces, offer comfort and guidance, and bring sunshine, joy, and laughter to my life.

Alex and Sarah, I love you! You are and always will be the bright lights of my life. I am so lucky that I get to be your mom. I have always aspired to set a good example of how finding purpose and doing fulfilling, impactful work make for a rich and meaningful life. As I wrote this second edition, I reflected on how young you were when I launched the Legal Lean Sigma Institute and found renewed appreciation for your support and sacrifices over many years. The time passes so quickly and now you are wonderful adults. I am immeasurably proud of you and grateful for every day with you.

Acknowledgements

Mom, you are my hero – strong, smart, fun, resilient, and the best kind of friend. Sondra and Tom Gibbons, thank you for being extraordinary parents, a beautiful couple, and two of my most loyal, unfailing supporters, and loudest cheering squad.

My sister Sue (a favorite co-creator), brother-in-law Barry, nieces and nephews-in-law Margot and Rob, Joanna and Brannon, and their kids (who are only second in intelligence, talent, kindness, good looks, and all-around awesomeness to my own two) and Amelia – I treasure you and times spent together.

My sister Lynn, you are remembered with so much love and you are missed. Thanks to you, we built a house of happiness, peace, and love. Wish you were here.

My grandmother Mary, I often hear your voice, encouraging "patience". I am still learning, but I have improved a lot (thanks at least in part to the frameworks of process improvement). You would be proud of your buddy.

To those who keep watch, thank you for the feathers. <3

Punkin, such a loyal companion, thank you for being by my side and at my feet as I wrote and edited this book. I'm glad for your presence. You did your mama Abbie proud.

Endless thanks to the friends who show up without fail in every way, whether in good times or the other kind. You always have my back, pick me up, make me laugh, and give unwavering support - and you are some of the best people I know – Allison Tuttle, Dominique Batt, Jan Cree, Jon Bradie (my Unit), Lucy Bean, Pam Konieczny, Roberta Montafia, and Ronna West Cross. Thank you to Bhavik Bhatt, for teaching me to follow my heart; Cathy Curtis, LMT, you are a magical goddess of love and light; my Seasons friends and MG&Gs, especially Carol Friend, Beth Ollum, Mike Ollum, Sue Pennisi, and Tammy Powell; and my many cherished friends and colleagues in the legal field, we have a shared history and enduring bonds forged over decades.

Mike, you are the gentle rock and steady rhythm that grounds and centers me. With love and gratitude, the highest of fives!

To my Legal Lean Sigma Institute teammates and scholars past and present – your brilliance, expertise, and generosity cannot be overstated. Your humble curiosity, passion for learning and sharing, and commitment to continuous improvement are incredible. You help me be a better person, scholar, leader, and practitioner.

This second edition is designed to help everyone in law. For that reason, the content has expanded to include references to behavioral economics, leadership, and knowledge management. A stronger focus for us has been change management – it is so integral to the success of a Lean Sigma program and unique in terms of how to use it effectively in law that a team of talented scholars has developed a certificate program on the subject that is offered by the Legal Lean Sigma Institute. I am indebted to my fellow designers and teammates. I gratefully acknowledge the significant contributions to my thinking and the content here by Legal Lean Sigma Institute scholars: Mo Zain Ajaz, Esq.; Ronna West Cross JD, LLS Green Belt; Frederick J. Esposito, Jr, MBA, CLM, LSS Green Belt; Scott "SJ" R. Jablonski, JD, LSS Yellow Belt, partner at Husch Blackwell; Jessica McBride, MBA, PMP, LSS Green Belt, certified change management practitioner; Jerry Rosenthal, LSS Master Black Belt of Good Thinking; Audrey Rubin, JD of Rubin Solutions; Kyla Sandwith, JD of De Novo Inc; and Rebecca Holdredge, JD.

Thank you to our clients and all who have embraced the work and mission of the Legal Lean Sigma Institute over the years. Teaching people about process improvement and working on projects and engagements has enabled me to cross paths and collaborate with so many bright, caring, and committed people. It is a privilege to be entrusted with such important work, a thrill to be a part of excellent teams, and an honor to have opportunities to do transformation work and learn with you.

Thanks to every Black, Green, Yellow, and White Belt certified in Legal Lean Sigma, and anyone who has earned a certificate or participated in a program or workshop. Each client, student, and program participant has helped us to improve our courses and consulting practice with feedback and ideas. Our success is because of you.

Silvia L. Coulter and Beth M. Cuzzone, my friends, collaborators, and Legal Sales and Service Organization co-founders and partners for more than 22 years now, you were early supporters of the exploration in how to bridge process improvement methodologies, encouraging me to create, incubate, and then run with the Legal Lean Sigma Institute "spin off". I am forever thankful for your willingness to take risks and try new things. Working with you is exhilarating and I wish others got to experience being on a team like ours.

Bill Flannery, you are gone, but you will never be forgotten as a pioneer, exceptional teacher, generous mentor, and my dear friend. Your lessons and legacy live on.

Thank you to my legal and financial team – Debra K. Mayfield, Esq., Karen VanKooy, Esq., Gabrielle Clemens, JD, LLM, AEP, CDFA, and Dawn Lapio of

Dusk to Dawn Tax and Accounting for the invaluable guidance, perpetual patience, and being my trusted advisors, advocates, and friends.

Thank you to Suffolk University Law School, especially Dean Andrew Perlman and Professor Gabe Teninbaum, Assistant Dean for Innovation, Strategic Initiatives and Distance Education, for the chance to teach the first combined process improvement and project management course in a law school. Being part of transforming legal education with you fuels me. I am thankful to every Suffolk Law student who took my class and became a certified Legal Lean Sigma Yellow Belt in Process Improvement and Project Management, starting with the first law school class in the world to take this course in the spring of 2014.

Whether it involves an experienced professional or a student, it is incredibly moving to see people go on to use the frameworks and tools and even pursue careers in the subject I love to teach. There's a profound sense of pride and fulfillment that comes with knowing I've played a part in shaping their journey and fostering their passion. When they choose to dedicate their careers to something I care so deeply about, it feels like a continuation of the work we've done together in a classroom or workshop setting – it's testament to the spark that has been lit, not just by the lessons, but by their own curiosity and determination. It's one of the most rewarding aspects of teaching, helping to guide and inspire their futures in ways that matter to them.

Not everyone appreciates the grain of sand that an oyster needs to make a pearl – I am the necessary irritant in this metaphor. It takes being comfortable being uncomfortable to be a disruptive force, especially when it means doing it over and over again There are those who don't fully understand that role or the value of constructive conflict, but most do value and come to welcome the chance to make a "string of pearls". Either way, I offer my thanks. Resiliency is a learned skill, albeit sometimes the hard way. That's why they call it experience, though, and I appreciate the many growth opportunities that have been afforded to me along the way.

So, cheers to the pearl makers, pathfinders, "firsts among equals", cat herders, and the catalysts, all those who are pushing water up the hill, leading horses, and grinding it out in law all over the world. It may be simple, this work, but it sure isn't easy. It takes discipline, optimism, and heart. It's brick-by-brick work, it is iterative, and it's hard to not skip steps. Let's keep learning and growing and going – collaborate and innovate wherever you can, whether incrementally or by leaps and bounds.

This book is dedicated to all who are working to improve the law for those in it and those we serve. I hope that what I've written here serves as a resource and contributes in some way to your great successes. Trust the process of process improvement (and don't skip steps). Stand on the shoulders of others to get a better view – we've got you. It's worth it. You've got this. I encourage you to share your experiences and have fun. I look forward to learning from you!

Catherine Alman MacDonagh, JD
February 2025

About the Legal Lean Sigma Institute

The Legal Lean Sigma Institute, LLC (LLSI) is the first and only organization to develop and bring to legal and business professionals in firms, offices, and departments a comprehensive set of process improvement (PI) and project management (PM) certification courses, training programs, and consulting services specifically designed for the law. LLSI holds a registered trademark in the term Legal Lean Sigma.

Legal Lean Sigma Institute faculty and consultants have worked on process improvement projects and delivered courses and programs all over the world for thousands of leaders in the legal profession, both privately and publicly.

In addition to visiting scholars, the LLSI Scholars in Residence include:
- Catherine Alman MacDonagh, JD, LLS Black Belt
- Mo Zain Ajaz, MBA, LSS Yellow Belt
- Ronna West Cross, JD, LLS Green Belt
- Frederick J. Esposito, Jr, MBA, CLM, LLS Green Belt
- Scott R. Jablonski, Esq., LLS Yellow Belt
- Jessica McBride, MBA, PMP, LSS Green Belt
- Jerry Rosenthal, MBA, LSS Master Black Belt
- Audrey Rubin, JD, LSS Yellow Belt
- Kyla Sandwith, JD, Masters in Law Firm Management, LSS Yellow Belt

Foreword

By Jordan Furlong

Whenever I'm meeting with the senior leadership or executive team of a law firm, a question that's always fun to ask is, "Who's your most productive lawyer?"

Invariably, the response to that question is something like, "Well, that would probably be Bob (or whomever). He billed (some staggering number of hours) last year and brought in (some equally breathtaking amount of money) as a result."

And that's my cue to say, "I didn't ask who was your highest-billing lawyer. I asked who was the most productive." And I go on to explain that there are several ways for a lawyer to contribute value to the firm and its clients, and generating a metric ton of billables is only one way to do it (and far from the healthiest).

I go through this exercise to help the leadership team understand that the way law firms define "productivity" is ridiculous and archaic. In the rest of the business world, productivity in its simplest form refers to the output (usually goods and services) that can be generated from a given set of inputs (primarily labor, capital, and resources).

Productivity is a measure of both the efficiency and the effectiveness of your business's production and workflow systems. The higher your productivity, the more "bang for your buck" you're getting – and the more your profit can increase.

Not in law firms, though. Productivity in this sector has been measured purely by volume of input, and there's only one type of "input" – the time and effort of lawyers. The most sophisticated industry reports produced by the most advanced legal information companies today routinely refer to a firm's "productivity" as the number of lawyer hours that are recorded, billed, and/or collected, depending on the measurement.

Among the many disadvantages of this approach, two in particular have long stood out. The first is that time-based productivity discourages efficiency innovations. If you are rewarded for hours billed, and someone develops a way to get an hour's worth of work done in ten minutes, you'll regard it as a threat rather than as a benefit. This is a big reason why law firms have lagged terribly in technological adoption.

But the other disadvantage of time-based productivity is even more acute – it places a hard ceiling over the law firm's profits. I don't care how many Bobs you have in your office or how many thousands of hours they can bill, there are physical limits to how many hours a lawyer can work and there are metaphysical limits to how many hours each day provides (24, last I checked).

A lawyer who takes an hour to deliver a service and bills $500 for their effort generates $500 of revenue in that hour. A lawyer who uses technology and systems to deliver six services in an hour, at a flat $250 for each service, generates $1,500. Which of these approaches seems better to you?

If you're reading this book, I already know which looks better to you. Either you're open-minded and curious about the advantages (financial and otherwise) of process improvements like Lean Six Sigma, or you've already bought into the concept and now you want to know how to make it work for your firm.

Either way, you're ahead of a very important curve – the productivity curve that's bearing down fast on the legal industry and will strike hard when it arrives. And the herald of this curve is Generative AI.

Gen AI – whether accessed through frontier model providers like OpenAI, Anthropic, or Google, or through legal-industry providers like WestLaw, Lexis, or vLex – is going to revolutionize productivity in the legal sector. Combined with non-AI automation and other technological advances, it's going to strip most of the value from time-based revenue models and force law firms to redefine what productivity means.

But technology, by itself, won't be enough to create a competitive edge for you. There might be benefits to early AI adoption, but within five to ten years, everyone will have roughly the same access to these tools. Your competitive advantage will come down to precisely how you reconfigure your own production system to take advantage of them.

And that's where this book really comes into play. Catherine Alman MacDonagh has updated her definitive guide to how law firms and legal businesses can use Lean Six Sigma and other process improvements to gain lasting competitive advantages and profitability enhancements. Myriad success stories and case studies, updated for this second edition, show how these methods are working in real-world legal settings.

By seizing the opportunities presented by process improvement methods, you can crank up your legal business' productivity to previously unseen levels, fulfill your business' potential, and deliver lasting value gains to your clients, your colleagues, and yourself.

Law firms that employ these tools and approaches now will see real benefits right away. But in the medium- and long-term, they also will protect themselves against the tsunami of disruption AI will bring. They'll begin the critical transformation of legal business models away from time-based productivity and towards, simply, productivity.

Who is your most productive lawyer? That's the wrong question. Ask yourself instead, "How productive, in every sense, is my entire legal business – and how can I make it even better?" The answer to those questions begins on the very next page.

Introduction

History – the creation of Legal Lean Sigma

I've always been good at organizing things and people, but my first real process improvement project might have been in an office, where I worked as a secretary during my high school years (I was also a summer camp counselor, where I developed skills that have been far more helpful than I ever would have guessed). After listening to the five people with whom I worked complain about how frustrating and disorganized it was, and how they wished it was set up, I completely overhauled the filing system. It was a big project, but everyone was very happy with the result.

My initial exposure to the practice of law was as a paralegal intern at the Legal Services Office at the University of Massachusetts at Amherst, where I handled consumer protection and landlord tenant cases. Paralegals were supervised by excellent lawyers, and we were extremely hands-on. We had significant responsibilities, such as intake and communicating with clients, drafting and sending demand letters, handling responses, and so forth. It was a great experience and the catalyst for convincing this former theater student to switch to a Legal Studies major and then go to law school.

That office served many students and was incredibly well managed and well run by smart, nice people who were extremely committed to the work we were doing and to teaching us too. It was a great culture. Like most people with limited knowledge of legal environments and how law offices are run, I did not fully appreciate the excellent law practice management or how many efficient processes were in place at the time. Certainly, I did as my career progressed.

My interest in finding ways to be more efficient and for people to work better together in a legal environment took root after I graduated law school in 1990. I worked as a corporate counsel in the law department of an insolvent insurance company. We represented the estate, meaning the policy holders. It was complex work that involved every state's Attorney General's Office and Department of Insurance, other insurance companies that held excess policies, reinsurance companies, and some massive cases, including large loss property and casualty and significant environmental matters.

Introduction

This was before the internet was born and we did not have the ability to send files electronically the way we do now because external email wasn't used then. Everything was so paper intensive. Fax machines were the fastest way to send things. Document productions involved Bates stamping thousands of pages. The way law was practiced in real life was perplexing. It was truly astonishing to discover that we, the client, were billed hourly by the law firm doing our work. How could it be that the longer the work took, the more our outside counsel got paid? This approach was so obviously misaligned with our goals, which included paying out as much as we could to our policy holders (not our law firm).

Because of this early experience practicing law, I would forever look at how legal work was performed and delivered from the client's perspective. As a business professional in several law firms, I learned more about how law firms operate, and my understanding and perspective expanded. It is somewhat obvious to state, but it's challenging to fully appreciate and empathize with someone if you haven't had the experience yourself. I saw a lot of missed connections, miscommunications, and misalignment, even though nearly every person I worked with really cared a lot about doing a good job and being a great teammate.

This made me curious about how to bring people together to make things better for all of us. Because of my work with client teams, I was already accustomed to working with a cross-functional team. Because I had been "Flannerized" by a man who later became a friend and who is remembered by many as the grandfather of legal sales, Bill Flannery, I also had an appreciation for diversity – different personality types, communication styles, experiences, etc. – and how important an element that was to leverage for a high functioning, high performing team.

Research led me to process improvement. While earning a Green Belt Certification in Six Sigma, I struggled, not only because I had to manually calculate standard deviation to pass, but because I could not quite articulate the connection between what I was learning and the realities of law. I understood intellectually that the concepts of controlling variation to produce greater predictability, reduce errors, and so forth applied to legal, but it took me nearly a year to bridge what I had learned in the safety of the classroom to something that was useful to my work as a director of business development in a law firm.

I continued to research and experiment. After finally trying some things in areas where there was a lot of repeatability (such as estate planning and trust operations), I finally figured out that adding the key ingredient of Lean to the mix was critical. I kept mentioning to my friend Wendy Duffey (in between discussions about the Boston Red Sox) that someone really ought to start teaching process improvement in the legal space. She finally said, "You keep talking about this, why don't YOU do it".

There was an undeniable gap in the marketplace, and I do love a challenge. One thing led to another and, thanks to Wendy's introduction, in 2008, I began to work with an expert who possessed deep experience in process improvement in various applications and industries all over the world – just not in legal. My goal was to design and deliver educational programs that taught process improvement in contexts that would be immediately relevant and useful to lawyers and the business professionals who work with them. The idea was novel and the approach and content so unique that the USPTO granted the application for a trademark in Legal Lean Sigma.

The first Legal Lean Sigma programs were offered in 2007 under the umbrella of the Legal Sales and Service Organization (LSSO), which was launched in 2003. With the support of my dear friends and LSSO partners, Silvia L. Coulter and Beth Marie Cuzzone, we unveiled our first White Belt certification course at the annual LSSO RainDance Conference. Very quickly, the success of those endeavors, combined with almost immediate interest in consulting services, created a need for a separate business structure. In 2010, the Legal Lean Sigma Institute LLC was formed.

In the same year, we began teaching our two-day Yellow Belt certification course as adjunct faculty at George Washington University's Master's in Law Firm Management program. This gave us the opportunity to introduce our take on process improvement to seasoned, accomplished professionals – lawyers, administrators, marketers, IT, HR, and finance students both learned and taught us about the application of process improvement in various legal settings. It demonstrated that these methodologies were scalable and applicable to any legal or business process in any size of organization.

In 2013, faculty were added and in 2014, LLSI expanded the certification offerings by including another option, which was completely unique to the legal profession – a combined process improvement and project management program. Tim Corcoran was instrumental in designing, developing, and teaching that content.

As of this writing in 2024, LLSI has delivered hundreds of White Belt and Yellow Belt certification courses, facilitated process mapping workshops, developed its own unique approaches to doing process improvement work, won awards for its groundbreaking methodology, the Legal WorkOut, helped organizations develop their architecture and programs, and led, facilitated, and supported legal and business process improvement projects all over the world. It has been awesome.

We have designed custom curricula and tailored programs, delivered keynotes, and certified and coached leaders in many different legal settings. Truly, the scalability and flexibility factors are astounding. Interestingly, our certification courses were routinely approved for continuing legal education credit from the very beginning – that is no small thing, considering that law practice management was just beginning to show on the legal radar when we first started.

Our consulting practice encompasses the full spectrum of services associated with introducing, developing, and implementing process improvement programs, including operational excellence assessments, strategy work, organizational development, and curriculum design and delivery.

We love what we do – and we really enjoy working with the talented, caring, driven, intelligent people that law seems to attract. More organizations than ever are offering privately delivered certification courses in their offices or remotely for their employees and clients. We have found there simply isn't a better experience than learning and working together as a team to make things better for everyone.

What we have discovered is that relationships deepen when we provide a framework for having structured conversations. Employing process improvement in law supports a culture of being truly client focused. Those who know understand that the best learn as they go and apply those lessons to improve all the time.

This philosophy explains why the Legal Lean Sigma Institute team members are not just faculty – we are scholars. We are learned experts, not only from our studies and experiences, but by improving all the time and gaining mastery through practice and continuous learning. We have found that legal and business professionals possess the characteristics and attributes that make them particularly well suited for process improvement work.

Once you know more about process improvement and what it can do, I hope you'll be eager to experience how transformative and powerful it is.

Chapter 1:
An introduction to Lean and Six Sigma for law (and some project management too)

The primary goal of this book is to introduce legal and business professionals in law to process improvement generally and the two primary process improvement methodologies (Lean and Six Sigma) in particular. We will explore the main concepts behind each, and the specific approaches and frameworks embedded within Legal Lean Sigma. In this way, readers will understand how these tried-and-true approaches that were born in manufacturing can be applied to law in any setting or organization regardless of size, location, or focus.

To begin, let's establish a foundational premise. Improving the way things are done is the key for making any business, process, person, team, or project more efficient.

Our definition of efficiency is something a bit more nuanced and sophisticated than "Do more with less". While that is one right answer, it is not *the* right answer. Sometimes, to be more efficient, we need to do less with more. Or more with more. Or less with less.

How do we know which is the right answer or approach? Who should decide? How, when, and where should we make the changes needed to successfully implement the improvement so that it produces the benefits we seek? What kind of structure and resources would we need? How can we get people to collaborate so that they can work better together? Can we develop competitive advantages while doing and delivering our work in ways that increase value to the client and our organization? In a nutshell, this is what Lean Six Sigma for Law is all about.

What is process improvement?
Most people can identify when there are "issues" with a process. Far fewer can thoughtfully respond to questions such as:
- Why are those issues occurring?
- How would you decide which problems are the most important to solve?
- Who should be involved and decide?
- How will you know when you have succeeded in improving a process?

Process improvement provides frameworks and tools to answer these critical questions.

In addition to an overview of process improvement, we will explore how to get started and structuring for success. I also hope to make the case for carrying out process improvements opportunistically and, eventually, carrying out process improvement systematically. Naturally, I aim to help the reader to make the case as well.

To begin, then, it is helpful to define what we mean by "process improvement". It is the systematic practice of first analyzing a process to understand how it is currently carried out, then searching for issues, problems, and opportunities in the process and prioritizing them. Then, tools and techniques are employed to solve priority problems and/or to capture significant opportunities. Finally, the new process must be controlled so that it delivers the anticipated benefits.

Process improvement helps us determine the best way to carry out a certain kind of work to achieve efficiency, excellent quality of work and service, high probability of successful outcomes, and predictability. When we develop the capacity to do process improvement work, we can employ project management skills to select the best processes, tools, and skills to be able to carry out our ideal process every time.

Process basics
W. Edwards Deming, who was known as the Father of the Quality Revolution and responsible for the first application of statistical quality control principles to a non-manufacturing environment, said it best: *"If you can't describe what you are doing as a process, you don't know what you are doing."*

A "process" is a describable, repeatable sequence of activities that generates an outcome. As such, to a process improvement practitioner, nearly everything qualifies as a process. Think of how many things we do that involve "steps" that we take without focusing intently on what we are doing, especially those actions we perform regularly. For example, consider the mundane routines of everyday life, like making coffee or tea. If you enjoy making one of these at home, you probably make it pretty much the same way every single time. This way, you have a consistently, predictably made beverage just the way you like it.

I love a great cup of coffee. I like a certain bean, ground not too coarse, not too fine, and a specific amount of water. I make my coffee in the same sequence nearly every day, almost without thinking. And then, when the coffee is ready, I add exactly what I want in it, in just the right amounts. Then, I drink it at the right temperature (not too hot or cold), and in my preferred vessel.

That's a process – a series of repeatable, describable steps that generates an outcome. Each time I make that perfect cup of coffee, I follow the same process to manage my project of making a wonderful cup of coffee. Because I am a fallible human who sometimes forgets to place the carafe in the machine, I made mistakes until I got a machine that would not allow the water to pass through the filter without a carafe in place to catch it. Now my process is practically error-proofed.

The incredibly complex processes of law (and, of course business and legal operations) are just like that. Each one involves many steps and tasks. Therefore, they also require good project management, because processes used in law involve a significantly greater scale and, often, much higher stakes. They usually involve multiple operations, people, organizations, and so forth (think everything from a simple will to a class action lawsuit). And if you, as someone working in law, cannot describe this work as a process, clients, teammates, and others may perceive that you don't know what you're doing.

Already, based on my experience, I anticipate that there are readers who are unconvinced (and may be bristling with the notion) that the legal work they do can be considered or distilled to "a process". One of the things I often hear from clients is that "we don't have a process for that". However, the reality is that if you are doing a particular kind of work right now, you have a process – albeit one that may not be terribly good or may radically differ from matter to matter, client to client, worker to worker, or office to office. Some organizations seem to think it's fine to let lawyers handle things as they wish. Please pause for a moment here to consider the magnitude and consequences of all that variation.

Processes are how law firms, departments, and offices create and deliver value to their clients. Thus, processes embody the knowledge of the individual, firm or office, department, practice group, or team. Our processes are the way we do and deliver our work. In effect, our processes are the best practices we have developed. As such, a great process can create excellent experiences for employees and clients and other competitive advantages.

Core business processes in law include:
- Intake;
- Conflicts;
- Timekeeping;

- Onboarding;
- Billing; and
- Pricing.

Naturally, various functions, such as management, finance, operations, marketing, business development, IT, HR/talent, knowledge management, etc. each have their own core processes.

Every practice area uses many processes as well. For example, Corporate might handle many mergers and acquisitions. That process involves many stages and tasks, starting with due diligence, followed by investigations, drafting, and negotiating agreements, regulatory compliance, closings, and post-acquisition work, such as integration. Within each of those processes are sub-processes and intersecting processes. All those processes and tasks are performed and operated by people who are typically acquiring and using a lot of knowledge that is not captured anywhere. Moreover, they are usually using information and technology in ways that are most effective for and familiar to them without much thought or understanding of how what they do affects others in the process.

To spark further thinking about what constitutes a process in law, consider all the people and steps involved in doing and delivering work in the following practice areas.

- *Corporate*. Bankruptcy, formation, restructuring, contracts, mergers and acquisitions, employment, finance, regulatory compliance, and many specialty areas, such as securities and tax.
- *Constitutional*. Advancing, protecting, or defending civil liberties, freedom of speech, freedom of religion, due process, equal protection, separation of powers, and the limits of government authority.
- *Employment law*. Compliance, mediation, litigation, drafting and negotiating agreements/contracts, workplace discrimination, wrongful termination, wage and hour disputes.
- *Family law*. Adoption, divorce, prenuptial agreements, alimony, child support, child protection, and guardianship.
- *Immigration law*. Completion and submission of required documents and forms, obtaining proper documentation.
- *Individual*. Bankruptcy, consumer protection, estate planning, trusts, probate, real estate transactions.
- *Intellectual property*. Copyright, patent, and trademark applications, portfolio management, and prosecution.

- *Litigation.* Prosecution or plaintiff work, defense work for every kind of matter involving a court, arbitration, or other authority, such as a tribunal.
- *Municipal law.* Local governance, land use planning, zoning regulations, finance, public contracts, administrative law, drafting ordinances and resolutions, contracts, and compliance work.
- *Military.* Enforcement and defense work related to court martial work, civil offenses, preservation of good order and discipline, legality of orders, and conduct.
- *Personal injury.* Auto/motorcycle/vehicle accidents, worker compensation, slip and fall cases, defective products, medical malpractice, auto accidents, as well as class action lawsuits (asbestos, for example).

In every example, there are high level steps that are taken to progress from start to finish and tasks that must be performed in each stage to complete that step and generate an outcome.

Processes always exist to serve a client. The word "client" has special meaning in law – in our work, we consider the users of the process to be "clients" as well. If the process isn't working well for the operators, it is not serving them as well as it could. In turn, it becomes more challenging, costly, time consuming, frustrating, and inefficient to serve "the client". If we are honest, most of us in law would agree this describes most of the processes we use.

Process measurement

To understand how well a process is working, we measure it. We are interested in two areas – "performance" and "efficiency".

Processes have a characteristic performance level, sometimes called process capability, that describes how well the process meets client expectations. This means, obviously, that we need to understand the client's expectations and requirements. In law, the client's requirements are very often not gathered, not specific enough, not documented, and not shared. In other words, most of the time, we have no solid data that tells us how well we are doing. Consider the implications of that statement, especially since most organizations declare themselves to be "client focused" or "client centered".

How can you say you deliver on this promise or measure how close you came to meeting the client's expectations if you haven't even established a range of what the client would find acceptable? Ronald L. Burdge, a leading "lemon law" attorney, points out the value of measuring client satisfaction:

> *"The legal profession frequently proclaims it is dedicated to providing legal services in a way that satisfies... But if we do not measure the quality of that service, then can we really say that we are able to provide excellent legal representation? If you don't know that you are doing good work, can you really be sure you are? If what you value is a satisfied client, then you must determine how to satisfy a client – and you will not really be able to know that until you understand how to gauge client satisfaction in the first place."*

We also measure process resource requirements, sometimes called process efficiency. This metric refers to the resources – time, people, equipment, money – required to carry out the process. There are many dimensions along which a process may be measured. Moreover, a process may perform quite well in some dimensions and poorly in others.

Who would not agree that nearly every process can be improved? This is why we will explore how we surface, select, prioritize, resource, plan, and support this work. We cannot work on everything at once, after all. We must plan for people's capacity to engage in this kind of thinking and work.

What are Lean and Six Sigma?
Now that we have process basics covered, we can delve into Lean and Six Sigma, two of the most commonly used process improvement methodologies.

In short, the two disciplines are about establishing the right things to do (Lean) and how to do things the right way (Six Sigma). Lean is about simplifying processes. With Lean, we focus on doing the right things and eliminating what is known as "waste" in a process. In this way, we ensure that we maximize resource efficiency. Six Sigma is focused on reducing errors and controlling undesirable variation.

While it used to be the case that practitioners might have argued that theirs was "the way", now the two disciplines are considered complementary and are used together. Some use the term Lean Six Sigma, others use Lean Sigma, which is actually an example of Lean in action, since it eliminates "six" as a superfluous word. That said, both terms are correct and are used interchangeably.

Lean

Lean concepts have been applied for centuries, but a major development in this line of thinking occurred in the Japanese automobile industry in the middle of the 20th century:

> "As Kiichiro Toyoda, Taiichi Ohno, and others at Toyota looked at this situation [of the automobile manufacturing process] in the 1930s, and more intensely just after World War II, it occurred to them that a series of simple innovations might make it more possible to provide both continuity in process flow and a wide variety in product offerings… and invented the Toyota Production System.
>
> "This system in essence shifted the focus of the manufacturing engineer from individual machines and their utilization to the flow of the product through the total process. Pause for a moment and consider how those of us in law might benefit from a similar shift in focusing on the flow of the product through the total process rather than the individual workers and things like staffing.
>
> "Toyota concluded that by right-sizing machines for the actual volume needed, introducing self-monitoring machines to ensure quality, lining the machines up in process sequence, pioneering quick setups so each machine could make small volumes of many part numbers, and having each process step notify the previous step of its current needs for materials, it would be possible to obtain low cost, high variety, high quality, and very rapid throughput times to respond to changing customer desires. Also, information management could be made much simpler and more accurate."[1]

I saw such a huge need in the law to make processes simpler and faster and committed to tackling the challenge of translating the concepts of process improvement so that they make sense in a legal context. It is not self-evident. After all, we are not manufacturing automobiles, medical devices, or silicon wafers.

This translation of these concepts from the manufacturing world to the legal space is why Legal Lean Sigma was created. The use of Lean and Six Sigma in law may be a simple concept, but that does not necessarily mean they are always easy to apply. Each law department or firm, practice group, legal or business professional, client, jurisdiction, matter or case, facts, judge, opposing counsel, and so on, is different and some are different every time.

So, one of our many challenges is ensuring that the desire to eliminate or change something in a process does not replace the exercise of good judgment or constrain our ability to do something that is in the best interests of the firm and its client for that particular engagement.

This is one of the reasons that Yellow and White Belt candidates in our certification courses find it easier to understand how to use process improvement in relation to business processes. Initially, it can be more of a stretch to think about how these concepts might be applied to legal work, since, in addition to all the differences between cases, matters, and the work itself, there can often be quite a bit of variation in terms of how lawyers like to do and deliver their work.

Once we start to focus on how we are working and the impact of all that freedom, we begin to realize there are so many reasons to change. For example, during a process mapping workshop, two partners were struggling to agree on one "best way" to handle an employment law matter. That is because each took a very different path to end up in the same place. The reality is that most legal professionals have no proscribed way of doing something on a more global basis, so it is mostly left up to the individual. And nearly everyone does something different. The partners turned to the paralegal who supported them, as well as three other lawyers, and asked how in the world the paralegal was able to keep track of all their preferences, saying this way of working was just not sustainable, it was wildly efficient, and so forth. The paralegal exclaimed, *"This is what I've been trying to tell you!"*

If we consider that every service offered in any area of practice contains a series of repeatable, describable steps – even if (and maybe especially because) there is variation in each one – we appreciate that each one is a process. Litigation is a process. Every transaction is a process. Every legal work product, every service delivered, is the outcome of a process. Accordingly, in each offering, there are abundant opportunities to apply Lean Sigma concepts and tools to make the process simpler and faster.

Lean's eight kinds of waste

Lean involves relentlessly searching for and then reducing or even eliminating what is referred to as "waste". This does not mean that we automatically cut something out of our process or that we consider it "trash". Instead, as we examine the series of repeatable, describable steps, we flag things as candidates for reduction or elimination that fall into these categories. In fact, without developing a far greater understanding about why steps are in the process, it is way too early to decide what to do with the candidates. For now, we simply identify them.

The eight kinds of waste are more easily recalled with the acronym DOWNTIME – see Figure 1.

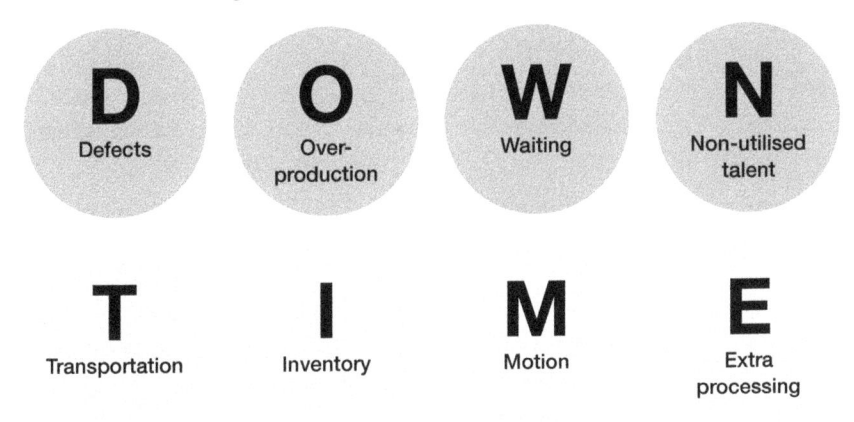

D	**O**	**W**	**N**
Defects	Over-production	Waiting	Non-utilised talent
T	**I**	**M**	**E**
Transportation	Inventory	Motion	Extra processing

Figure 1: DOWNTIME. Source: Legal Lean Sigma Institute LLC.

Understanding that Lean came from the auto manufacturing world, these "categories" of waste make sense. But how do they translate in a legal context?

Let's go through each in turn:

1. *Defects and all related waste, including inspection, testing, and correction.* Examples of defects include missing a filing deadline, incomplete forms, bad drafting, data entry errors and omissions.
2. *Overproduction.* Examples include starting work before clearing conflicts, printing too many hard copies, and drafting a ten-page memo when only a one-page summary was requested.
3. *Waiting.* Examples include awaiting responses from clients, employees, or opposing counsel, starting a call or meeting late due to late arrivals, waiting for technology such as boot up/restart times.
4. *Excess capacity.* For example, not using the lowest cost resources such as clients, paralegals, and assistants that are capable of doing tasks, when partners are doing associate level work, or over-staffing a matter.
5. *Transportation (this type of waste refers to things moving as opposed*

to people moving, which is considered "motion"). Examples include moving files from one place to another and sending hard copies rather than emails.
6. *Inventory.* Examples include work in process (WIP), unread email, marketing materials (such as collateral, brochures, and promotional items, or event materials).
7. *Motion (which refers to people moving as opposed to things).* Examples include people spending extra time getting from one place to the next due to travel or poor office layout, delivering files rather than mailing/emailing them, extra keystrokes/clicks to find documents.
8. *Extra processing steps.* Examples include conducting too much research or double and triple checking (e.g., approvals of expenses without any real review).

Waste is present in virtually every process. In its Lean management guide, *Lean for Legal Staff – The Seven Hidden Wastes,* legal services consultant and trainer Levantar gives examples of how work in progress (WIP) is created through waste:

"One department found that 40 percent of the inputs (paperwork and forms) it received from clients contained errors or omissions. To correct these, the legal staff had to call the clients; we know from our work in call centers that only one in three outbound calls is successful... Imagine therefore that for every 100 matters being processed there were 180 activities generated."[2]

Lean uses many tools to help us determine what are the right things to do in order to have a simpler, faster process, where all the activities are closely linked together with no DOWNTIME kinds of waste.

Six Sigma – getting to error-free
Lean is an excellent methodology all on its own and is especially well suited for law. It becomes even more powerful when we add Six Sigma. The term "Six Sigma" refers to a statistical measurement of standard deviations from the mean in a normal distribution.

Six Sigma thinking is a natural for law. The more experienced the legal or business professional, the easier it is to answer Six Sigma questions:
- What are the key factors that affect outcomes?

- What is the "best way" to do something (i.e., how can we increase our probability of a positive outcome)?
- What are the benefits of consistency and standardization?
- How carefully does a process need to be controlled to give the results desired by the client?

Imagine error-free law. That's what Six Sigma inspires us to do – get as close to perfect as we can. This is accomplished by using a set of tools and techniques that were used originally to improve business processes and manufacturing quality and are employed in legal to reduce undesirable process variation, errors, and defects.

This methodology was developed at Motorola in the 1980s to make improvements on the manufacturing floor. The company was among the first to receive the Malcom Baldridge Award. Later, other companies adopted it, including Allied signal, Boeing, and General Electric, where CEO Jack Welch famously led the adoption in 1995 and saved billions of dollars.

In 1999 alone, Six Sigma delivered $320m (£213.3m) in productivity gains – more than double the original goal of $150m (£100m). Six Sigma was rolled out in the GE in-house legal team in 1996 and the team applied the principles across the legal function in all group divisions. All GE lawyers, globally, were required to reach the Green Belt level, which required two to three weeks of training and completion of at least two Green Belt projects.

Elpidio Villarreal, counsel litigation and legal policy adviser with GE in the US, is a Six Sigma Green Belt. He is the architect of the Early Dispute Resolution (EDR) process, which was introduced after applying the program to litigation. In an interview[3] with Law.com in 2001, he admits that the lawyers were initially skeptical about how the strategy would work, saying:

"There was a question about how one can apply the quantitative mathematical approach, which is geared to the manufacturing process, to the arts and liberal graduates in the legal function. We came to rest at the fact that although we cannot apply Six Sigma strictly in the same way, it does not mean that the central insights do not apply. Almost everything we do in the legal department is a process that can be broken down into components and we can assess the improvements."

The key to applying Six Sigma is to identify what the client wants – a process that Villarreal says has benefits in itself:

> "The business people had probably been telling us for ages, but we simply did not listen. Six Sigma requires you to do so and the inevitable result is that it makes you more responsive."

Villarreal has no hesitation in recommending Six Sigma to other in-house departments. He says:

> "GE lawyers are now thinking in terms of the process and how we can measure the value. It has made us better lawyers because we no longer simply accept things. For instance, I can no longer accept the analysis from outside counsel that we have a 'pretty good case'. I want to break that analysis down."

Villarreal's advice for all in-house counsel is to consider applying the principles to their legal functions. He says:

> "If I was made general counsel of a major company tomorrow and the company had not implemented Six Sigma, I think I would try to take the lead. The management can then see what is possible."

Our focus is on understanding relationships between inputs and outputs of the process. Those include exploring the key factors that affect outcomes, and the "best way" to do something (i.e., how can we increase our probability of a positive outcome). We question how carefully a process needs to be controlled to give the results desired by the client, and we ask what are the benefits of consistency and standardization?

While Lean is focused on resource efficiency, with Six Sigma, our focus is on process capability and alignment with requirements. In other words, we find out how capable the process is of delivering what the client requires. Usually, clients have a range of acceptability with lower and upper limits – the same way I am when I make my coffee. Too light or dark? That won't work – there is some place in the middle of those limits that will.

Once we define the client's requirements, we can work toward a more repeatable, predictable process where we are doing things right and have created something very capable. That does not mean we gratuitously standardize anything. In fact, some aspects of the process might be locked down tight while other steps might have more flexibility built into them. This way, professionals can bring their experience and best thinking to bear.

A Six Sigma process is one in which there are only 3.4 defects per million opportunities (DPMO) – see Figure 2. We define "opportunity" as any chance to not meet the required specifications. This standard makes perfect sense in the context of a manufacturing environment where Six Sigma was originally developed.

SIGMA LEVEL	DEFECTS PER MILLION OPPORTUNITIES
1	691,462
2	308,538
3	66,807
4	6,210
5	233
6	3.4

Figure 2: DPMO in Six Sigma Processes.[4]

At its core, Six Sigma revolves around a few key concepts. The first is "critical to quality", which are the attributes that are most important to the client(s). A "defect" is any failure to deliver what the client wants. We must always keep in mind that variation is what our clients experience, what they see and feel – clients want to be pleased, not surprised, so it is important to have "stable operations", which ensure that we have consistent, predictable processes to improve what the client sees and feels.

Case study – NovusLaw

NovusLaw offers document review, management, and analysis for lawyers. It offers a stunning case study in the applicability of Six Sigma to the document review process. It also serves as an example of an industry driver and innovator:

"Six Sigma is what we use to eliminate defects as we measure and analyze our work processes. Typically, undocumented processes will yield 20,000-

60,000 defects per million opportunities. Six Sigma is designed to get that down to fewer than four per million. On our most recent document review we performed at Five Sigma, or approximately 200 defects per million. By the way, that's about 200 times better than the average in the legal industry today."[5]

This type of work used to be routinely performed by law firms. Now, law firms may do very well to partner with an outsourced provider that can deliver greater predictability and much higher quality work at a predictable price.

Not every step or part of every process should be standardized or controlled as tightly as another step in the same process – this is why legal process improvement is both art and science. There may be plenty of steps that require us to allow for a lot of latitude as we need to build in room for variation based on the lawyer's experience and knowledge. Other steps require little to no judgment and are therefore good candidates for controlling variation. Every case or matter does not need to be approached as though we had never done this kind of work before – this is inefficient, and it also actively contradicts what we say to our clients, prospects, and referral sources about working with us to enjoy the benefits of our great experience.

Mapping process improvement
The foundation of process improvement is to describe (map) the process. Then, we measure the process. Each process has a characteristic performance level and characteristic resource requirements. The process performance (also called process capability) describes how well the process meets client expectations, while the process resource requirements (also called process efficiency) refers to the resources (time, people, equipment, and costs) required to carry out the process. There are many dimensions along which a process can be measured; a process can perform well in some dimensions and poorly in others.

To know whether the process is capable of delivering what clients require, we must determine that client's range of acceptability. Let's illustrate this using a simple example. I like half-and-half in my coffee, but I don't want it too light or too dark. I have an ideal "color" coffee, but I'd accept it if it was a little too dark or a little too light. Anything outside that range is not acceptable and does not meet my requirements. I also do not want variation – I want my coffee to be within the range of acceptable limits every day.

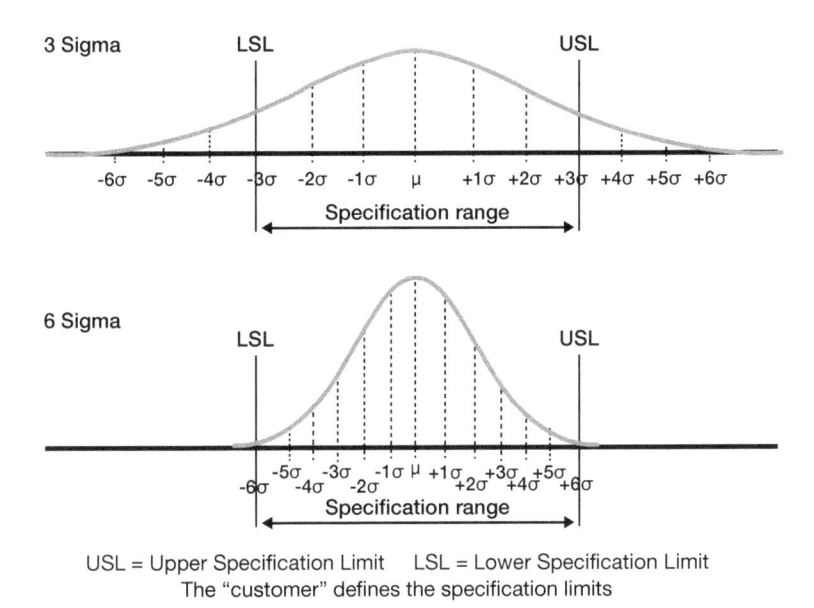

Figure 3: Sigma level limits. Source: Adapted from Quora.com.[6]

Sometimes, therefore, there will be a narrow and other times a wide range between the Upper Specification Limit (USL) and the Lower Specification Limit (LSL). The customer/client defines the specification limits. Where the range is wide, a lower Sigma level process is perfectly adequate. However, as the standard of quality increases, less variation and greater consistency in the process is essential. In other words, the closer to perfect the output must be, the higher the Sigma level must be. A process must be instituted to produce outputs that meet the specified range of acceptability between the USL and the LSL, which means we have to know what the client expects in the first place. When we are measuring in this manner, we can truly claim that we know that we produce quality work product and service that meets the client's requirements. To accomplish this, we must also employ good project and client management. See Figure 3, which explains the Sigma level limits.

Project management
There is a direct connection between process improvement and project management (also called legal project management or LPM). What is the

benefit of having the ability to manage projects very well if our underlying process is not the best it can be? Conversely, what is the value of having an excellent process that is not being managed well?

Essentially, project management is a role and set of skills that ensure that, for a particular engagement, we review and select the right processes and then apply them appropriately to each matter. Then, project management involves actively managing schedules, staff, and deliverables to deliver high quality work on time and under budget to achieve specific goals.

At the Legal Lean Sigma Institute, we define project management as the process and activity of planning, organizing, motivating, and controlling resources, procedures, and protocols. So, even project management may be considered a process.

Our PM model contains six steps (see Figure 4):

1. Define the objective. What constitutes a win for the client?
2. Define the scope and constraints, e.g. budget, timeline, quality, what is on/off the table.
3. Establish the project plan. Identify standard, variable, and volatile tasks, and establish task timelines and budgets. What is on the "critical path"? What resources are necessary, *including a project manager*?
4. Execute the plan. Track efforts, time, budget, results.

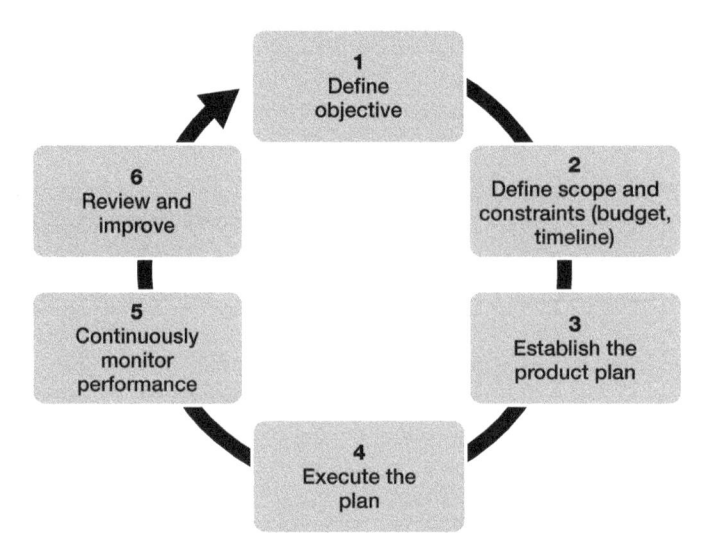

Figure 4: Project management six step model. Source: Legal Lean Sigma Institute LLC.

5. Continuously monitor performance and change management, including regular communication and establishing a continuous "feedback loop" to adjust as needed, as close in time to when they are needed.
6. Review and improve. Learning organizations focus on improvement over time.

Like PI, PM is not "one size fits all". There are different approaches to PM, such as Waterfall or Agile, that can be employed. The way we carry out the steps and the tools we use vary greatly from one organization or team to the next. There are many platforms and technology used to support PM, from simple to extremely robust. Like every process, we use the People, Process, Platform to determine our own requirements and then (and only then) do we select the approaches and technology tools we will use.

Many Legal Lean Sigma Institute clients ask, "In which should we invest and engage first – process improvement or project management?" The lawyerly answer is, of course, "It depends". The truth is that there is no one "right way" to begin. That stated, my bias and standard suggestion is for firms to learn the two disciplines at the same time and employ them together. This is exactly why the Legal Lean Sigma Institute developed the first and only certification courses for law that combine Lean, Six Sigma, and project management. Secondarily, I recommend engaging in process improvement first, so that a firm begins to improve processes and simultaneously to develop project management skills. After that, the firm can train project managers and others using optimized processes.

Whether you and your organization begin with process improvement or project management, eventually, both must be employed to fully realize the benefits of either one. We attain a multiplier effect when we combine process improvement and project management. That is because we have better, more standardized processes that are well controlled. In turn, that enables us to achieve a high level of performance.

Do the right things (Lean) the right way (Six Sigma) the first time, every time (project management).

When you begin to do process improvement work, you find out quickly that whatever you decide to do will impact one or more of the other "Ps" in the P+ Ecosystem (explored further in chapter eight), including planning, pricing, performance metrics and management, profitability, practice management and innovation, and, most important, people.

No matter what the situation or strategy, the sequence is *always* this:

People. Process. Platform.

The art and science of legal process improvement
We established that the concept of process improvement is simple – identify what is working or not working, capture or fix it, and enjoy the benefits. But, while the idea is clear, the work itself requires commitment, patience, resiliency, and a symphonic combination of art and science.

The methodologies contain proscribed, scientific methods with specifically sequenced activities to be followed in a disciplined manner. Selecting the right approach, applying the concepts and tools, and carrying out those activities as we work with a cross-functional, diverse team of people? That's the art of process improvement.

In law, my ballpark estimate of the balance is about 35 percent science, 65 percent art. This explains why having a skilled and experienced practitioner involved in the design and build of a program or in any project or other effort is so critical for success. Follow the proscribed method and it's practically fail-safe because the framework is considered scientific for a reason. As with all things in PI, it's iterative. Do a good job with each step and the next one is easier. However, the artful selection of different formats and ways to engage a team that bring out the best in people changes with every project and each team. Getting that right is so fundamental to successfully harnessing and unleashing the power of a cross-functional diverse team. People are first in the sequence, then process, then platform.

All of us use processes every day. We may not recognize what we are doing as a process and it may or may not be a good one, but the things we do involve a series of repeatable, describable steps and activities that are taken each time to complete it. All our processes can be improved, whether through simple fixes or by taking a more robust approach.

Since lawyers and those working in law the world over appear to be more easily persuaded by precedent and more motivated to be first to be second than they are by the idea of being the first to innovate, this book contains compelling case studies as to how Lean and Six Sigma have been applied in law.

The combination of Lean and Six Sigma, as well as the art and science involved, gives us some of the most powerful, effective approaches to employing process improvement. There is no question that opportunities for improvements and even innovation in law are virtually everywhere. When we start looking through the Lean Sigma lens, we cannot help but see many chances to make so many things so much better in our processes for the client, our organizations, and ourselves – with no tradeoffs. In fact, we begin to understand that there is greater risk in continuing to operate the way we are now than there is in changing the way we work and how we work together.

Lean Sigma offers us the methodology and frameworks for success.

References
1. Lean Enterprise Institute; see www.lean.org/WhatsLean/History.cfm.
2. First published in March 2012 and updated in February 2013; see www.levantar.co.uk/index.php/lean-consulting-training-strategy-reviews/lean-management-process-improvement-free-lean-guide-to.
3. www.law.com/international-edition/2001/01/24/management-how-general-electric-plugged-into-six-sigma/
4. www.sixsigmaonline.org/defects-per-million-opportunities-dpmo-six-sigma/
5. Adam Smith, Esq. LLC, "Conversation with Ray Bayley of NovusLaw"; see www.adamsmithesq.com/2008/06/a_conversation_with_ray_b.
6. www.quora.com/Why-is-6-sigma-called-6-sigma

Chapter 2:
The five key principles of Lean Sigma

Maintaining the client's perspective
Lean Sigma is both an approach and a toolkit. The methodology consists of investigating a process and improving it by using a set of five principles in a particular sequence.

There are variations of the five key principles. For example, Womack and Jones defined the five principles of Lean manufacturing in their book, *The Machine That Changed the World*.[1] The five principles are considered a recipe for improving workplace efficiency and include:
1. Defining value.
2. Mapping the value stream.
3. Creating flow.
4. Using a pull system.
5. Pursuing perfection.

The five key principles identified and used by the Legal Lean Sigma Institute are:
1. Specify value.
2. Reduce waste and variation.
3. Make value flow at the pull of the client.
4. Align and empower employees.
5. Continuously improve in pursuit of perfection.

See Figure 5 on the next page, on the five key principles of Lean Sigma.

1. Specify value in the eyes of the client
To better understand the first principle of defining customer value, it is important to appreciate what value is. Simply put, value is what the customer is willing to pay for. This means we must discover the actual or underlying requirements of our client(s). In law, the less sophisticated or knowledgeable the client is, the more likely it is that the client may not know what they need, want, or value, or are unable to articulate it in terms of work

Chapter 2: The five key principles of Lean Sigma

1	2	3	4	5
Specify value in the eyes of the client	Reduce waste and variation	Make value flow at the pull of the client	Align and empower employees	Continuously improve in pursuit of perfection

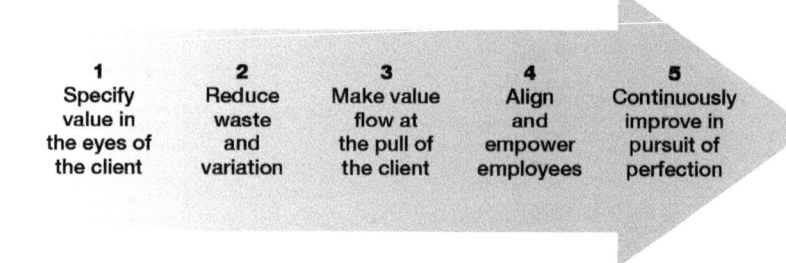

Figure 5: The five key principles of Lean Sigma. Source: Legal Lean Sigma Institute LLC.

product. However, more experienced clients will tell us in very clear terms what they want in requests for proposals (RfPs), outside counsel guidelines and in interviews, intake and strategy discussions, and project planning. Often, all we need to do is ask.

We can employ a wide range of techniques such as interviews, surveys, demographic information, and web analytics that give us answers to the question of what our clients find valuable. In law, they are often very clear as to the way they want to be served.

In this step, we use the client's perspective to evaluate whether an activity is value-adding (activities that work to create a feature or attribute the client is willing to pay for) or non-value-adding (activities that take time and resources, but do not create additional value for the client). All non-value-added activities are priority candidates for elimination or minimization.

Of course, we do not just indiscriminately cut anything or anyone from a process. In fact, there are many occasions where we may need to do more with more, or less with more, where additional people/resources are required to make a process efficient. Further, just because value is not clear to the client, that does not necessarily mean that the step should be eliminated. It is an opportunity for a discussion about why something is necessary, advisable, or important to do from the lawyer's perspective. Even after discussion, the client might not find the activity valuable – this is an even greater reason to be highly efficient.

For any processes, we consider:
- What is the value of the process in the eyes of the client?
- How do you establish this (or how would you find out)?
- What do you do that your clients might not consider valuable?

- What waste is there in the process?
- What are the effects of variation in your processes on your firm and on your clients?

2. Reduce waste and variation

Waste and variation are Lean and Six Sigma terms, respectively. In this step, we identify tasks as one (or more) of the eight kinds of waste and flag it for potential reduction or outright elimination. At the same time, we are cognizant of the fact that processes are harder to operate and require more resources if they vary. Moreover, when processes vary, sometimes the results will be outside the client's acceptable range.

This second principle is where we identify and map the workflow. In this step, we use the client's definitions of value as a reference point. We identify all the activities that contribute to those values. Activities that do not add value to the end client (as opposed to the users of the process) are considered waste and therefore become candidates for reduction or elimination.

The waste that we identify can be either non-value added but necessary or non-value added and unnecessary. Anything that is non-value but necessary should be reduced as much as is possible. Activities that are non-value and unnecessary are considered pure waste and should be eliminated. This is an excellent way to get quick wins and achieve immediate improvements.

Another benefit to mapping the workflow is that it gives us a visual aid. Often, when we do even basic process mapping, it the first time anyone has shown – rather than just "talked through" – all the high-level steps and tasks. With a map, we can also see which processes are owned by what person or functional area or teams. We can also employ the RACI model (Responsible, Accountable, Consulted, Informed) and start discussing who is responsible and accountable for measuring, evaluating, and improving the process and who needs to be consulted and informed.

This principle reinforces that, by reducing and eliminating unnecessary processes or steps, we can ensure that our end-user clients are getting exactly what they want while at the same time producing benefits to ourselves, such as reducing our cost of producing the work or delivering the service.

3. Make value flow at the pull of the client

When a process has "flow", the steps are closely linked together with no DOWN-TIME waste (see chapter one). It means we are moving from one value-adding activity directly to another, without stopping or waiting. Non-value-added steps have been eliminated and activities are completed with little to no lag time. This means there is no waiting or batching and the process takes the shortest possible time from the beginning to the end.

The idea of "pull" is that an individual, team, or organization is able to create value directly in response to actual client demand. Providing exactly what the client wants and acting exactly when the client wants (and at the last possible moment) requires all process steps to be closely coordinated to work together seamlessly.

This is the promise of Lean Sigma – simpler, faster processes that are predictable and meet client requirements. A shorter cycle time where we do things right allows us to be very responsive to the client. Responsiveness is something that every single one of the Legal Lean Sigma Institute clients cares about and has prioritized.

This makes sense. After all, we are all consumers and we are living in an "on demand" world, where every one of us wants – and expects – frictionless interactions. Reflect on your own customer experience and how much we value a seamless, no hassle interaction with a brand throughout the entire journey. This is why we do journey mapping, to understand all the touchpoints we have, both seen and hidden with our clients. By eliminating unnecessary barriers and making every step feel effortless, we can give clients what they want, when they want it, the way they'd like to receive it.

Often, increased attention to this results in the integration of technology tools. Even simple applications, such as chat boxes and calendaring, can greatly reduce the friction that clients experience in working with us. What impression does it make on a client working with various firms when one is focused on making value flow and the other isn't? Let's say Firm 1 offers online polling about availability to a larger group so we can quickly reach consensus about when to meet. It also offers individual online calendaring with a link in every email so that clients can simply schedule an appointment without any humans being involved. In comparison, Firm 2 requires going back and forth by email, often with an assistant. We've all been there: "Dates 1, 2, and 3 work for me." "Sorry, what about 4, 5, or 6?" "Unfortunately, no, what about…" "Are you Ok with just person A and C meeting so we can move forward?" (Oops, did that step on someone's toes?) and so on… So much effort and attention, just to schedule a meeting or appointment when the actual work will be done.

4. Align and empower employees

To successfully, continuously improve, we must harness and unleash the power of great teams. There are teams of grouped individuals, where each member of the team is carrying out separate aspects of a project. Other teams that act as an extension of the leader. The third type – the integrated, true team – is able to leverage individual strengths to achieve extraordinary capacity for coordinated action. This is the kind of team we are aiming for, not only when we deliver process improvement projects but in the teams delivering client work and service.

Aligning and empowering employees are two key aspects of effective leadership and management that contribute to a positive workplace culture and improved organizational performance. Here's what they mean.

Aligning

Aligning employees refers to the process of ensuring that everyone in the organization understands and supports the company's mission, vision, values, and strategic goals. It involves creating a shared sense of purpose and direction across all levels of the organization.

The key components of aligning employees are:
- *Clear communication.* Leaders must clearly communicate the organization's goals, expectations, and how each employee's role contributes to these objectives.
- *Goal setting.* Aligning individual and team goals with the overall strategy ensures everyone is working towards the same outcomes.
- *Consistent messaging.* Reinforcing the organization's mission and values through regular updates, meetings, and internal communications.
- *Leadership example.* Leaders must embody the values and behaviors they want to see in their employees, setting a standard for alignment.
- *Feedback and adjustment.* Regularly reviewing progress and providing feedback to ensure that everyone stays aligned with the organizational goals.

Law is deeply entrenched in the war for talent – and that is not restricted to laterals in firms. It extends to the top business talent as well. In recent years, we have seen marketing and business development departments leave firms en masse. Imagine losing an entire department, and all its (undocumented) knowledge, overnight. How long and how much effort would it take to recover?

Aligning employees is an incredibly powerful response to the employee experience that delivers unparalleled benefits and advantages. Those include improved collaboration and teamwork, greater focus and efficiency, and higher levels of investment as well as improved morale, experience, and satisfaction levels. Finally, it produces demonstrably better overall organizational performance.

Empowering

Empowering employees means giving them the autonomy, resources, and confidence they need to take initiative, make decisions, and contribute to the organization's success. It involves trusting them to do their jobs effectively and supporting them in their professional growth.

Empowering employees involves:
- *Autonomy.* Allow employees the freedom to make decisions related to their work, encouraging innovation and ownership. My own interpretation of this includes the notion that legal professionals (partners) should defer to the expertise of business professionals in law, get out of their way, and let them run things.
- *Access to resources.* Provide the tools, training, and support needed for employees to succeed in their roles.
- *Encouragement and trust.* Build a culture of trust and inclusion where employees feel valued, heard, and seen, and are encouraged to take risks without fear of failure. Easier said than done in law, but it is possible!
- *Recognition and rewards.* Acknowledging and rewarding contributions and achievements to reinforce the behaviors we want to encourage.
- *Professional development.* Offer opportunities and reward employees for learning and skill-building. This includes career advancement to help employees grow within the organization – so many business professionals are not afforded this opportunity and feel they have to leave a firm they like just to advance in their careers.

The benefits of empowerment include increased motivation and job satisfaction, higher productivity and creativity, and enhanced problem-solving and innovation. The organization realizes greater employee retention and loyalty and is more dynamic and responsive.

When employees are both aligned with the organization's goals and empowered to take action, they are more likely to be engaged, productive, and committed to the company's success. This principle also happens to directly support diversity, equity, inclusion, and accessibility initiatives.

Whether the principle is applied in the context of process improvement or as a standalone, the combination of alignment and empowerment fosters a strong, cohesive workforce that can adapt to challenges and drive the organization forward. That, in and of itself, is a competitive advantage.

5. Continuously improve in pursuit of perfection
Because changes in the business environment are constant and rapid, they create requirements for higher process capabilities and efficiencies. If we do not continuously improve, we lose our ability to compete and function.

As such, this last principle may be the most important one. We should make sure that employees on every level are involved in continuously improving processes. Becoming a learning organization is a strategic objective worthy of inclusion in your plans.

There are "breakthrough" and "incremental" improvements. Where employees are encouraged and motivated to find ways to get better with each day, they will not only achieve process improvements, but also directly contribute to creating a culture of continuous improvement, our ultimate goal.

The "laws"
There are four other "laws" that are useful for us to consider.[2]

The law of flexibility
The law of flexibility states that the speed or velocity of any process is correlated to its ability to adapt to changing requirements. If you want to deliver fast, you need to decrease the time it takes for your process to changeover from one specification to another. Any time that is spent on changeover is essentially lost or unproductive time. Building a process that is agile and flexible will allow businesses to meet delivery requirements and expectations despite changing demands. This is especially crucial for complex businesses that offer various product and service options.

The law of focus
The law of focus takes its cue from the Pareto Principle. This law states that 80 percent of the delays experienced in any business process are caused by 20 percent of the process activities. To increase gains from any process improvement initiative, businesses must focus on improving and optimizing those 20 percent activities. During your Lean Six Sigma project implemen-

tation, you'll get to recognize that these 20 percent activities are mostly non-value adding. Eliminating or reducing the time spent on non-value adding activities will allow your business to focus its resources on value-adding activities. This results in higher levels of cost-efficiency.

The law of velocity
Also known as Little's Law, the law of velocity states that the speed of a process is inversely related to the amount of work-in-progress (WIP) items at any given time.

$$\text{Lead time} = \frac{\text{Number of WIP items}}{\text{Average completion rate}}$$

Our metric for speed, in this case, is the *lead time*, which is the amount of time it takes for a product or service to be completed from the time the customer/client request is triggered. Average completion rate is the number of work items that get finished within a given period.

Using this formula, we know that, the more WIP items in your process, the slower it gets. By limiting the number of WIP items in your system, you can lower your lead time and deliver faster to customers. Kanban,[3] one of the pillars of the Toyota Production System,[4] complements this law. One of its key properties is to limit work-in-progress[5] to avoid tasks from accumulating at any point in the process.

The law of complexity and cost
In Lean Six Sigma terms, process complexity can be described by the different types of products, services, variations, parts, options, or features that your processes handle. While some complexity or variation is beneficial as this provides options to customers and can cater to varying preferences, too much complexity can only become costly for businesses. The law of complexity and cost pushes businesses to find the balance in terms of process complexity, cost, and speed.

Applying the Lean Sigma principles
The five Lean Sigma principles provide a framework for creating an efficient and effective organization. They encourage creating better flow in work processes and developing a continuous improvement culture. By practicing all five principles, an organization can remain competitive, increase value

delivered to customers, decrease the cost of doing business, and increase its profitability.

References
1. Roos, Daniel; Womack, James P.; Jones, Daniel T.: *The Machine That Changed the World: The Story of Lean Production*, Harper Perennial (November 1990).
2. https://kanbanzone.com/2020/5-laws-of-lean-six-sigma/
3. https://kanbanzone.com/resources/kanban/
4. https://kanbanzone.com/resources/lean/toyota-production-system/
5. https://kanbanzone.com/resources/kanban/wip-limits/

Chapter 3:
DMAIC – a data-driven, problem-solving framework

After a project is prioritized and resourced, a good process improvement methodology must be used to deliver results reliably. Lean Sigma uses a disciplined, data-driven problem-solving approach known as DMAIC (pronounced Da-MAY-ic). That stands for Define, Measure, Analyze, Improve, Control.

This acronym is practically a mantra for process improvement practitioners everywhere because it can be used for projects as well as strategy, and it can be implemented as a standalone quality improvement procedure or as part of other process improvement initiatives.

Using DMAIC for projects
Following the DMAIC framework significantly improves the probability of project success. That is because it provides us with a proscribed sequence of steps that includes change management components and helpful ways of thinking through and analyzing many different questions and situations.

With DMAIC, we are encouraged to specifically Define the problem or opportunity, Measure the process performance and find out what is happening, Analyze why those things are occurring, and only then to decide on solutions that Improve the process.

A more typical approach for most people seems to be that we leap from having a fairly vague notion about the current state to selecting a solution (and getting a bit entrenched) very quickly. As most people realize, this approach involves a great deal of guesswork. While it is inexpensive to guess, it can be very expensive (and a colossal waste of time) to guess wrong.

At first, it is challenging for "fix it" type people who are experienced and intelligent (and who often have pent up grievances and easily implementable ideas) to be patient. Typically, teams are ready to start "solutioning" right away. Following DMAIC can be particularly challenging for those who are untrained and new to process improvement.

It may also be somewhat difficult to restrain lawyers – we are trained to issue spot, and then jump right into falling in love with our favorite answer in a very short period of time. When we liken this to a more extended version of IRAC – Issue, Rule, Analysis, Conclusion – that most of us learned in school, it feels and sounds more familiar. This is an example of the "art" aspect of process improvement, where we experience a small victory and build a bridge and experience small victories along the way.

Incidentally, I strongly prefer CIRFAC – Conclusion, Issue, Rule, Facts, Analysis, Conclusion – which is a more effective presentation for all personality types and communication styles. It can be used in oral and written communications, and CEO types in particular appreciate the "no scroll" approach and getting the conclusion right at the top of the message.

However, without exception, by the time we have moved through the D, M, and A phases, project teams agree that it was worth not skipping steps and delaying our problem-solving until we had a deep understanding of what, exactly, we are solving for.

Why DMAIC is effective

DMAIC contains highly effective safeguards that help the team and project be successful. This includes the all-important meetings where a project team presents to a small group of decision-makers appointed as a steering committee. These toll gates or gate reviews take place at the conclusion of each phase. The team presents its work and requests the steering committee's permission to move on to the next phase. This ensures that we are communicating as we progress with our projects and that we are employing good change management techniques.

Thus, after (and sometimes during) each phase, the process improvement project team meets with the project sponsor and a steering committee that is typically comprised of cross-functional leaders in the firm to pass through "gate reviews" or "toll gates". In these meetings, the steering committee holds the team responsible for completing specific deliverables that are required in each phase and ensures the team has addressed all the important considerations. They also offer additional perspective, information, suggestions, and feedback.

Thus, rather than complete a project from start to finish and then deliver the results, the approach demanded by process improvement is for our cross-functional and diverse team to regularly check-in with its project sponsor and engage in gate reviews with a group of decision makers that stays with the project from start to finish. This format builds in regular and ongoing communication for the duration of the project and provides a forum for the team to share its work as it progresses from diagnosing, measuring, and analyzing the process to finally developing improvement ideas. The shareholders also have opportunities to contribute their diverse perspectives, expertise, and resources on an ongoing basis – this is built into the process of process improvement.

DMAIC builds in failure avoidance due to its design and rigor. It incorporates change management principles to ensure consensus is built as the project team progresses through each phase. Thus, there are numerous benefits to following the framework and to never skipping steps.

The five steps of DMAIC

Define	Define the problem and why it needs to be solved
Measure	Measure the current performance of the process
Analyze	Analyze the opportunities to reduce waste or variation
Improve	Improve the process by identifying, implementing and validating process changes
Control	Control the process by implementing methods to ensure improvements will be sustainable

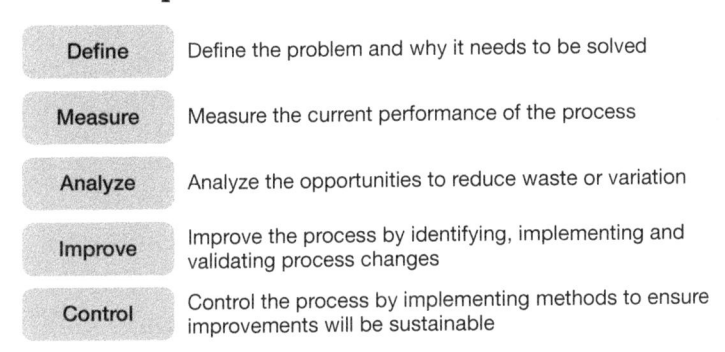

Figure 6: DMAIC – the framework for PI projects.

The five DMAIC steps of Define, Measure, Analyze, Improve, and Control are always performed in that exact sequence, without ever skipping steps – see Figure 6.

1. Define the problem and articulate why it needs to be solved.
2. Measure the current performance of the process.
3. Analyze the opportunities to reduce waste or variation, identify root causes.
4. Improve the process by developing solutions to address root causes, then identify, implement, and validate process changes.
5. Control the process – ensure improvements achieve project goals, will be sustainable and monitored, and are translated into benefits.

Step 1: Define
At the end of each phase, the team is required to produce written deliverables. The Define phase requirements are:

1. Project charter.
2. Documented client requirements.
3. Document the process.

It is vital to not shortcut this phase. Everything else is dependent on the work we do here. Expert facilitation by an experience Lean Sigma practitioner is critical. Because everything else will be built on this foundation, it must therefore be strong.

In this phase we initiate the project, form the team, and have a kickoff "Define" phase workshop. We start out with good project management and strong facilitation, which are employed before and throughout every phase. We assign roles, explain responsibilities, develop a project charter and a project management plan, and agree on project implementation details, such as tracking, responsibilities, a repository for our work, file, and email naming conventions, and establish ground rules for working together. We ensure that there is strong sponsorship and ownership and determine the most useful problem-solving approaches for the problem.

In Define, we begin our journey through DMAIC. The tool we use first is important to master – the project charter. As we work through the elements of the charter, we develop a solid document with an overview of the project. It clearly states the project's goals and objectives, articulates the business case, sets the scope and boundaries, identifies resources and participants, establishes target dates, and documents issues, concerns, and anticipated outcomes of the project.

By engaging in deep thinking, listening, and a series of discussions, our cross-functional, diverse team begins its work to explore and understand where we have issues. Stakeholders are identified, and voices and requirements of the clients are gathered, understood, and documented. Since the primary goal of this phase is to ensure that the team members involved in the project focus on the business problems, the team ensures that the needs and requirements of the clients are aligned with the project goals.

Accordingly, we typically conduct a stakeholder analysis first. It is essential to understand stakeholder interests, power, and influence on the project so that we may carry it out in the most effective, thoughtful, and appropriately inclusive manner. We do not want to inadvertently reorganize someone else's process for them – in law especially we are likely to get massive, passive resistance at best and outright refusal to change at worst. Important stakeholders are identified; their needs and requirements are properly documented.

One of the important decisions a team must make in this phase is whether it has a serious business issue to work on, one that truly is worthy of allocating resources to address at this time. If not, it may recommend to the steering committee that it pauses or ends its work. Due to solid pre-project planning, it is unlikely but possible that a team working on a project is unable to convince itself that the project it has been asked to deliver is addressing something important enough to prioritize and resource. When and if that happens, however, realizing this fact early saves the organization more than time and resources – it prevents a poor outcome, negative experience, or failure.

The team reaches consensus about the real nature of the problem or opportunity, how it really knows it's a problem or opportunity (meaning, what evidence does it have), why it should pay attention to it, and what could happen if it doesn't. That last question can often be the most compelling reason to do anything and can be highly motivating. It also taps into something lawyers are very good at, which is imagining worst case scenarios. They are far more likely to change when the team makes a good case that it is less riskier to do so than to continue operating as it is now.

Because it is so important, Lean Sigma Principle 1 – "Specify value in the eyes of the client" – is addressed at the very beginning of the project. It is imperative that we understand both "Product" requirements, which are the features of the final product delivered to the client, and "Experience" requirements – how the client expects to be treated and served during the relationship with the individual, team, or organization.

One of the tools we use to determine client requirements is Moments of Truth. A Moment of Truth is any opportunity to make an impression (good or bad) on a client. It is a specific point on the customer journey, where the customer forms an indelible impression of the product, brand, or service, which influences a later decision.

Let's use a simple example to illustrate what is meant by a "specific point". What is it like to visit your office for the first time? Parking alone could involve a dozen Moments of Truth.

- Is it easy to find parking?
- Does it cost money to park?
- Can I pay with my phone/cash/credit card?
- Is it expensive to park? (And do you validate parking if so?)
- Are there spots close to the entrance?
- Is there good signage?
- Is it in a garage?

- Is the garage part of your office building?
- Is the garage bright and clean or dark and dirty?
- Are the parking spaces tight?
- Is it a multi-floor garage?
- Are there visual cues so that I'll remember what floor I'm on?
- Are the spaces numbered?
- Are there charging stations?
- Is there a card at the elevator with the floor number on it so I don't have to try and remember?
- Is the parking area safe?
- Is there security?

This relatively minor step can greatly impact someone's impression of you and your organization – and it has nothing to do with the reason they are visiting you. Also, it's just one touchpoint in their journey. Everything we do touches our clients in one way or another. Paying attention to Moments of Truth is an absolute must for any organization claiming to care about clients or that it is client-centered (which is every organization!).

There is usually not one "most important" client concern, but, rather, several "more important" concerns. These are called "critical to quality" (CTQ) and are the quality for which the client pays.

CTQs must be 1) limited in number and 2) measurable to be useful to us. They are linked to a specific product, service, or event ("Moment of Truth"). Typically, a CTQ involves a single performance criterion, such as cost, speed, or quality, which is measurable, based on real data, and validated periodically. Most importantly, the CTQ distinguishes between acceptable and unacceptable performance.

One universal CTQ is quality. Embedded within that is the idea that the first sign of quality is constancy. Clients typically do not notice the average performance, but they do notice variation.

After we document the client requirements, the last thing we will do in Define is to start mapping the process. This helps set process boundaries, identifies input and output variables, and begins to familiarize team with process. A useful high level process mapping tool is the IPO Diagram (Inputs – Process – Outputs). Some organizations use the more robust SIPOC, which stands for suppliers, inputs, process, outputs, customers/clients.

The team then prepares its required written deliverables for the first gate review or toll gate with the steering committee:

- Create and approve a project charter.
- Identify client requirements.
- Identify and document the process.

Everyone should be present during each gate review. We work as a team. We also clearly demonstrate to the steering committee that we have established a level playing field and that each person is an equal and a respected and valued member regardless of position or title outside of the project.

When we get approval, we are ready to move on to the "Measure" phase.

Step 2: Measure
In the "Measure" phase, we concentrate on Lean Sigma Principle 2: "Identify waste and variation" by measuring the process. Thus, one of our first tasks is to do more robust process mapping, using one or more of a variety of process map types.

In this way, we gain a thorough understanding of the current state of our process (how we do things now); therefore, the team must have the ability to do both basic process mapping (IPO, block, top-down, detailed) and specialized mapping (swim lane map, spaghetti diagram, information flow diagram, time-value analysis), each of which shows the same process from a different vantage point.

A block diagram, for example, shows the whole process in just a few, key steps. A top-down map shows sub-tasks under the main blocks. A detailed map shows all the steps with their relationships to all the other steps, including those that are wasteful, such as waiting and re-work.

Specialized process maps are created to highlight particular kinds of issues or waste. In law, we usually develop a top-down map to show the sequence as well as a swim lane, which shows how all the functions involved in a process do their work as well as interact with one another. This means we can clearly see where we have handoffs. Since waste always accrues at boundaries, wherever there are handoffs, we are likely to find one or more of the eight kinds of waste – and those become candidates for reduction or elimination.

Process mapping is engaging and fun. It's an opportunity to bring in some of the stakeholders who aren't on the team to contribute. It makes for an excellent day of team building and seems to open people up to conversations that were maybe considered "difficult" before. More law departments and clients are collaborating with their law firms in process mapping workshops – the experience produces interactions and results that are unmatched by other activities.

Process mapping has many benefits, including being able to see the actual process (often for the first time) from start to finish. We all know that pictures are worth a thousand words. This makes process improvement, identifying issues, and changing processes much easier. In fact, visualizing processes makes the problems clearer from the start. And "show me" is better than "tell me". One of the hardest things for a team is to resist the temptation to fix anything as we are mapping, but to capture the current state in all its beauty or ugliness. So often, there are "facepalm" moments, such as, "I had no idea what I did here affected you at a different point in the process" or, "Wow, why can't we just do this earlier / later / differently". Those reactions are precedent to making any changes, whether they are small or dramatic.

Besides project work, process maps are excellent tools for communications with clients and teams and project management. A map can support relationship, client, or business development efforts not only by engaging people in conversations that elicit potential points of collaboration and differentiation, but because a client, prospect, or referral source can see you know what you're doing, because you have a process. Activities like onboarding, training, and teamwork are far more effective through visualization.

In the Measure phase, the team establishes a baseline of performance against which to measure progress. It will usually gather a significant amount of data to learn how the process is working (or not) and to identify waste and variation, defects, and causes of defects. Using good project management techniques, it develops a measurement strategy and plan.

First, the team needs to generate ideas about what it wants to know and what it wants to measure. To do this, it employs tools such as an issue diagram and/or a measurement assessment tree, which help a team think through and organize a complex problem.

To create an issue diagram, the team starts with the problem / opportunity statement in the project charter. Then, it can take one of two approaches. In the top-down approach, it brainstorms major categories of issues that are or might be related to its problem / opportunity and explores each category down to one or two levels of detail. The bottom-up approach involves having the team brainstorm issues individually – I often have them work quietly on sticky notes for this, which is ideal for anyone with a preference for introversion. Then, we talk about the issues they thought of or suspect they exist. We group them by affinity and start to see certain areas of inquiry emerging, such as process, communication, policy, or training issues, just to name a few common categories.

A Measurement Assessment Tree is another effective tool for planning data-gathering to answer key questions about the process. It uses two concepts – critical-to-quality outputs (the things in which the client is most interested) and stratification. We start by identifying one key output. Then, we think about the factors that might influence the type or amount of the output. Next, we identify specific types of data to collect that would answer the question of how the stratification factor did or did not affect the output. This tool supports logical and linear type of thinking, so it is quite effective for use in the law.

Next, we put together a data collection and sampling plan, deciding what we will measure, how much of it will be helpful, where we can get it, what format we want, who is responsible for hunting it down, and when it is due. It is important to measure variations (range, deviations), averages, patterns, trends, and comparisons to competitors. The team will think about how it measures, selects what to measure, and identifies data sources.

We sometimes describe this gathering step as a big "fishing expedition" where we cast a net to see what can be learned and what is (or is not, which is also valuable to learn) available. It is an iterative process, since a team might be (and often is) surprised by what is and what is not currently available in a firm, either in terms of ease of access, quantity, or quality. The Measure phase is like swimming in murky waters. Team members who prize clarity will need to get comfortable being uncomfortable until things become clearer.

There is a hierarchy of data with respect to its usefulness and validity:
1. Reliable data that can be extracted from a system in electronic format.
2. Data that exists, but not in a convenient format (for example, paper files), which requires the team to figure out where it is, extract it, and then put it in a useful format, such as a spreadsheet.
3. Data that does not yet exist, but can be created using observation worksheets, surveys, and log sheets.
4. Externally available data, which usually is not specific to the firm, but may still be useful.
5. Estimations and opinion, which is better than nothing but not ideal. Usually, this involves asking several knowledgeable people and collating opinions.

6. Anecdotes, which might be useful as a last resort. However, we have to be sure to understand the frequency of any occurrence rather than relying on one person's perception or experience.1

While the deep analysis of our data will take place in the next phase ("Analyze"), long before that the team will need to understand what the data means and whether it has answered the questions raised so far in the project. Remember, we are hoping to learn how the current process is performing, so we want to gather and analyze benchmarking data in two dimensions – process capability and process efficiency.

Creating a visual representation of data is a powerful first step towards understanding. Graphical data analysis is the process of making sense of the data, determining if it is adequate, and representing it in a way that informs and highlights key information. Each data point collected will be displayed in charts and graphs (like Pareto charts, run charts, and histograms). This can be a laborious process for some organizations. Others have business analysts and data in formats that make it easier.

Now that the data tells the story, the team can begin describing the current state of the process very clearly and accurately; this is usually the first time a firm has ever truly understood how a process has been performing with such depth and accuracy. Typically, it is very eye opening. It can also be alarming; it is more likely than not that the process is performing even more badly than people thought.

The good news is that at this point in the project, a team will have a lot of data about the process, including process maps showing steps and waste, characterization data showing overall process capability and efficiency along several dimensions, and stratification data showing patterns and providing clues to causes.

At this point, the team knows what is happening in the process – in fact, it knows more about the process than anyone ever has. The team are experts. They are ready to summarize and prioritize the areas of opportunity into a limited number of "focus areas". These are the things the team has become most interested in analyzing in greater detail in the next phase.

Finally, we use our graphical displays to help us create a storyboard that explains our logic to the steering committee. Now, the team gets ready for another gate review. If it is meeting in person, at this point in the project, the walls of the room in which the team is working are covered with graphics, charts, flip chart papers, and sticky notes.

As such, we want to assemble the relevant data points and organize the analyses into a logical order that tells a story. We are taking data, turning it into information, and then translating that into knowledge and even wisdom that is shared with the steering committee. The first and last displays in the story should summarize the key points. It is best if the steering committee is able to be on site for this gate review and to view all the required written deliverables:
- All critical processes have been thoroughly and appropriately mapped.
- The team has thought through the questions it has about the process and the potential process issues and created a measurement plan.
- Stratification data has been gathered to look for patterns and causes.
- Focus areas have been identified and supported by data; a storyboard explaining its logic has been started.

Now that we know what is happening in the process, it is time to explore the focus areas and see if we can learn why those things are occurring.

Step 3: Analyze
In "Analyze", we examine each focus area to identify and verify waste, defects, and determine root causes. Root cause analysis takes place in three steps:
1. Exploring.
2. Generating hypotheses.
3. Verifying causes.

The team uses the data gathered in the measure phase to find patterns, trends, and other differences that suggest or support theories about the causes of waste or defects. Naturally, it may need to gather further data to complete its analysis.

The first step is to explore each focus area. The team begins by assembling all the process maps and analyses that relate to each focus area. Using the Lean perspective, the team annotates each process map with notes, highlighting non-value-added steps, waste, potential causes of problems, and ideas for further exploration. All process maps are useful for asking whether steps are non-value-add. In particular, the team looks for disconnects, decision points, inspection points, redundancies, and rework loops.

The team takes a similar approach to the graphical analyses, annotating each one with notes about interesting observations, patterns, and trends.

Finally, the team determines whether other tools or analyses might be useful in exploring the focus areas. To complete the Explore step, for each focus area, the team creates a summary of interesting observations and questions.

The second step is to generate hypotheses for the causes of the waste or defects. At the end of the explore step, the team has a list of interesting observations, waste, problems, and questions. Two commonly used tools for root cause analysis are the fishbone (or cause and effect) diagram and the Five Whys technique.

A Fishbone Diagram, also known as an Ishikawa diagram or Cause-and-Effect diagram, is a visual tool used for identifying, organizing, and analyzing the potential causes of a problem. It's called a "Fishbone" diagram because its structure resembles the skeleton of a fish, with the problem at the "head" and the causes branching off like bones. A Fishbone diagram is used to systematically explore the possible causes of a problem to identify its root cause(s). It is widely used in quality control, project management, and process improvement.

1. *The Problem (head of the fish)*. The problem or undesirable effect the team wants to analyze is placed at the "head" of the diagram. This is usually a clear and concise statement of the issue.
2. *Major Categories (bones of the fish)*. These are the main branches that extend from the central line (the "spine" of the fish). Each branch represents a category of potential causes. Common categories include:
   - *People*. Human factors, such as skills, training, or behavior.
   - *Process*. The procedures or steps followed in completing a task.
   - *Equipment*. Tools, machinery, or technology involved.
   - *Materials*. Raw materials or resources used in the process.
   - *Environment*. External conditions like temperature, lighting, or cultural factors.
   - *Methods*. The techniques or approaches used to perform tasks.
   - *Measurements*. Data, metrics, or measurement systems involved.
3. *Sub-Causes (smaller bones)*. These are smaller branches that stem from the major categories. They represent specific factors within each category that could contribute to the problem. Each sub-cause is explored further to identify its impact on the problem.
4. *Root Cause Identification*. By examining the diagram, teams can identify which causes are most likely contributing to the problem. The goal is to drill down through the layers of causes to uncover the root cause(s).

The Five Whys technique is a problem-solving method used to identify the root cause of a problem by asking "Why?" multiple times – typically five, though it can be more or less, depending on the situation. The idea is to move beyond the symptoms of the problem and uncover the underlying issue that is causing it. It can be used with the Fishbone diagram or on its own.

The way it works is to:
1. *Identify the problem.* Start with a clear and specific statement of the problem we are facing.
2. *Ask the First "Why".* Ask why the problem is occurring. This leads us to an initial cause.
3. *Ask the Second "Why".* Once we have the answer to the first "Why," ask "Why?" again to dig deeper into that cause.
4. *Continue asking "Why" (third, fourth, and fifth Why).* Repeat the process, each time asking why the previous cause happened, until we reach a root cause.
5. *Identify the Root Cause.* By the time you reach the fifth "Why", you should have a clearer understanding of the fundamental cause of the problem.

The Five Whys is an effective technique, especially in law, because it feels very natural to us. It is simple, easy, and it can be done quickly, so it leads to immediate insights. Be careful to not stop too early. That only leads to addressing symptoms and not resolving things at the root cause. Also, beware of biases. The answers in Five Whys depend heavily on the knowledge and experience of those involved. Done well, the Five Whys technique helps teams address problems in ways that lead to lasting improvements and reduce the likelihood of issues recurring.

In the last step of the Analyze phase, the team uses data to verify or discard its hypotheses about causes. Then, it prepares for its gate review. It confirms for the steering committee that it has:

- Examined focus areas for bottlenecks, disconnects, and redundancies that might contribute to waste.
- Analyzed data to understand potential root causes of problems and defects.
- Developed root cause hypotheses for the problem.
- Investigated and verified root cause hypotheses to isolate the "vital few" root causes.

The team then gets permission to move on to the next phase. Finally, the team gets to improve the process! At this point, it is (hopefully) clear how important it is to never skip steps in the DMAIC approach. If we were to begin to develop or get stubborn about solutions too early, we would not identify the best or even right answers. How could we without having conducted any root cause analysis?

Step 4: Improve
In the Improve phase, the team generates and develops creative solutions that address the root causes confirmed in the Analyze phase. It will follow a specific series of steps in this phase, being careful not to skip any.

The first thing it will do is write a new problem statement. Now that it has identified focus areas and root causes for each one and has data to show its knowledge about the effects of those things and their impact, its problem statement will be quite different to the one it developed for the project charter. The Improve Phase problem statement will clearly document the problem with the team's deeper understanding so that every team member has the same appreciation of what must be improved.

Next, the team will create solution specifications, also known as solution filters. This gives it a mechanism with which to evaluate potential solutions. To be effective, the specification describes how a good solution looks and feels, or what it can do, but not what the solution is. A good example is, if you were looking for a new home, you would have a list of "must have" and "nice to have" attributes you give to your real estate agent so they can determine which properties to show you. Good solution specs identify target performance or important constraints, such as budget, timing, and what it will enable or be capable of doing.

Once the filter is done, the team is ready to brainstorm! Solutions must address root causes and support the team's original goals. The team must generate a quantity of creative solution ideas and then prioritize the best solutions to avoid taking on too many activities. Also, the solutions must be cost effective and must not be so disruptive that those involved in implementation fail to support them.

We teach structured brainstorming techniques:
- *Channeling* is where we brainstorm categories of solutions and then ideate within a category before "switching channels" to the next one. This expands the types of ideas generated.
- *Anti-solution* helps us when the team is not generating ideas or is

stalled. This one gets people laughing, because the approach is to think of the worst or silliest ideas to solve the problem – in other words, the opposite of a good solution. It is very easy to switch gears and figure out how to build on those anti-solutions and make them workable.
- *Analogy* moves the team's minds to a more creative place. We think of situations or problems from a completely different field, analogous to the one we are working on, and discuss how the problem is solved in that field. Then, we determine whether and how to translate any of these solutions to our situation.

Another way to engage in structured brainstorming is the Billboard approach, which we now think of as crowdsourcing. That's highly effective for geographically disperse teams.

Now we are ready to analyze and select solutions. The team understands the solution ideas it has generated and has some sense of which solutions have great potential and are a fit – in this step the team will first filter the solutions through the filter we developed. Then, we select the vital few to pursue.

Again, PI offers us an assortment of tools to choose from. Depending on the team's preference, we might use a force field analysis, where we consider what driving and restraining forces exist within the organization that will support or sabotage an alternative. A simpler tool, with which everyone is familiar, is the straightforward pros and cons analysis. For a very robust approach, we might use a weighted decision matrix of our solution specifications and evaluate our solutions against each of the requirements. Alternatively, we could use a PICK (Possible-Progress, Implement, Consider, Kill) chart also known as an impact / ease matrix – it is a square with four quadrants with an Impact axis and an Effort axis. For each solution, we determine the level of effort and the likely impact, then place it in a quadrant. We may determine that we are only going to propose medium to high impact projects that are an easy- to medium-degree of difficulty to implement, for example.

At this point, the team will meet with the steering committee to present its recommendations. Because we have brought the team along in our thinking every step of the way, the committee understands the reasons for the proposals and is more likely to approve piloting. Once the team get approval, the selected solutions must be tested before full-scale implementation to ensure they are effective and implementable.

Testing our ideas by conducting a pilot involves creating a pilot planning checklist and making sure we are as contained as we can be so that we are trying out our ideas in a safe environment. After all, we won't have a second chance to get it right the first time. Also, risk makes lawyers extremely uncomfortable.

Options include a limited pilot where we test for a limited time, with a limited group of employees, clients, and issues, or a partial solution where we break the solution into parts and test some components. A different way to pilot is to conduct a real-life simulation where we create a dummy operation and test the solution on it. Similarly, we could also try a modeled simulation by creating a scaled version of the problem concentrated in time and space to test the solution. A tech / computer / AI simulation allows us to rapidly test many different conditions.

To capture our learnings, we always conduct After-Action Reviews where we document details about what we did and who was involved, what we wanted to accomplish, what we planned to do, what we actually did, what we accomplished and what we will do next time. This information will be shared with the steering committee and, when there is agreement that the solutions are ready for prime time, we will get ready to roll them out.

Full-Scale Implementation is like piloting, but with much less control and also much more at stake. Because of that, we will need to plan in detail all elements of communication, training, documentation, troubleshooting, measurement, and performance management.

When we are ready for our Improve phase gate review, the team will rewind a little to prepare the presentation to the steering committee, even though it has met with them at several key points in this phase.

- A prioritized list of potential solutions.
- High-potential solutions further developed and analyzed; recommendations agreed to.
- Pilot planned, executed, and debriefed.
- Solution(s) have been further refined based on pilot results.
- A full-scale implementation plan has been developed and includes plans for all major elements of implementation.

Though it may be tempting to declare victory and move on, the project is not quite over. The steering committee approves the team's move to the "Control" phase to make sure it locks in the new process.

Step 5: Control
In the "Control" phase, the process improvement project team develops approaches to maintain a process with an operation that is stable, predictable, and meets client requirements by doing four things
1. Documenting the new process.
2. Designing controls.
3. Instituting process ownership.
4. Translating improvements into benefits.

Documenting the new process involves creating and publishing standard operating procedures or statements of work that describe how each step in the process will be performed. Ideally that will be done in a standardized way. The team should have clear and complete documentation of the new process to help ensure that all who participate have a way of getting on the same page. For example, standard operating procedures describe how each step in the process will be performed, ideally in a standard way.

One of the Toyota Production System Rules is that "All work shall be highly specified". When people understand exactly what they are supposed to do, they generally will do it that way. Careful design of the work for each worker should include detailed work procedures that explain the sequence of work, offer support for the worker including information, tools, supplies, and materials, taking into consideration ergonomic, safety, and human factors. Standard work will allow the team to maximize productivity of people and equipment, minimize variation, errors and defects, improve predictability of schedules and outputs, and create a basis from which the process can be improved. It also allows it to train new employees more effectively, which is important if the firm is growing by acquisition.

We will clean up our project repository and make sure to include the artifacts that can and should be available as appropriate. This practice ensures widespread availability of information about what has been done and what results were achieved.

Second, we design the controls. We need to determine which variables must be controlled to produce the stable performance required. Most of the time, the focus is on measuring the final product or outputs (lagging indicators of performance), such as customer satisfaction, cycle time, or errors / defects. However, better organizations move toward measuring the process (leading indicators of performance) such as progress toward completion, speed, or quality and consistency. Regardless, we will need to define metrics, assign responsibilities, and decide how and when to take corrective actions.

The third step involves instituting process ownership and discipline. It is critical to clearly identify an individual who is responsible for the overall health of the process. The process owner has ultimate responsibility for maintaining the improvements achieved. The owner also educates others of the reasons for maintaining the improvements and the benefits derived from the improvements. The owner manages control but does not personally execute all the control work (e.g., obtains and posts control charts, but may not create the charts). In short, the owner is the one who knows whether a process is performing adequately and is responsible for planning improvements if it is not.

The last step of the Control phase is to ensure the team translates improvements into benefits. Making process changes doesn't necessarily translate into improvements in the desired metrics or the bottom line. Often, managers need to get involved to translate a process improvement into a financial benefit. It is likely that a process improvement will generate more than one kind of benefit.

It is important to note that it is neither the process owner's nor the project team's responsibility to decide what to do with the benefits. For example, if eliminating a wasteful activity means an employee has extra time, management bears the responsibility of turning that into a benefit to the organization.

At this point, the team will turn to data to tell the success story of its project, showing that it accomplished its project goals and delivered solid returns on investment.

All key project materials and artifacts should be preserved in a project repository, which ensures appropriate and ongoing availability of information about what has been done and what results were achieved by the project. Processes will always relate to, or overlap with, others in the firm, so those involved in other, future projects will undoubtedly find the team's work of interest. A project repository will explain the thought process behind the team's process improvements and should follow the DMAIC flow of the project so that it can serve as a knowledge resource for the firm.

Finally, the team prepares for its final gate review. We compile results data, confirm that we have documented the new process, completed control design, and instituted process ownership. Most important, we proudly share the achievement of the project charter goal. It will be important to report accomplishments, to raise ongoing issues and opportunities with management – and to celebrate success!

The Kaizen approach

In addition to DMAIC for full-scale projects, Kaizen is a variation that works very well in law. In the Lean Sigma world, this has come to mean a focused, accelerated, structured process improvement methodology. It is well suited for problems of limited scope and we can usually complete a project in about four to six months.

We still go through the normal DMAIC sequence, only in a condensed period. That makes it an ideal approach for organizations that need or want to move fast. It is also excellent for those who work in law as they are almost always working at full-capacity, and it is easier for them to work on a shorter duration project. For those who work in different locations, it's an opportunity to collaborate with others without needing to commit to a lot of travel.

One team member involved in a project where we used this approach reported that:

"Overall, the process worked well. I liked the Kaizen approach. The time frame / commitment worked well for me. After hearing tales of the prior (full-scale DMAIC) projects and time involved in those I was very pleased to be involved with a Kaizen approach."

The way we structure our Kaizens is to prepare and get organized, then have a kickoff meeting, where we carry out the "Define" stage work and plan the "Measure" stage. The team then spends a couple of months collecting and analyzing data, then comes back together for a Kaizen event.

For three days, we will carry out as much of the remaining DMAIC sequence as we can in long workshops. We review all the data and select focus areas on the first day (Measure). Next, we discuss causes and interrelationships, then engage in root cause analysis (Analyze). We move rapidly into developing solution alternatives and recommendations, as well as pilot and implementation plans as far as possible in the workshop (Improve). Gate review takes place at the end of each day. The team continues to work on piloting and implementation as well as developing control schemes (Improve and Control phases) after the workshop, when working together effectively is less dependent on being in the same room at the same time. Steering committee and other meetings such as gate reviews continue to take place as we bring the project to completion.

In DMAIC we trust

In addition to providing us with a logical sequence of steps that have plenty of change management and communications built into the process, the DMAIC framework helps us to minimize or even eliminate typical project failures. It also helps us avoid the typical causes of poor achievement of promised results. To illustrate the point:

- "Define" helps us avoid picking the wrong problem to solve in the first place by having the team carefully define what it is trying to solve, determine the scope and so forth.
- The "Measure" phase greatly improves our chances of selling our recommendations.
- "Analyze" safeguards against making poor recommendations.
- The "Improve" phase helps to ensure we develop the right solutions and avoid poor implementation.

Team members who started out as Six Sigma Yellow Belts and then earned their Green Belts after successfully completing their projects have this to say about the DMAIC framework:

"Working as a team to improve a process allows you to collect a large amount of data, see different perspectives and complete tasks more efficiently. DMAIC works."

"Breaking down the project using the Define, Measure, Analyze, Improve, and Control process really does work. It seems a bit overwhelming at first, but it gives a great result."

In summary, rather than complete a project from start to finish and then deliver the results, the approach demanded by process improvement is for our cross-functional and diverse team to regularly check-in with its project sponsor and engage in gate reviews with a group of decision makers that stays with the project from start to finish. This format builds in regular and ongoing communication for the duration of the project and provides a forum for the team to share its work as it progresses from diagnosing, measuring, and analyzing the process to finally developing improvement ideas. The stakeholders also have opportunities to contribute their diverse perspectives, expertise, and resources on an ongoing basis – this is built into the process of process improvement.

DMAIC builds in failure avoidance due to its design and rigor. It incorporates change management principles to ensure consensus is built as the project team progresses through each phase. Thus, there are numerous benefits to following the framework and to never, ever skipping steps. Trust the process.

Reference

1   "Outlining the problem of long delays, CIO Kevin Divine of the Hunoval Law Firm asked supervisors and staff in the firm's North Carolina default department how long they thought it took from file intake to sending out a notice of hearing to launch the foreclosure process. Anecdotally, they saw it as 14 to 20 days. But the crunched numbers tallied 69." See Carter, T., Foreclosure firm goes statistical to improve speed and quality, *American Bar Association Journal*: www.abajournal.com/magazine/article/foreclosure_firm_goes_statistical_to_improve_speed_and_quality.

Chapter 4:
Additional process improvement methodologies

While DMAIC is perhaps the best-known and often used framework, there are other powerful methodologies that are routinely employed and well suited for use in law.

Legal Lean Sigma practitioners believe in liberally combining all PI, PM, Design Thinking, and innovation concepts. In every case, we use every approach and tool at our disposal, flexibly and appropriately, to advance team and PI project objectives.

That is because we believe that practitioners are always learning and becoming masters of the art and science of PI. This does not mean we recommend skipping steps – we do not. We will always recommend adhering to the framework that was selected, but, since we believe even PI can be improved, we encourage experimenting with tools that could be effective for the situation at hand. This is how we have developed our own unique approaches, such as the Legal WorkOut and Legal Lean Sigma Design.

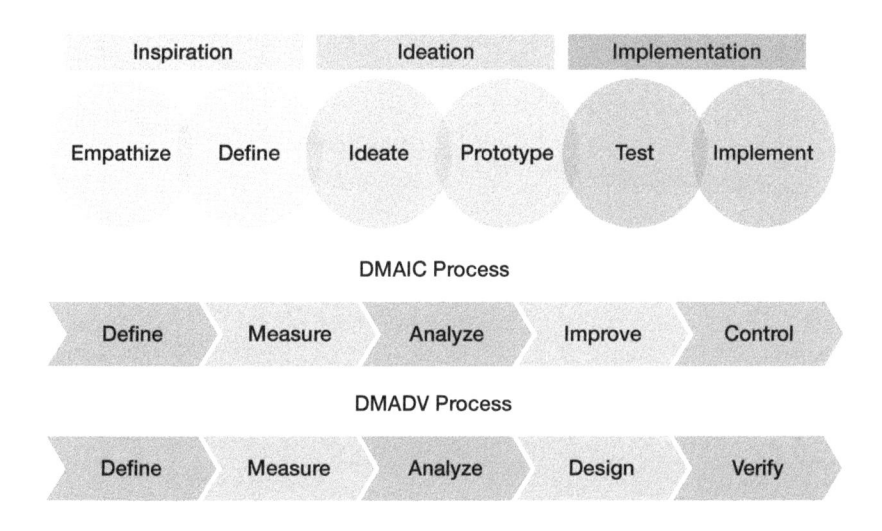

Figure 7: Design Thinking, DMAIC and DMADV.

DMADV

DMADV is a robust methodology for designing high-quality processes and products from the ground up, with a strong emphasis on meeting customer needs and minimizing defects. It is best used for the following:

- New product or service development that must meet specific customer needs and quality standards.
- Process design, where we are creating an entirely new process.
- Process redesign, when an existing process is so flawed that incremental improvements aren't enough.
- When the current process or product doesn't meet the required standards, and a new design is necessary to achieve closer to Six Sigma quality.

The acronym DMADV stands for Define, Measure, Analyze, Design, and Verify. The first phases of DMADV mirror those in DMAIC. Define involves defining the goals of the project, the scope, customer requirements, and the success criteria. Measure is where we quantify customer needs and expectations, and then translate them into measurable specifications.

In DMADV, the Analyze phase involves developing design ideas and alternatives, identifying potential risks, evaluating the feasibility of each option, and then selecting the best design that meets the CTQs and client expectations.

The next phase, Design, is where we create detailed designs for the selected process or product, ensuring that it meets all requirements. We develop detailed process maps, workflows, and prototypes. We also optimize the design to meet performance, cost, and quality requirements. Then, we use the same pilot testing options as in DMAIC, such as simulations and modeling to test or validate the design. Finally, we refine the design based on testing and feedback.

In the last phase, Verify, we validate that the final design meets client requirements and performs as expected in the "real world". This involves thorough testing and validation against the original requirements, collecting feedback, and making adjustments. We also document the process and ensure a plan is in place for continuous monitoring and improvement.

Like DMAIC, DMADV also maintains a focus on the clients, ensuring that the final design meets their needs and expectations. It is more geared to Six Sigma thinking than Lean, as our goals involve reaching high levels of quality and minimizing defects and variability. It is an excellent approach for identifying and mitigating risks early in the design process, and, despite the more statistical sounding approach, encourages the creation of innovative designs that can lead to competitive advantages.

Legal WorkOut®
The Legal WorkOut is a fusion of methodologies, concepts, and tools used in process improvement, project management, and Design Thinking. This methodology was invented by the Legal Lean Sigma Institute in response to taking what we have learned over many years about what works well in a legal environment. It is particularly effective for organizations that choose a collaborative, accelerated approach to improving legal and business processes. Our workshops are effectively designed to remove silos, break through barriers, and build bridges between people and organizations.

Our award-winning approach enables us to access knowledge and harness the power of teams quickly and effectively. In just our first day of working together, we build skills, facilitate highly productive discussions, and produce specific and effective ideas that get approved and executed quickly.

To accomplish this, we take cross-functional, cross-organizational, diverse teams of people and invite them to two focused workshops. The goal is to get the work out of a process – fast. Most of the time, the people performing tasks in a process or project possess a lot of knowledge about performance gaps and pain points and, many times, they keep it to themselves. At the same time, they have excellent ideas about "quick fixes", "low hanging fruit", and "no brainers" that don't require a lot of time to analyze or implement.

In the Legal WorkOut, we assemble a cross-functional team to focus on a specific process. Through a "hackathon" type of workshop, we facilitate discussions that produce eye-opening insights about how work is being done and delivered. With a new understanding of the process, we engage in creative problem solving and develop ideas and recommendations that "get the work out" of the process – and that are easy for leadership to approve the same day.

Next, the ideas are piloted. Our accelerated and proven approach produces measurable results in just 30-90 days that will benefit the organization, teams and individuals, and customers/clients. Then, the team regroups, share its progress, and drafts short-term and longer-range work plans. This second workshop adds to the effectiveness of the Legal WorkOut because follow up and accountability are built into the process.

The Legal WorkOut is a silo-busting, barrier breaking, and bridge building approach that produces impressive, sustainable results and significant returns on investment. In addition to the convincing metrics, teams report that they have "never worked better together". With the Legal WorkOut, there is no trade off; everyone wins. This is the primary reason many practitioners enjoy this work – to help people work even better, together. Because of the design, speed, and results of this approach, it is an excellent starting point for any organization.

We have seen that is particularly effective for use between law departments and their internal clients and/or their outside counsel. Audrey Rubin, JD, vice president and chief operating officer at Aon Global Law Department says:

"The Aon Law Department works with our preferred law firms on process improvement. In joint workshops with the stakeholders, actual processes involving both of us are mapped and simplified. It is proving to be a most valuable endeavor. Lean Six Sigma is the right approach for all law departments... the multifaceted initiative has resulted in reduced legal costs, increased budget predictability, improved legal outcomes, and greater employee satisfaction."

Aon's award-winning Legal WorkOut case study is included in chapter 14.

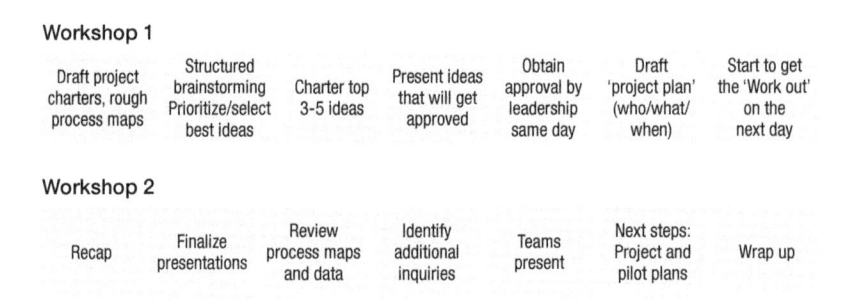

Workshop 1

| Draft project charters, rough process maps | Structured brainstorming Prioritize/select best ideas | Charter top 3-5 ideas | Present ideas that will get approved | Obtain approval by leadership same day | Draft 'project plan' (who/what/when) | Start to get the 'Work out' on the next day |

Workshop 2

| Recap | Finalize presentations | Review process maps and data | Identify additional inquiries | Teams present | Next steps: Project and pilot plans | Wrap up |

Figure 8: Using Legal WorkOut workshops for change. Source: Legal Lean Sigma Institute LLC.

Plan, Do, Check, Act

Plan-Do-Check-Act (PDCA) is a cyclical, iterative, problem-solving process used for continuous improvement of processes, products, or services. PDCA is widely used and is akin to a "mother sauce". In cooking, this term refers to a basic sauce that serves as the foundation for other sauces, called derivative sauces, daughter sauces, small sauces, or secondary sauces. In other words,

PDCA concepts and steps can be found in many derivative works. PDCA is also known as the Deming Cycle, named after W. Edwards Deming, who popularized it.

The phases of PDCA are intended to be continuous – Plan, Do, Check, Act, Plan, Do, Check, Act, Plan, Do, Check, Act.

In Plan, the objective is to identify a problem or an area for improvement and develop a plan to address it. We gather data to understand the current situation, analyze it to identify root causes or opportunities for improvement, and develop a plan that includes specific actions, resources, timelines, and metrics for success.

The objective of the next step, Do, is to implement the plan on a small scale to test its effectiveness. We ensure that the implementation is done as planned and document any deviations or unexpected issues that arise during the implementation.

In Check, we evaluate the results of the implementation to determine whether the plan worked as intended. This is accomplished by measuring the outcomes of the implementation using the metrics defined in the Plan phase, compare the actual results with the expected results, and analyzing the data to understand the impact of the changes. Then, we identify any gaps, successes, or areas for further improvement.

Then, we Act. Based on the results from the Check phase, we take action to standardize the successful changes or to address any remaining issues. If we are successful, we standardize the changes by incorporating them into regular operations. If we did not achieve the desired results, we identify what went wrong and decide whether to repeat the cycle with adjustments. As always, we document lessons learned and share them with the team or organization.

Then, we Plan the next cycle of improvement if further actions are needed.

PDCA supports continuous improvement because the model itself encourages ongoing refinement and improvement. This alone makes it a key tool in Lean Six Sigma methodologies. The structured approach provides a clear, systematic process for problem-solving and process improvement. It's also got the kind of flexibility that makes it well suited for law and everywhere else. The iterative nature allows for continuous adjustments and improvements, adapting to new information or changing circumstances. Finally, testing changes on a small scale in the Do phase helps minimize risks before full-scale implementation, appealing to the risk aversion that is prevalent in the law.

Pure technology

While we are big fans of technology, as PI practitioners, we preach, on repeat, People, Process, then – and only then – Platform. So, it might be somewhat surprising to read about "pure technology" as a process improvement methodology. It is not a widely recognized or standardized term like Lean, Six Sigma, or PDCA. However, the concept is useful in the context of using technology as the primary or sole driver of process improvement.

In the context of process improvement, pure technology as a methodology generally means leveraging technology to optimize, automate, or completely transform business processes without relying heavily on other, traditional process improvement methodologies. The focus is on using advanced technological tools and systems to achieve efficiency, reduce errors, and enhance productivity.

This approach involves keeping up with new tools and technologies that match with organizational needs and user requirements. It does not mean getting new technology on a whim and/or forcing people to work in a new and different way to support the technology.

Examples of pure technology in process improvement that are most useful in law include automation, data analytics, AI and machine learning, and digital transformation. There are many excellent publications addressing generative AI in the law and it is a giant area to explore. Clients should ask, and law firms must be prepared to respond to client inquiries, about their use of AI. In "Questions to Ask Your Law Firms About Their Use of Artificial Intelligence", William T. Garcia, Matthew D. Coatney, and Julie D. Honor, write:

> *"Even the most casual observer of current news appreciates the projected use of artificial intelligence (AI) to improve service delivery across a variety of industries. AI techniques such as natural language processing, machine learning, and deep learning have been commercially available for several years and are incorporated into some of the more widely adopted software applications (for example, Lex Machina, which analyzes court dockets to predict case timing and judges' penchants). The more recent maelstrom involves the use of a species of AI called 'generative AI' (GenAI). GenAI is a subset of deep learning (a sophisticated subfield of machine learning) that, based on a user 'prompt' (i.e., query or request), creates new images, computer code, video, audio, or natural language based on enormous amounts of data analyzed to train the algorithm. GenAI is designed to generate content – it is not an editor, not an analytic tool (yet), and not a*

web browser. It does not necessarily operate in 'real time'– it may be basing its work off ingested materials that are years old. Failure to understand this limited functionality (which concededly GenAI performs brilliantly) is the genesis of much of the criticism and concern about the use of these applications.

"Clients need to understand the technology being utilized to support their representation and seek competent legal advice on the issues that might arise. When considering a law firm's use of AI, it is essential for clients to ask relevant questions. Remember, the goal is to gain a clear understanding of how the law firm incorporates AI, ensuring that it is used responsibly, ethically, and in the best interests of the client. This article offers a list of a few of the questions that a client might ask its lawyers about their use of AI and GenAI."[1]

In fact, the questions they include in the three categories of the firm's use of AI, benefits and considerations, and risk and compliance offer a roadmap for important conversations by and between law firms, office, departments and their clients.

Automation includes RPA, Robotic Process Automation (RPA), which many law firms, service providers, and law departments have done successfully. Deploying software robots to automate repetitive and rule-based tasks frees up human workers for higher-value work and more strategic activities. Another example is workflow automation, where we use software to automate and streamline complex business processes, ensuring consistent and efficient execution. For example, most organizations use some form of project management or ticketing type system to support intake, assignment, tracking, monitoring, and reporting.

Data, "Big Data", and analytics must be part of an organization's strategy and plans, and all organizations have prioritized privacy, security, compliance, and accessibility. A welcome evolution is that we are seeing more business analysts in law – whether they are on a PI team or available to us as a resource, especially during the Measure phase, it is a function and skill set that is valuable in process improvement. Data is literally everywhere, in every process and in every corner of our business. We have untapped opportunities to leverage analytics tools and gain insights from vast amounts of data, leading to better decision-making and the kind of process optimization that produces higher quality work product and service.

Analytics includes real-time monitoring systems to track process performance and identify areas for improvement instantly. Law firms that compete for work through responding to requests for proposals, take note – this is what clients want and they expect to get it.

Predictive analytics with artificial intelligence (AI) and machine learning (ML) are here, not some "wave of the future". Law is already using AI and ML algorithms to predict future trends and outcomes, allowing for proactive adjustments to processes, including legal practice and operations. Intelligent process automation (IPA), where AI is combined with RPA to create more adaptive and intelligent automation solutions, is also being employed.

The below AI generated piece explores the types of law that stand to benefit the most from AI integration.

AI and the transformation of law

AI is transforming many areas of law, but some legal fields stand to benefit more than others due to the nature of their work, reliance on data, and potential for automation. Here are the key areas.

Contract law

AI is revolutionising contract law by enhancing document review, drafting, and risk analysis. Legal professionals can leverage AI-powered tools to analyse contracts with greater speed and accuracy, significantly reducing the time spent on manual review. These tools can also identify potential risks, inconsistencies, and unfavourable clauses, ensuring stronger contractual protections. Additionally, AI-driven platforms assist in contract negotiations by comparing terms against industry standards and suggesting optimised language. This not only increases efficiency but also minimises legal disputes arising from poorly drafted agreements.

Intellectual property law

Intellectual property law greatly benefits from AI's ability to streamline patent and trademark searches, enforce rights, and enhance filing processes. AI can quickly scan vast patent databases to detect existing claims, reducing the risk of infringement and improving the efficiency of patent applications. Moreover, AI-powered monitoring tools help track copyright and trademark violations online, allowing for swift enforcement actions. The automation of IP filing assistance also simplifies the submission process, ensuring that applications comply with legal requirements and reducing errors that could lead to rejections or delays.

Litigation and dispute resolution
AI is transforming litigation by enhancing legal research, case prediction, and dispute resolution. Advanced machine learning algorithms can analyse case law, statutes, and judicial decisions to provide lawyers with relevant precedents and arguments. AI's predictive capabilities also help assess the likelihood of success in court by identifying patterns in past rulings, allowing firms to make more informed strategic decisions. Additionally, AI-powered mediation tools offer alternative dispute resolution options by facilitating negotiations and proposing settlements, reducing the need for prolonged litigation and court proceedings.

Compliance and regulatory law
In the highly regulated corporate environment, AI is proving invaluable for ensuring compliance with evolving laws and regulations. AI-powered platforms can continuously monitor legislative changes, alerting businesses to new compliance obligations and helping them adapt policies accordingly. In sectors such as finance, healthcare, and data protection, AI can conduct automated audits, detect irregularities, and assess regulatory risks, reducing exposure to legal penalties. By automating due diligence and compliance reporting, AI enables companies to meet legal requirements more efficiently while minimising human error.

Legal research
Legal research, traditionally a time-consuming task, has been significantly enhanced by AI's ability to process and analyse vast amounts of legal data within seconds. AI-driven legal research tools can identify relevant cases, statutes, and legal principles with greater accuracy, providing lawyers with comprehensive insights in a fraction of the time it would take manually. Additionally, natural language processing (NLP) enables AI to understand complex legal queries, delivering precise results tailored to specific legal arguments. This not only streamlines research but also enhances the quality of legal analysis, allowing professionals to focus on higher-value strategic tasks.

The above was assisted by an AI engine and reviewed, fact-checked, and edited by the author of this book, who has most certainly used RPA and AI to facilitate the updating of the original *Lean Six Sigma for Law Firms* in this second edition, more expansively and inclusively entitled *Lean Six Sigma for Law*.

For insightful commentary on how Gen AI will further impact the legal profession, readers need look no further than Jordan Furlong's Substack on the topic.[2]

We have all seen the power of digital transformation, including the implementation of Enterprise Resource Planning (ERP) systems to integrate and manage core business processes in real-time. It was not that long ago that cloud computing was brand new. Now, law (and everyone else) utilizes cloud technologies for scalable, flexible, and efficient process and project management.

Using pure technology for process improvement produces several advantages. Scalability is one. Technology solutions can be scaled up or down quickly to meet changing business needs. Another is consistency. Automated processes reduce the variability that often comes with human intervention, leading to more consistent outcomes. Speed is critical for supporting the imperative to be responsive, something that law cares a lot about. Technology can significantly speed up processes by handling tasks faster than human workers. There is also cost efficiency to be found. While there may be upfront costs, technology-driven processes can lead to long-term cost savings by reducing labor, errors, and waste. Finally, pure technology delivers on the innovation promise. Leveraging cutting-edge technology can lead to the development of new business models and revenue streams.

Ideal applications include high volume, repetitive tasks, and data-intensive processes, where decision-making can be improved through data analytics and real-time insights, when we need to quickly scale processes without proportional increases in labor costs, and where innovative solutions are the best response to the demands of modern business challenges. While pure technology offers significant benefits, it also requires careful planning, investment, and management to be successful.

Business process redesign / reengineering

BPR is a sort of "clean sheet of paper" type methodology that involves fundamentally rethinking and redesigning or reengineering business processes. It often involves automation. The goal is to achieve significant improvements in critical performance measures such as cost, quality, service, and speed. BPR aims to help organizations radically restructure their operations, often leading to transformative changes that can improve efficiency, reduce costs, and enhance client satisfaction.

Unlike incremental improvement methodologies like Lean or Six Sigma, BPR advocates for radical redesign – a complete overhaul of existing processes.

It involves questioning the very fundamentals of how business processes are conducted, often leading to new, innovative ways of operating. This approach is obviously better suited for any organization in law that is not permanently tethered to tradition. BPR shifts the focus from optimizing individual tasks or functions to improving the entire, end-to-end process

The idea is to look at how work flows across departments and how value is delivered to the client. In this way, the objective of BPR is to achieve dramatic improvements, not just minor tweaks. It aims for significant, breakthrough results, such as cutting costs by 50 percent, reducing cycle times by 90 percent, or improving quality tenfold. Because BPR emphasizes understanding client needs and redesigning processes to better meet those needs, it can enable an organization to deliver more value to the end user client while simultaneously improving organizational efficiency.

As you might expect, technology often plays a critical role in BPR. The reengineering of processes typically involves leveraging new technologies to automate, streamline, or completely change the way tasks are performed. Again, we do not purchase the technology first. Rather, we follow a series of steps – technology and other solutions, as with DMAIC and DMADV, are not considered until we are ready to design the new process.

There are five steps in BPR.

1. *Identify processes for reengineering.* Identify key business processes that are critical to the organization's success but are underperforming or outdated. These are the processes that will benefit most from radical redesign.
2. *Understand and analyze current processes.* Conduct a thorough analysis of the current processes to understand how they work, identify bottlenecks, inefficiencies, and redundancies. This may involve mapping out the entire process flow.
3. *Design the new process.* Develop a new process that addresses the weaknesses of the current one. This design should be innovative, leveraging best practices and new technologies to achieve the desired improvement goals.
4. *Implement the new process.* Roll out the redesigned process, full-scale, across the organization. This may involve significant changes in workflow, documentation, employee roles, and technology. Training, communication, and change management are critical at this stage to ensure smooth adoption.
5. *Evaluate and improve.* Monitor the performance of the new process

against the goals set in the design phase. Continuous improvement should be encouraged even after the initial implementation, as further refinements may be needed.

BPR is powerful and it can deliver excellent results. However, employ this approach with caution in a legal environment. Radical changes can be met with resistance from employees and management who are accustomed to existing processes, and that is particularly true with legal professionals. It is especially true for those who have practiced a certain way for many years.

In other words, BPR involves significant changes, which can be very risky. If not managed properly, it can lead to significant disruptions in operations, a lot of upset people, and even dramatic failure. BPR requires careful planning, execution, and change management to be successful and it is recommended very rarely and only when an organization has demonstrated innovation maturity and readiness.

Theory of Constraints
Dr Eliyahu Goldratt's Theory of Constraints (TOC) is a process improvement methodology that emphasizes the importance of identifying the "system constraint" or the bottleneck in a process. Since every process has a limiting factor or constraint, reducing this constraint is usually the fastest and most effective way to improve "flow" and profitability.

Often, the chain analogy is used to describe TOC. Just as no chain can ever be stronger than the weakest link, every process has a constraint that limits the output. For our purposes, a constraint is any factor that limits the performance of a system relative to its goal. It could be a physical constraint (like a bottleneck in getting information or documents) or a non-physical one (like a policy, mindset, or lack of available staffing for a matter).

There are usually many constraints in the processes used to do and deliver legal work as well as produce the outputs of our business processes in law. When we identify, then alleviate or even remove constraints, we "make value flow at the pull of the client". Implementing the Theory of Constraints also produces better control over operations, less inventory waste, and drastically reduced firefighting. Often, we generate additional capacity from our existing resources (meaning, we free up people's time) so that we can redeploy them.

A big challenge to employing this methodology in law is to keep that which is good about the processes while removing the constraint. Be careful not to act without understanding why the constraint exists in the first place. Usually, it is there for good reason (think compliance), so though it may appear to be something we can just cut out, there are always reasons to measure more than twice and cut once. Another challenge to using this in law is that, in complex systems, it can be challenging to accurately identify the true constraint, especially if it is not a physical bottleneck.

TOC starts by defining the primary goal. Then, it emphasizes maximizing throughput by focusing on the constraint. TOC encourages reducing unnecessary inventory (one of Lean's eight kinds of waste) to free up resources and improve cash flow and operating expenses by making the process more efficient.

TOC provides a systematic approach to identifying and addressing constraints through these five steps:

1) *Identify the constraint.* Determine the single most critical factor that limits the system's ability to achieve its goal. This could be a machine, a person, a policy, or any other factor.
2) *Exploit the constraint.* Make the best possible use of the constraint by ensuring it is fully utilized and not wasted. This may involve prioritizing tasks that involve the constraint, minimizing downtime, or reallocating resources.
3) *Subordinate everything else to the constraint.* Align all other processes, resources, and activities in the organization to support and optimize the performance of the constraint. This means adjusting workflows, schedules, or policies to ensure that the constraint operates at its maximum potential.
4) *Elevate the constraint.* If the constraint's capacity is still insufficient, take steps to increase it. This could involve investing in new equipment, hiring more staff, or changing policies to remove the constraint.
5) *Repeat the process.* After addressing the current constraint, reassess the system to identify any new constraints that may have emerged. The process is iterative, as removing one constraint often reveals another (note – this a variation of PDCA).

By addressing constraints, TOC can lead to higher production rates, faster project completion, and better overall system performance. It ensures that critical resources are used efficiently, reducing waste and operating expenses, and provides a clear framework for prioritizing actions and making decisions that align with the organization's goals. It can be a powerful methodology for improving organizational performance by focusing on and addressing the most critical limiting factors. Finally, its structured approach helps organizations achieve significant and sustainable improvements by continuously identifying and managing constraints.

5S

The 5S methodology is used to improve workplace efficiency and productivity by creating a clean, organized, and safe work environment. It is an excellent way to eliminate waste, reduce errors, and increase employee satisfaction by providing a clear and structured system for organizing workspaces and materials.

The 5S method was adapted by Japanese companies after Toyota representatives visited Ford in the 1950s to learn about automotive mass production. More recently, the "KonMari" became more widely known as a home organization system invented by Marie Kondo. The KonMari method transforms cluttered homes into tidy and simplified living spaces. The 5S principles are similar to KonMari.

Imagine setting up every conference room in the same, consistent manner, with every cabinet labeled, Wi-Fi and directory information within arm reach or sight, your most used and/or needed supplies readily available and easy to find and access. How much time would be saved by visitors to your office if they were able to start working productively because of a more organized work environment? 5S delivers frictionless interactions.

The 5S workplace organization method involves following a five-step process translated from Japanese words, which is often used in manufacturing to help reduce waste, downtime, and inventory. There is tremendous potential for employing this in law.

1) *Sort (Seiri)*. Remove unnecessary materials to make space for important items.
2) *Set in order (Seiton)*. Organize the important items.
3) *Shine (Seiso)*. Clean the workspace.
4) *Standardize (Seiketsu)*. Update procedures to reflect changes to the work environment and job duties.
5) *Sustain (Shitsuke)*. Assign responsibility and track progress to ensure the new procedures are followed.

One of the best things about the 5S method is that it is a highly effective way to communicate information to people visually. Everyone can see that there is a place for everything and that everything is in its right place. This improves working conditions and reduces waste, downtime, and inventory. 5S also serves as a foundation for deploying more advanced Lean tools and processes.

In law, 5S is a low-investment, high-impact approach that is people-centric. It engages workers in "owning" their workspace and helps to instill a culture of quality, productivity, and improvement. Reducing clutter is an ongoing battle in most legal environments, but there is ample evidence to suggest we would benefit from employing 5S, or KonMari, in our offices at home and at work.

Reducing clutter and working in an organized space can have a wide range of benefits, both for individuals and organizations. These benefits extend across physical, mental, and even financial aspects of life. That includes increased productivity and efficiency due to finding what is needed more quickly and reducing the time spent searching for documents, tools, or other items.

5S reduces stress and anxiety overall, so it supports workplace wellness and offers something that every person working in law needs more of – a sense of calm. An uncluttered space is more conducive to clear thinking and focus and can lead to a sense of control. Who would not benefit from enhanced focus and concentration? Clutter can be visually distracting, making it harder to concentrate on the task at hand. By decluttering, you minimize distractions and can better focus on what's important and make better decisions. A clean environment allows for better cognitive function, as your brain doesn't have to process as much visual noise. It also supports enhanced creativity and innovation!

An organized space delivers other benefits, such as sustainable practices that are better for the environment, better space utilization, improved health and safety, and better first impressions (remember, Moments of Truth!) on clients, partners, and employees, since it projects a sense of professionalism and competence. Employees are likely to feel more motivated and valued in a well-organized, clutter-free workplace, leading to higher morale and job satisfaction.

Finally, less time will be spent cleaning and organizing. Once a space is clean, organized, and maintained, it's easier to keep it that way. This saves time on maintenance tasks and leaves more time for meaningful work that delivers value to the client and the organization.

Gemba Walk

A Gemba Walk is a workplace walkthrough that involves observing employees as they work, asking about their tasks, and identifying productivity gains. This highly effective management practice is where leaders visit the "front lines" of an operation to observe and engage with employees and identify areas for improvement. It is a very simple yet powerful way to promote continuous improvement.

Gemba Walk is derived from the Japanese word "Gemba" or "Gembutsu", which means "the real place" or "the place where value is created". It is a very different approach than meeting in some sterile conference room or calling someone to your office. It is often literally defined as the act of seeing where the actual work happens, where the value is delivered. It is a demonstration of respect and appreciation for the worker too.

It is entirely possible to have virtual Gemba Walk using video conferencing tools. Virtual Gemba Walks are usually conducted via one-on-one video calls, online focus group discussions, and shadowing exercises, where a worker shares his/her screen while working and his/her manager quietly observes then asks questions as appropriate.

Gemba Walks help eliminate incorrect assumptions about the workforce and drive changes with a lasting positive impact. Developed at Toyota, Gemba Walks can empower organizations to sustain continuous improvement efforts. They help identify and resolve disconnects between leadership vision and the implementation of processes in operations.

This is different to "management by walking around". Instead, the main goal of Gemba Walks is to observe, listen, learn, and help. Leaders can easily observe what is and is not working for workers. They can identify issues and gain valuable insights into how to improve them, reduce existing waste (waste, bottlenecks, non-value-added steps, etc.) and discover where continuous improvement opportunities exist. They can and should discuss goals and objectives with employees and build stable relationships with those who actually do the work and create value.

This supports inclusion and is a demonstration of values in action for organizations that are focused on the employee experience. It demonstrates management and organizational commitment toward professional development, boosts employee morale because it shows someone cares about them and values their work, and is an excellent way to introduce changes that can be easily accepted by them.

Finally, a Gemba Walk is a stellar way to cultivate a culture of improvement, openness, collaboration, and teamwork while streamlining operations across different levels in organizations, saving time and money.

References

1. https://admin.thompsonhine.com/wp-content/uploads/2024/07/Questions-to-Ask-Your-Law-Firms-About-Their-Use-of-Artificial-Intelligence.pdf
2. https://jordanfurlong.substack.com/p/level-the-playing-field-give-consumers

Chapter 5:
Process improvement projects

Some organizations begin their explorations by developing skills and establishing a common language. This is not just helpful for feeling more cohesive and on the same page, it saves time and can accelerate progress toward doing something that delivers real results.

When we privately deliver our certification courses, we select processes for each team to use during the workshop components of the program. This way, they are learning about process improvement (PI) and project management (PM) and getting a chance to apply the concepts and tools in the context of something that is meaningful and immediately useful. It also gives us a chance to get some draft work done. In turn, this helps us evaluate the processes that would be good starting points for an organization.

Process selection
To help the organization or team select a process for either course work or as a potential project, we uncover:
- What is causing frustration?
- What are clients and employees saying / requesting / demanding?
- What are our drivers for:
  - Efficiency?
  - Excellent quality of work and service?
  - High probability of successful outcomes?
  - Predictability?
- Where is work at a high volume? What is repeatable?
- What is trending?
- Where are you experiencing pricing pressure, high write offs, and/or write downs?
- What is paper intensive and/or form driven?
- What seems to be taking longer than it should?
- Where do we have opportunities and demands to expand our capacity and/or capability to handle particular kinds of work?
- Consider how we are currently doing the work:

- Process capability – how well does the process meets client expectations and/or requirements?
- Process efficiency – what are the resources (time, people, equipment, money) required to carry out the process?

Starting with "quick wins" is an effective approach, since these projects typically involve low to medium degrees of difficulty and medium to high impact, deliverables, and results. It is equally true that focusing on core business processes such as intake or onboarding also produce the kinds of data and results that contribute to greater understanding of the methodologies and the current state of processes that are central to any firm, office, or department's operations.

Intake is one of the best places to start – it can be scoped expansively or narrowly to focus on specific areas. Obviously, it is a process that captures a lot of data that is used in many other areas.

Case studies – intake

Rivkin Radler LLP
Rivkin Radler's chief operating officer, Fred Esposito, knew he wanted the firm to start its process improvement program by working on a process critical to the business - intake. In an interview with Thomson Reuters,[1] Esposito explained the client intake process was selected:

> "Because it not only touches every part of the firm, it also produces outputs that affect and inform those other processes and strategic decisions. I believe that client intake may be one of the most critical areas on which a firm can focus its process improvement efforts, simply because it's a contact point with almost every part of the client's interaction within the firm."

As the project team leader, Esposito selected partners, associates, managers, directors, and administrators – such as those in finance, billing, and IT – to work on the project, cherry-picking ten individuals who now have been working on this project for more than two years. There have three partners from different practice areas, the firm's director of finance, director of IT, director of marketing communications, billing manager, and a lead legal assistant.

Three equity partners form the project steering committee (SC). Their guidance, buy-in and communications with the project team are instrumental to the success of the project. In the Define phase, the project team developed a project charter, part of which work involved making a business case with the firm's data to illustrate the inefficiencies. Once the steering committee reviewed the data presented, it was convinced that it had picked the right project, was tackling the right problems, had the right team, scoped the project well, and that the goals that had been set could be achieved.

At each phase of DMAIC, the project team and the steering committee learned more about what was happening from the data that was collected, measured, and analyzed. The team chose three focus areas in the Measure phase – False and Missed Conflicts, "Parked Time" (meaning time recorded using a "holding area" code), and Inaccurate and Incomplete Data. In the Analyze phase, the team explored why those things were occurring, identifying root causes in common – priority, policy, protocol, communication, and training.

By the time the team made its recommendations in the Improve phase, the steering committee was fully on board and innovation began to take shape. One idea was to undertake a collaboration between the firm's general counsel, new business committee (NBC), and client intake process improvement project team to develop a training manual with clear protocol for all NBC report reviewers and newcomers. The aim was to provide ongoing education and training to supplement the manual and provide information about why checking for conflicts is important, how to review the new NBC report, what to look for to discern potential conflicts, and when and how to add additional party information.

The modified report was easier to read and highlighted more targeted information for conflict review. It also provided a clear protocol to follow when reviewing the NBC to ensure clarity and consistency. The solutions were piloted with firm personnel, giving them an opportunity to weigh in on some of the solutions being considered and to offer ongoing feedback.

With a project goal of reducing the value of time parked by at least 50 percent, the team would address key stakeholders' highest priorities. Time would be available sooner to include on bills, fewer items would be rejected or appealed due to the length of time that had elapsed between when the work was done and when it was invoiced, and, finally, the firm would be able to collect earlier if the items were billed sooner, which meant that the profits would be distributed sooner too.

They changed the timing and format of the report distribution, sending it electronically mid-month rather than along with pre-bills at the beginning of the month. They followed up with targeted emails asking about specific items, included legal assistants on those communications, and continued to modify the approach to improve on the success of this approach.

The result? The value of parked time was reduced by 74 percent, exceeding the project goal of 50 percent.

Esposito explained:

"We saw a lot of things from the lawyers' perspective that have been very useful. The project team delved into not only the procedural process of how the firm was conducting client intake – measuring and analyzing the different steps of the intake process – but also identified what was being missed or overlooked.

"For example, a large part of the intake process is determining whether potential clients have conflicts that should be known to the firm. With the ability to focus on this one specific area, the team was able to find a way to better identify conflicts around adverse parties or relationships between parties, which often get missed in routine conflict checks. They also determined whether there were false conflicts being raised that may have caused needless problems.

"Solutions considered for this area included reformatting of intake and conflict check protocols and forms. All of the proposed solutions for piloting were vetted by the SC and the firm's new business committee. The DMAIC framework is so useful because the building blocks of transformation are built right into it. Working with attorneys and staff at all levels was the key to success because you cannot make substantive change to any process without gaining the knowledge and experience of those who are working with the current and proposed process.

"When the pandemic hit, we wanted to see what the impact of a virtual law firm would be on these processes. So, we regrouped and revised our project charter and scope. In fact, we actually did the Measure and Analyze phases twice. That was because team members had worked the conflict process to a certain point, then decided to expand the scope to capture these missed and false conflicts. There was enough information that had been gathered to tell us this is something we should be considering."[2]

While the firm is still working through the more robust Improve phase solutions, especially on the technology aspects for the new process, it is beginning to plan for the Control phase work, such as instituting process ownership.

The results were so impressive that the firm won the Transformation of the Year Award from the Legal Sales and Service Organization (LSSO).[3] The judges were struck by what the team accomplished, noting how impressive it is that the firm "addressed something that rarely gets solved" and how the team tackled improving the intake process.

They also noted that the transformation involved "people who perform different functions and have competing priorities and that everyone worked together to get it done". The process improvement project focused on assessing the current state and exploring how and what changes will streamline and make the individual and firm processes related to a massive, business critical process, more efficient. The team also engaged leaders and various stakeholders inside and outside the firm, including partnering with several software providers.

By taking the time, following the process improvement framework, and using the tools of Legal Lean Sigma, the team gained a deep understanding of the current process and tasks needed to carry it out. They identified areas where they could eliminate waste and unnecessary variation and create a more efficient process that could be monitored and controlled for favorable performance.

Finally, the judges said that the work focused on *"a really, different thing – and is focused on clients – anyone who has worked inside can see that it would make a difference. It's the unicorn project."*

Florida Rural Legal Services Office

Like most other legal aid organizations, people who called or walked into one of Florida Rural Legal Services' (FRLS) offices – in Belle Glade, West Palm Beach, Lakeland, Punta Gorda, Ft Pierce, or Ft Myers – sometimes waited a week or more between their initial call, appointment with an eligibility screener, and chat with an advocate. The length of time varied depending on the office. Yet, some clients had a pressing need for legal services quickly.

With the goal of reducing wait time between a potential client's first contact and their first conversation with a legal expert, Melissa Moss, who was then deputy director for strategic initiatives at The Florida Bar Foundation, thought FRLS would benefit from the application of process improvement methodologies and tools.[4]

She was right. Within the first quarter, FRLS increased intakes and the amount of people served by 30 percent, and the lag time from a client's first contact to an attorney chat was reduced to under 48 hours. With the training they received during the project, they also retained *"the continuous improvement mindset, to move clients to answers even more quickly, so that even more people can be served".*

Because of the important role FRLS played in 13 South Central Florida counties, it was awarded a federal Legal Services Corporation Technology Initiative Grant to centralize its intake and install a new digital call center and phone system. Management supported the idea of focusing on the workflow first and committed to the process improvement project.

A Gemba Walk was performed by a consultant to observe the receptionist at work. He tracked walk-in visits and hotline calls, counted steps from desk to door, and watched case transfers. The data he captured showed that it took between five and seven days total from the time of contacting the receptionist to screener, and from screener to legal advocate.

With four main offices and satellite offices, and each one with its own screener, there was a lot of variation – not only in terms of what the screener and the office did on intake but the kind of services sought and provided. There was an overall lack of standardization as well as differences in capacity, with some offices overbooked while others had availability.

The most important tasks – the ones that served the customer – were fairly simple:

> *"The first question is, 'Does that client meet their criteria?' If so, the next step is for that client to meet the advocate. Everything else in between is not value-added."*[5]

By observing without bias or assumptions how the existing intake process worked for clients and employees, it became clear what was happening and why it was occurring.

The consultant observed that being tied to the phone was a constraint, especially when the receptionist had to let visitors in through a door down the hall that was locked for security reasons. In that case, he suggested the receptionist use a wireless headset (an excellent example of a quick fix/Just do it solution) to avoid interrupting the flow of any call.

The new phone system allowed for the centralization of calls. But that was just the beginning. Clients wanted to speak with an attorney on the day they made contact. Why wasn't that happening?

First, they needed to be screened to see if they met the eligibility criteria for legal aid services. That was one holdup – a process to standardize. Then, a consultation with a legal advocate could be scheduled.

But some advocates had expertise in housing, some in family law. Area managers had concerns about asking a landlord-tenant expert to discuss a child support payment problem. Even if they couldn't answer all questions, couldn't adding a rotating attorney-of-the-day to field emergency calls help some of the cases get addressed quickly? Testing out the proposals made sense.

Eligibility appointments were centralized, and then the attorney-of-the-day was added. The results were immediately successful.

Civil legal aid intake infrastructure in Minnesota

Anyone looking to improve intake, especially in legal aid, would do well to review the comprehensive 27-page report entitled "Analysis of the Civil Legal Aid Intake Infrastructure in Minnesota Final Report Objective".[6]

The 2017 report captures impressive work done in response to the Chief Justice's directive to the Legal Services Advisory Committee (LSAC) to investigate *"possible improvements to coordinated infrastructure and centralized intake with 'no wrong door' for clients as a central value"*.

The project goal was *"To deliver recommendations for a collaborative system among LSAC funded programs that increases client access to civil legal aid by improving the efficiency of intake and advice processes statewide"*. The project scope focused on the level of coordination and on the avenues and barriers to access across the statewide system. The analysis considered the intake processes in each of 19 LSAC direct service grantees that range in size from two to 103 full-time employees.

To gain an understanding of these systems individually and collectively, the study team engaged in an extensive collection of data regarding the current infrastructure and processes for intake and referral of applicants for service. They discovered ten "disconnects":

1. Lack of knowledge about legal aid (lack of awareness that programs and their services exist; perception free service is inferior).
2. External bounce (contacting and being referred among social service organizations, governmental agencies, courts, and others before being referred to legal aid, if ever).
3. Within system bounce (applicant contacts and is referred to successive legal aid programs, none of which provide service).

4. Within program bounce (multiple contacts within program before application decision reached).
5. Online intake does not collect all information needed to determine financial and substantive eligibility.
6. Information collected by online intake can be inaccurate or incomplete.
7. Applicant is not available when callback from online intake is made.
8. Timing of case acceptance meeting meetings delays response to applicant.
9. Attorneys spend time on initial intake duties that may not be the highest and best use of their time.
10. Intake not available for potential applicants who cannot seek assistance during business hours because of work or otherwise.

Based on this extensive and thorough examination, the study team developed a future state process map and recommendations. Finding that *"fundamental changes are in order to supplement and expand the system's accessibility and to address the disconnects identified"*, several focus areas were identified and three sets of recommendations (with detailed explanations) were offered:
- Immediate adjustments to develop a clear referral policy among LSAC funded programs and to expand intake hours for persons who work or otherwise cannot access services during business hours.
- Ongoing marketing and publicity to increase knowledge about the law and the legal system and to direct people with legal needs to the appropriate source of help.
- Staged development of a centralized capacity through which persons with legal needs can access the system and be transferred to an appropriate source of help, or be told at the earliest opportunity if no assistance is available (Triage and Channeling).[7]

The above two projects produced artifacts such as reports, playbooks, and process maps that are freely available.[8] The author of this book is a member of the team.

PI practitioners
To be a PI practitioner, it helps to have certain attributes. It is important to have credibility amongst your peers and leaders. If you are driven to improve, are results-oriented, optimistic, and persistent, you're more natu-

rally suited for this work. Emotional intelligence is extremely important. Skills are obviously vital as well – these can be developed formally and informally. It is beneficial to have good people, communication, teaching, facilitation, presentation, problem-solving, and analytical skills. People who can influence without authority and possess business acumen will also be suitable.

There simply is no substitute for experience. Obviously, the only way to get that is to do the work and be in a state of continuous improvement yourself. I am always cautious about appearing self-serving, but it is a basic truth that, while we encourage people to experiment with PI concepts and tools, when you are ready to do this work for real, it is critical that you work with a highly skilled and experienced practitioner. There is too much at stake when you first get started to not do things right. In law, failures are long remembered, and you are not likely to get a second bite at the apple.

In addition to the attributes, skills, and experience mentioned, a project facilitator must be excellent at meeting management, team, and organizational dynamics, change and conflict management, and project management. The ability to flexibly and masterfully select the right tools and approaches that are most effective for the people and situation at hand is artistry that is developed and refined over many experiences and years.

PI project roles and responsibilities

We employ project management in the delivery of every PI project, starting with identifying people who will serve in specific roles and carry out proscribed responsibilities.

Management's role is to establish a good process to select projects – another relatively straightforward concept but one that is structured differently in every organization. Strong sponsorship and support and an agreement to follow a robust methodology are critical success factors as well. Management is also responsible for good resource planning and allocation – there must be the right organizational support reward systems in place as well as enough time and resources for anyone to be successful.

A PI team of about eight people is likely to spend about 20 percent of its time overall on a PI project. Management must ensure they are given the time, space, capacity, and rewards to do this work. Subject matter experts must participate and outsiders (consultants, experts in Lean Sigma, data science, etc.) are often required. In the law, that means some of our highest fee earners and most important VIPs must participate and contribute at some level. If the performance review, management, and compensation systems are not aligned, it is nearly impossible for law firm partners to justify the time spent on a project. Doing this work is an investment that delivers significant returns when done right. This is one reason that picking the right project is important. It must be worth it.

The project steering committee is a small group of decision makers to whom a PI project team reports. They represent senior leadership. Usually three to five people in total, the steering committee's role is to approve the project objective(s), scope, and team recommendations, remove barriers, guide and direct the project, and conduct what are called gate reviews. It is worth noting here that a process improvement program steering committee is a different role. That steering committee is a key body in managing and guiding process improvement initiatives within an organization. Its primary role is to provide oversight, direction, and support for process improvement projects to ensure they align with organizational goals and achieve desired outcomes.

Gate reviews, or toll gates, are formal and critical checkpoints or decision points in a Lean Sigma project as the team works through the phases of the DMAIC (Define, Measure, Analyze, Improve, Control) framework. These reviews are where the progress of the project is evaluated before it can move on to the next phase. Each phase of DMAIC has its own gate review, ensuring that specific objectives and deliverables have been met before the project proceeds.

Gate reviews are conducted to ensure quality and completeness. This implies that the steering committee must be trained either in advance or in conjunction with a project, since their role is to help to confirm that all necessary steps have been thoroughly completed, and that the team is ready to advance to the next phase. They also facilitate decision-making, providing an opportunity for project sponsors, stakeholders, and leaders to assess the project's status and decide whether to continue, revise, or halt the project. Finally, they mitigate risks – something near and dear to every lawyer. By assessing progress at each gate, potential issues can be identified early, reducing the risk of failure later in the project.

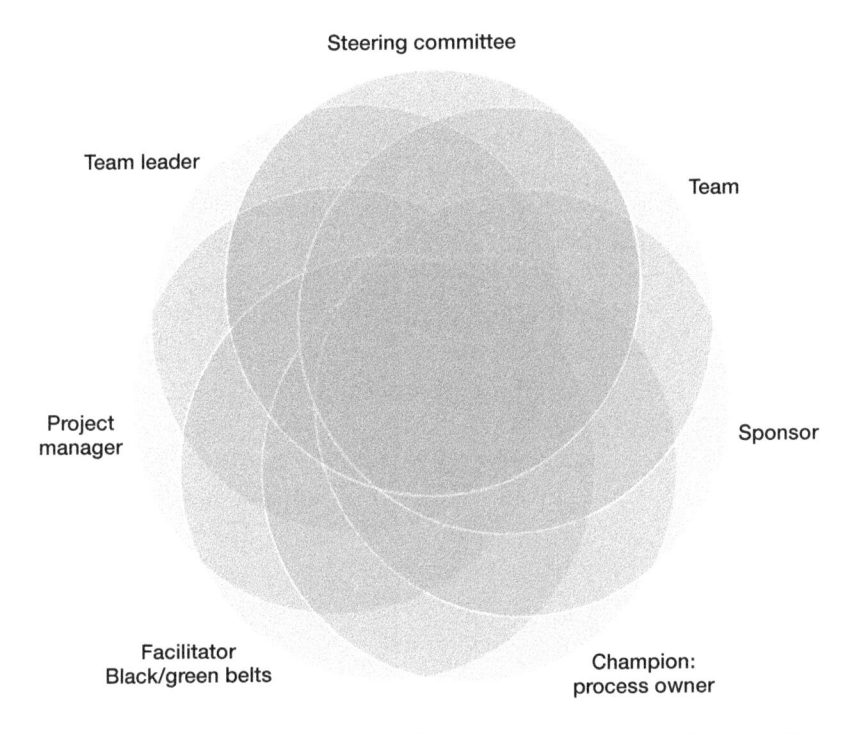

Figure 9: PI project role and responsibilities. Source: Legal Lean Sigma Institute LLC.

The PI project team is usually composed of six to eight members. It is always cross-functional and diverse. We also require different experiences, personality types, and communication styles. In addition to subject matter experts, often it can be helpful to include someone who knows little about the process, as they have few, if any, preconceived notions about how it works or should be operating. As we move through the DMAIC phases, we will draw on the varied skills of team members as well, being mindful of selecting people who can help the team be well rounded in every possible way. The team members must represent priority stakeholders, be credible, and capable of serving as ambassadors for the project. It also helps if they have demonstrated abilities to be part of a high functioning and high performing team (see Figure 9).

Each team member must commit to remaining on the project for the duration. This includes attending – and being fully present at – team meetings and being an active participant by sharing their knowledge, experience, ideas, and concerns. For the success of the project, they must also complete tasks for which they are responsible. They will also seek opportunities to apply continuous improvement principles and tools elsewhere.

The project team leader and manager work hand-in-hand, though their roles are different. The leader is more than "the face" of the project team, usually working behind the scenes and out in front before, during, and after a project to communicate and connect the dots. Sometimes, this involves negotiating with managers and supervisors for resources and "socializing" solutions and other aspects of the project. Of paramount importance for the person who is leading is to ensure the team stays focused and disciplined and that the project objective is achieved and delivered within budget, on time, and in scope.

Together, they handle setting up project meetings (kickoff, event, check-in, report out, project updates) and getting approval of the project objective, scope, recommendations, plan changes, and deliverables from the sponsor, champion, and steering committee. They will also coordinate communications, including leading and managing check-in, report out, and project update meetings. They will refer difficult issues to the sponsor, champion, or steering team and help the champion and facilitator complete their responsibilities.

The sponsor, or project owner, provides visible and vocal support for the project and resources (staff, budget, consultant, equipment, etc.). Responsibilities include approving the project objective(s), scope, and team recommendations, participating in the kickoff meeting, attending any check-in, report out, and project update meetings, and supporting the champion, steering committee, and project lead and manager. The sponsor may be on either the project team or the steering committee (but no one can be on both).

The champion, or process owner is a role that can be performed by the sponsor or project manager. Responsibilities include helping to obtain resources, making sure the right people are involved (engage facilitator, project manager, team), and removing barriers to the project. The champion will attend kickoff, check-in, report out, and project review meetings. Generally, is a good practice to include the process owner on the steering committee.

The facilitator must be an experienced Lean Sigma practitioner and, particularly in the early stages, should be familiar with law and the unique issues, structures, and culture. The facilitator's role is to coach and educate the sponsor, champion, steering team, and team members about continuous improvement methods and tools and determine the best method and tools to use for achieving the project objective. Responsibilities include designing (or really co-designing with the lead, sponsor, and process owner) the project. The facilitator develops agendas, facilitates the kickoff, check-in, report out, and project meetings, as well as events and workshops, and manages team dynamics during them. Responsibilities also include helping the project lead, manager, sponsor, and champion complete their responsibilities.

Team success factors
A focused and disciplined process improvement team is successful when it effectively identifies, analyzes, and implements changes that lead to measurable improvements in a process. Several factors contribute to a team's success.

Clear goals and objectives give the team purpose and a clear understanding of the problem they are trying to solve and the objectives they aim to achieve. Successful teams also have the backing of senior leadership, which provides the necessary resources, removes obstacles, and ensures alignment with broader business goals. A capable team leader or facilitator is essential to guide the team, keep them on track, and resolve conflicts.

PI projects and other work must be performed with cross-functional representation. Teams must include members from various departments or functions that are involved in or impacted by the process. This not only ensures we understand the process as a whole, but also fosters collaboration. Having individuals with deep knowledge of the process and related areas can help in identifying root causes and developing effective solutions. We also require diversity in experience, skills, and viewpoints, which lead to more innovative and comprehensive solutions.

Regular and transparent communication among team members is critical for sharing ideas, updates, and feedback. It is also necessary to keep stakeholders informed and involved throughout the process. This ensures their support and addresses any concerns early on and later. A key element of communication includes proper documentation of findings, decisions, and progress. This is essential for continuity and knowledge transfer.

The team must adhere to a data-driven approach. Successful teams rely on accurate data and the right metrics to identify problems, measure performance, and evaluate the impact of improvements. Moreover, we engage in fact-based decision making, meaning decisions should be based on data analysis rather than assumptions or opinions, ensuring that solutions are targeted and effective. Everyone must agree to follow a structured methodology and proven frameworks. Utilizing methodologies such as DMAIC (Define, Measure, Analyze, Improve, Control) or PDCA (Plan-Do-Check-Act) helps to structure the improvement efforts and ensures that all critical aspects of the process are addressed.

Teams should adopt a mindset of ongoing improvement, recognizing that processes can always be optimized further. They must also have autonomy. Teams that are empowered to make decisions and take ownership of their work are more motivated and engaged. A key component of this is to build in accountability measures. Clearly defined roles and responsibilities, along with regular progress reviews, help ensure that everyone contributes effectively and that the project stays on track. At the same time, successful teams are adaptable and flexible. They anticipate and manage resistance to change by involving stakeholders early, communicating benefits, and addressing concerns. They are also willing to pivot or adjust their approach based on new information or changing circumstances. After completing a project, successful teams reflect on what worked well and what could be improved in future efforts, fostering a cycle of learning and growth.

Finally, the team must be recognized, something that is not always done well in law. Celebrating the team's achievements boosts morale and reinforces a culture of continuous improvement.

By focusing on these factors, a process improvement team can navigate challenges, drive meaningful change, and achieve lasting improvements that contribute to the organization's overall success.

References

1. www.thomsonreuters.com/en-us/posts/legal/leveraging-process-improvement-client-in-take/
2. *Ibid.*
3. www.legalsales.org/2023LSSOAwards
4. www.floridabar.org/the-florida-bar-news/lean-lawyering-a-legal-aid-office-test-drives-the-toyota-way/
5. *Ibid.*
6. www.mncourts.gov/mncourtsgov/media/scao_library/documents/Minnesota-intake-study-Final-Report-6-14-17.pdf
7. www.mncourts.gov/mncourtsgov/media/scao_library/documents/Minnesota-intake-study-Final-Report-6-14-17.pdf
8. www.legalaidprocess.org/resource-pages/from-the-field

Chapter 6:
Mastering key PI tools

Mastering tools such as Six Sigma or Lean often involves certification, which adds to a professional's credibility and can enhance job prospects in industries that prioritize efficiency and quality. Whether you intend to pursue a career as a practitioner or participate in or lead a project, mastering even a few of the key tools used in process improvement is crucial for anyone in business. They are especially helpful to those in law, who are under ever increasing pressures in today's competitive and efficiency-driven environment. As has been mentioned several times already, nearly every lawyer will state rather emphatically that responsiveness and client focus are core values.

PI Tools Overview-By Phase

Define	Measure	Analyze
☐ Project Charter	☐ Process Observation	• UDEs
☐ SMART objectives	☐ Process Mapping	☐ Pareto Chart
☐ Business Case	☐ Logical Process Flow	☐ Five Whys
☐ Stakeholder Analysis	☐ Physical Process Map (Spaghetti Diagram)	☐ Cause-Effect Diagram (Fishbone)
☐ Project Schedule (Gantt Chart)	☐ Swim Lane	☐ Weighted Matrix
☐ Voice of the Customer	☐ Value Stream Map	☐ Reality Tree
☐ Moments of Truth	☐ Value-Added / Non-value Added	☐ Root Cause Analysis
☐ Critical-To-Quality	☐ Time Value Analysis	☐ Impact / Ease Chart
☐ Customer requirements	☐ Data-gathering planning	☐ Data Stratification
• Kano Analysis (Basic, Core, Breakthrough)	☐ Issue Diagram	☐ Correlation and Regression
• Customer Loyalty Grid	☐ Storyboard	• Hypothesis testing
• QFD	• Characterizing Processes	
• Takt Time	• Takt time	
☐ IPO Diagram	• Waste Summary	
	• UDE List	
	• Process Capability Summary	
	• Process Efficiency Summary	
	• Process Scorecards	☐ = Covered in yellow belt course
	☐ Focus Areas	

Figure 10: PI tools overview – by phase. Source: Legal Lean Sigma Institute LLC. (continued on next page)

PI Tools Overview-By Phase

Improve
Lean Sigma Solutions
- Simplification
  - PQ Analysis
  - Product-Process Matrix
  - Product Families
  - Cells
  - Block Layout
  - Monument strategies
- Lean Process Design
  - Takt time
  - Activity of the product / service
  - Employee load charts
  - Basic material positioning
- Work Design
  - Activity of the employee
  - 7-cycle analysis
  - Elimination of NVA and motion
  - ☐ Standard work
  - Standard operations routine
  - Standard work combination
  - Ergonomics
  - ☐ 5s
- Equipment Optimization
  - Many tools, but applies minimally to law firms

- Process Capability Improvement
  - Defect Analysis
  - ☐ Process capability
  - Cost of Poor Quality
  - Measurement Systems Analysis
  - ☐ Cause and Effect Diagram (Fishbone) and Five Whys for Root Cause Analysis
  - ☐ Stratification
  - ☐ Measurement assessment tree
  - Defect reduction (PF /CE/CNX/SOP)
  - Analysis of Variance
  - Error-Proofing
  - Design for Six Sigma
  - Testing / inspection elimination
- Work Control
Many tools – most applicable to law firms are:
  - Flow and pull
  - Point of use
  - Level loading
  - Just-in-Time
  - Make-to-Order

- Self-Improving Processes
  - Lean Metrics
  - Visual Controls
  - Dynamic visual workplace
  - ☐ After-Action Reviews
  - Value Stream Organization
  - Culture
  - Support processes
- Structured Problem-Solving
  - ☐ Problem Statement
  - ☐ Solution Specification
  - ☐ Alternative Approaches
  - ☐ Recommendation
  - ☐ Modeling and Simulation
- FMEA
- ☐ Pilots

Control
- Visual displays and visual controls
- Dynamic Visual Factory
- ☐ Closed-loop process control
- Statistical process control
- Control Systems Assessment

☐ = Covered in yellow belt course

Figure 10: PI tools overview – by phase continued

While there are many useful Lean, Six Sigma, project management, change management, and design thinking tools, there are a couple of tools used with such frequency that they should be mastered. Project charters in general and all their elements are particularly important because they apply to PI and every other kind of project.

Project charters

A project charter serves several essential purposes, providing numerous benefits. For one thing, it clearly defines the project. All human beings tend to get into fire-fighting mode in a work environment. The project charter makes sense in a business or process improvement context, but it can be used in other ways as well.

Surprisingly, legal practitioners often seem to dive right into doing work without really thinking about how to approach it (or not). Assigning and relationship partners or executives may not spend enough time sharing the background, relevant information, or context that helps workers understand the basics, such as the objectives, or the time or budgetary constraints. Much of the waste we see in law comes from a lack of planning.

A charter, even done quickly, is something a lawyer might use as part of intake with clients, for example, to document and ensure that they and the client are (literally) on the same page. The bigger the team, the more complex the matter or project, the more reasons there are to have a document that can be referred to throughout the course of a matter. This helps us avoid things like "over-lawyering" and, instead, continuing to stay aligned with the client. Every matter or case is a project, after all. Ask any associate or paralegal if they agree – it is rare that partner figures out and then communicates how long a task should take or detail exactly what the work product should look like or contain. Usually, that information is divulged in the critique that comes after the (initial) work has been performed.

Productivity would dramatically increase if only projects were clearly defined at the outset. Usually, we have a vague idea of the purpose of the project, but typically the scope and objectives are fuzzy at best. The project charter clearly outlines the scope, objectives, and goals of the project. This provides a shared understanding of what the project is intended to achieve, helping to align all stakeholders. It details the key deliverables, ensuring everyone knows what the project will produce, and what are the target dates.

A charter establishes authority and accountability since it officially authorizes the project and the project manager to start work. When it is approved, it grants the project manager the authority to allocate resources, make decisions, and direct the project team. It also defines the roles and responsibilities of the project team, stakeholders, and other involved parties, clarifying who is accountable for what.

Stakeholder analysis
Whether or not you are using a project charter, it is always helpful to identify the stakeholders. Stakeholders are defined as people, groups, and/or organizations that have an interest or concern in the process / project who can either affect or be affected by the process or project, directly and/or indirectly.

They help make a project successful because they provide valuable information regarding needs, resources, realistic objectives, and practical considerations. They also recognize hidden items that might not be obvious in the planning stage, identify points of opposition, and prevent problems during implementation.

A rough stakeholder analysis can be done in three to five minutes, so it's not time-consuming. Once we see how many functions, positions, and people are identified (and so quickly!), we begin to understand why no one should start another project without spending the time to identify who they are and how they might help or impede our progress.

Stakeholders may cause us to re-define or refine the objective. We can consider the potential legal and business objectives and the potential losses from all stakeholder perspectives, as well as the relative likelihood of outcomes and the factors that might influence each one.

Once they have been identified, a stakeholder power grid, also known as a power/interest grid or influence/interest matrix, is used to categorize stakeholders based on their level of power (influence) over the project and their interest in the project's outcomes. See Figure 11 overleaf. This grid helps project managers and teams prioritize stakeholders and develop appropriate strategies and tactics for engaging them throughout the project lifecycle.

The stakeholder power grid is typically a 2×2 matrix that categorizes stakeholders into four quadrants based on two dimensions:

1. *Power (influence)*. The ability of the stakeholder to affect the project, either positively or negatively. This can be due to their authority, expertise, control over resources, or influence within the organization.
2. *Interest*. The degree to which the stakeholder is concerned with or affected by the project's outcomes. High stake interest indicates that the stakeholder cares deeply about the project, while low stake interest means they are less concerned.

A high power, high interest stakeholder is one to manage closely. These are the key stakeholders who have both significant power and a strong interest in the project. They could be senior executives, key customers, or critical team members. It is imperative for these stakeholders to be closely managed and regularly engaged. They need to be kept fully informed and involved in decision-making processes to ensure their support and buy-in.

A high power, low interest stakeholder is one to keep satisfied. These stakeholders have significant power but may not be highly interested in the day-to-day details of the project. They could be high-level executives. We must provide them with sufficient information to ensure they remain

```
High
         ┌─────────────────┬─────────────────┐
  I      │   High power,   │   High power,   │
  N      │   Low interest  │   High interest │
  F      │  Keep satisfied │  Manage closely │
  L      ├─────────────────┼─────────────────┤
  U      │                 │                 │
  E      │   Low power,    │   Low power,    │
  N      │   Low interest  │   High interest │
  C      │     Monitor     │  Keep informed  │
  E      │                 │                 │
         └─────────────────┴─────────────────┘
Low
                      INTEREST
         Low stake                    High stake
```

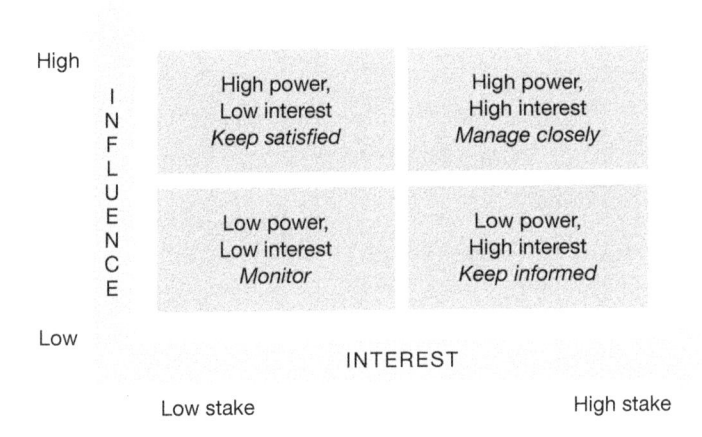

Figure 11: The stakeholder power grid. Source: Legal Lean Sigma Institute LLC.

supportive of the project yet engage them selectively, focusing on key milestones and high-level updates.

A low power, high interest stakeholder is one to keep informed. These stakeholders have a high level of interest but relatively low power to influence the project. We must keep them informed and engaged, ensure they have access to project updates, and encourage their input, as their insights and feedback can be valuable, even if they lack decision-making power.

A low power, low interest stakeholder is one to monitor. These stakeholders require minimal effort and the least amount of communication. They can be updated occasionally or only when necessary.

The prioritization of stakeholders based on their influence and interest helps us focus on those who matter most to the project's success. Once we know that, we can develop and deliver specific communications and engagement opportunities for each stakeholder group. In this way, the right information is delivered in the right way at the right time to the right people. This exercise also helps us identify stakeholders who might derail our progress or who could pose risks to the project if not managed properly. This enables more proactive mitigation strategies and assists in allocating resources (time, attention, communication efforts) more effectively.

Overall, by identifying the stakeholders and documenting the project's purpose, objectives, and scope, the charter helps manage stakeholder expectations and avoid project killers, like scope creep. Sustained alignment encourages a sense of ownership in the project and involvement. This effort pays off, especially during the implementation stage, and ensures the focus of a project remains on the people it is meant to support/serve. Sometimes the term "Single Source of Truth" is used to describe the project charter. That is because it acts as a central document that can be referred to throughout the project. It ensures that all communications are consistent and based on the same set of facts and objectives.

There are so many benefits that an entire book could be written about project charters; to point out one more, it provides a reference for future projects. We can use our template for successful future projects, especially in organizations that either plan to or regularly undertake similar types of projects. The insights gained from the project charter can be used to improve future charters, incorporating lessons learned to enhance project success. Because we have defined the criteria for project success, we can use that during project closure to assess whether the project has met its objectives.

In summary, a project charter is a foundational document that provides clarity, authority, and direction for a project. It aligns stakeholders, facilitates communication, supports planning, and helps ensure that the project is successful and aligned with organizational goals. Mastering the creation and use of a project charter is essential for effective project management.

This is critical work that sets us up for success in any project, yet too often we give it short shrift. At the Legal Lean Sigma Institute, Ronna West Cross is known for saying "proper planning promotes peak performance!" Plan, plan, plan, plan, plan, then execute.

Process mapping

If there is only one other tool to master, it might be process mapping. Behold, the power of sticky notes and markers! We nearly always develop a top-down map and very often a swim-lane diagram as well. Value stream mapping is also helpful in identifying and eliminating waste, leading to more streamlined processes and increased productivity.

Maps are fundamental and contribute so greatly to a team or individual's success. The vast majority of people are visual learners, so seeing the process from end to end is, as we almost always hear in these sessions, "eye opening". It's a great way to get everyone engaged, and to learn and show what each function is doing, when they are doing their work, and where we have loops and missed connections.

Also, process maps have applications outside of process improvement as they support project, team, law practice, and people management as well as innovation, training, communication, teambuilding, strategy, planning, marketing, and business and client development activities. We have yet to experience a more powerful tool to forge and further relationships than developing a process map or using it to talk about how we are going to use our process and apply it to a particular engagement.

Try mapping your workflow, starting with the first and last steps (to scope the process) and then filling in the high-level steps in between. Use sticky notes and do not draw lines because once you start filling in the primary tasks required to complete each step, it is likely you will move those sticky notes around. Everyone struggles with capturing the current rather than the ideal state, because once we start to see how we are really doing something now, we want to change it. So, as you are using this tool, it's likely you'll move things around and add tasks and steps as you map.

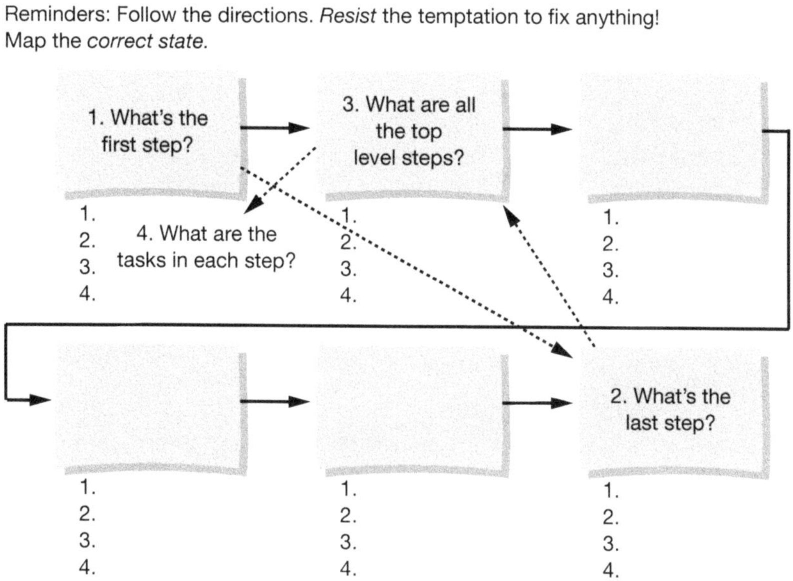

Reminders: Follow the directions. *Resist* the temptation to fix anything! Map the *correct state*.

Figure 12: Process mapping. Source: Legal Lean Sigma Institute LLC.

One of the tools our students seem to like a lot is the Kanban. This is a visual tool that helps manage and optimize workflow by using cards or signals to represent work items, making it easy to identify bottlenecks and manage work in progress. It is commonly used in Agile methodologies but can be applied to various types of work to help teams visualize tasks, track progress, and identify bottlenecks. The board helps ensure that work flows smoothly from start to finish by making the status of tasks visible to everyone involved.

By limiting the amount of work that can be in any phase of the value stream, before any new item can be introduced in that work step, there must be capacity. If there is no open space, work downstream must be completed to create open capacity. In this way, work is pulled through the system by available capacity, not pushed. This is apparently a novel concept in law, where people are expected to give it their (impossible) "110 percent". Using this methodology, you need to finish what you are doing before you can start something new.

The Kanban board (see Figure 13) is typically divided into vertical columns,

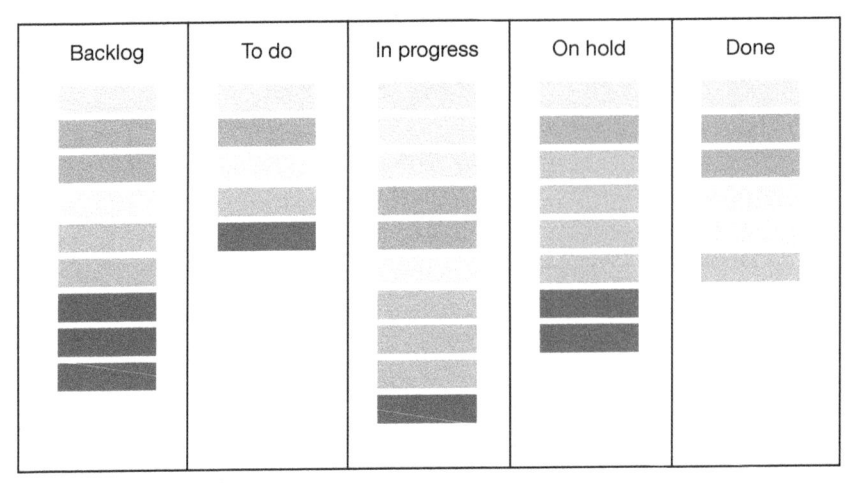

Figure 13: The Kanban Board. Source: Legal Lean Sigma Institute LLC.

each representing a different stage in the workflow. Common columns might include:
- *Backlog:* Tasks that need to be done but haven't been started yet.
- *To Do:* Tasks that are ready to be worked on.
- *In Progress:* Tasks that are currently being worked on.
- *On Hold:* Tasks that cannot be progressed.
- *Done:* Tasks that have been completed.

The columns can be customized to fit the specific workflow of a team or project, and more stages can be added if needed.

Tools like Kanban boards, fishbone diagrams, and SIPOC or IPO charts are great for visualizing things and communicating with stakeholders. Another tool – the Failure Mode and Effects Analysis (FMEA) – helps to identify potential failures in a process before they occur, allowing for proactive risk management. Finally, conducting an After-Action Review (also known as the cheerily termed "post-mortem" – see Figure 14) and capturing, analyzing, and learning from what went well and what can be improved can be a game changer. When we can implement preventive measures, we reduce the likelihood of costly errors or failures. That's always a good thing.

After action review – what did we learn?

What we wanted to accomplish	Participant group
What we planned to do	

What we actually did	What we actually accomplished

What we'll do next time

Figure 14: The After-Action Review. Legal Lean Sigma Institute LLC.

Many process improvement tools require collaboration across departments. When you have a solid understanding of how to use the right tools in the right way at the right time, it facilitates better communication and cooperation among teams. That usually leads to more cohesive efforts and allows for faster identification of inefficiencies, which reduces the time spent on trial and error when solving problems. Moreover, you'll deliver improved quality and consistency, cost reduction, and competitive advantages, while fostering a culture of continuous improvement.

Mastering just a few of the tools we use will no doubt enhance your problem-solving and team building skills. This is because they provide structure for analyzing and solving complex questions. Every individual will benefit from the ability to systematically identify root causes and implement effective solutions as a response to why things are occurring (especially as opposed to guess work).

In summary, proficiency with even select tools used in process improvement provides a solid foundation for improving efficiency, reducing costs, enhancing quality, and driving continuous improvement. Whether for personal development or organizational success, these tools are essential for anyone looking to make lasting improvements in how work is done and delivered.

Chapter 7:
The case for process improvement

Most processes fall short of their potential

Even if a process does not need to be redesigned or reengineered, most people agree that their processes could be improved, by a lot. Lean Sigma practitioners usually find one of several scenarios. One is that the process people think is in place does not really exist. Another is that each person has his or her own process (highly likely in law). Nearly every process takes much longer and has way more steps and handoffs than people might guess. This is one of the reasons that process mapping is so impactful.

Everyone in law benefits from optimized processes. It is better for practitioners, staff, and clients. Most people working in law firms, legal aid offices, law departments, government and military law offices, and legal service providers yearn to fulfill their purpose and be more productive, more efficient, and less frustrated.

As Henry Ford famously said, *"Most people spend more time and energy going around problems than in trying to solve them".*

In law, our experience is that most people are spending more time and energy struggling heroically, trying to cope with things that don't work well. They are also expending more effort in trying to solve problems created by ineffective processes than in trying to improve them. When that happens, it is inarguable that they are not doing things that are value in the eyes of the client.

In many cases, we have seen that what started out as a decent practice or way of working has changed considerably over the years. Usually, this is due to well-intentioned actions taken by workers who employ "workarounds" to compensate for the failure of the process. The result is that law firm processes often, by lack of attention or intention, wind up looking like one of those collections of farmhouse type buildings you might see in the countryside that were constructed over time. It is apparent they were adding to the main building, one after another as the years passed by. If we were to design it now, it is likely that an architect would draft the plans with the current requirements in mind and it would look quite different.

The processes we use in law, by analogy, are just like that collection of buildings; it is unlikely that we would design legal and business processes today that look like what we have (mostly) unknowingly and unintentionally developed over the years. Those who have employed Lean and/or Six Sigma will attest to the fact that, as soon as we start to describe and measure a process, we will begin to see things that could be improved, either in the client's eyes or the eyes of the firm/department – or both.

In fact, most of our processes fall far short of their potential and improving them will benefit *both* the client and the law firm, office, or department. The reality is that if we continue to operate our processes as we always have while the expectations of clients, owners, regulators, etc. rise, we will inevitably experience a performance gap. However, if we improve our processes *before* those expectations rise, we will develop significant advantages.

The profession is a business, and it has changed
Law firms began changing their views and recognized that law is both a profession and a business because they were forced to, not necessarily because they chose to accept this reality. One of the reasons is that general counsel and their leadership teams are on the front lines of legal industry transformation. The C-suite is intensifying pressure on them, not just to reduce spend but also to operate as business units and to morph from cost centers to value creators while proactively serving as enterprise defenders.

The 2021 EY Law Survey,[1] conducted in collaboration with the Harvard Law School Center on the Legal Profession, identified several fiscal and operational challenges faced by corporate legal functions. Here is a sampling of the data:
- 75 percent of GCs are having difficulty handling current workloads.
- The workload is projected to increase by 25 percent during the next three years.
- 88 percent of GCs report plans to reduce their budgets in response to escalating pressure from the C-suite and board to do so.
- Among large corporations (>$20bn annual revenue), the C-suite mandated legal cost takeout has jumped from 11 percent in 2019 to 18 percent in 2021.

A 2021 Gartner Report[2] projects law's accelerating transition from lawyer and labor-centricity to tech-enabled scalability. Here are some highlights:
- By 2025, legal departments will increase their spend on technology threefold.

- By 2024, legal departments will replace 20 percent of generalist lawyers with non-lawyer staff.
- By 2024, legal departments will have automated 50 percent of legal work related to major corporate transactions.
- By 2025, at least 25 percent of spending on corporate legal applications will go to non-specialist technology.

A study by The Digital Legal Exchange[3] revealed the C-suite's changing legal remit is broader than financial and operational issues. The research found that 97 percent of business respondents said they wanted the legal function's success metrics to be aligned with business goals. Nearly three-quarters (74 percent) of business respondents said it is important/extremely important for legal to create revenues and new market opportunities.

"To meet the expectations of business requires general counsel to "reimagine the art of the possible", not only for their internal teams but also for their entire supply chain. Most GCs are initially focusing on changing their internal team's culture, mindset, and ways of doing things before tackling the supply chain. That has provided sourced providers – notably law firms – with a temporary reprieve that will not last.[4]

A global pandemic certainly has a way of changing things fast. We were all forced to change the way we worked, the way we thought about working, and the way we worked together. Law firms were forced to recognize they are vendors, part of the supply chain. And they are not exempt. The innovators and early adopters benefited from leadership wisdom and foresight, coupled with their commitment to act. As they usually do. While law firms continue to do well financially, the attention paid to pricing continues to increase.

As consultants Adam Smith Esq.[5] succinctly put it:

"We [the legal profession] are being squeezed on the top line:
- *By clients exercising pricing pressure; and*
- *By the increasing visibility and acceptability of 'substitutes' for at least some of what BigLaw has traditionally done.*

"We have overcapacity, as an industry, to the order of seven percent of our headcount:
- *Citi Private Bank has estimated that if all the 70,000+ lawyers in their*

> sample of firms were working as many hours per year as they did five years ago, 5,000 of them would not be needed.
> - Yet we continue not only to prevent attrition from taking its natural course, but we are adding to [the] headcount.
>
> "Expense growth has again begun to outpace revenue growth:
> - Our #1 time-tested technique for increasing revenue is to raise rates; we can do that until the cows come home, but clients will take it right back in decreased realization – now at an all-time historic low for the industry.
> - Our #2 time-tested technique for increasing revenue is to load up on lateral partners; but in this environment they may be adding more to expense than to revenue.
>
> "We are completely unserious about taking the shortest route between two points in terms of attacking both overcapacity and expense growth in a single stroke. We have not even begun to address our equity partner headcount.
> - Evidently, we lack a sense of urgency.
> - The tepid, "no longer in free fall" economy has become the enabling economy, coyly inviting us to postpone for tomorrow what no longer seems a matter of great urgency today.
> - We have, in short, committed the classic and so-oft-repeated sin of wasting a crisis."

Attitude is a choice. We can and should choose to view these increased pressures and changes as opportunities to seize.

Whether you work in a law department or law firm or office of any size, these concepts apply. The truth is that all of us in law (and everywhere else) are experiencing serious financial and operational pressures.

Because we now have alternative options for getting work done rapidly and at greater value, efficiency and pricing pressures are increasing. We need good processes more than ever. From single corporate counsels, solos, and small firm practitioners to legal aid and other offices to the world's largest firms and law departments, the pressure to do better and be better is intense.

Regardless of your setting or position, it is essential to determine what clients find valuable in a process, select the lowest cost resource capable of handling each task in the process every time, and then do and deliver the work with the highest standards of quality every time and profitably overall.

There is no better time than now to embrace process improvement. At this point, conversations about this subject have become much more commonplace between law firms, offices, and departments, and their clients. It is important for lawyers and business professionals to be able to talk about why process improvement is important to them and what they are doing to build their capability. These are conversations to have, regardless of type or size of team or office. These discussions help build and enhance relationships and allow people to directly contribute to their organization's vision, mission, goals, and success.

The risks are greater than the challenges

Some are skeptical about the ability of their leaders to adapt and lead their organizations through the changes that are going to be required for survival. I have had the repeated good fortune to work with many extraordinary CLOs and GCs, managing partners, practice group leaders, and business professionals who have embraced process improvement. What I have seen is that their teams do not just "adopt and adapt" – they also develop high-functioning teams and significant competitive advantages.

Making the necessary changes will never be easy. As Ray Worthy Campbell explained in the *New York University Journal of Law and Business*:

> "The business literature on innovation, which has been largely ignored by scholars addressing legal markets, helps make many things clear. Successful incumbents cannot easily change their business model; their resources, processes, and values are optimized to their current clients and will resist change. Incumbents can use radical new technologies to sustain their business model, but tend to leave alone new technologies or business processes that do not enhance their offerings to their current clients."[6]

However, the risks associated with standing still while competitors (even those who have yet to appear on the scene) move forward will be far greater than the challenges firms will inevitably face in embracing process improvement.

> "Disruptive entrants can enter the low end of the market with new technologies or business processes, and disrupt the market through a sequence that sees them improving their offerings in an iterative manner, eventually allowing them to challenge for the incumbent's best customers."[7]

As an accredited partner of the Smart Collaboration Accelerator, I often quote Heidi K. Gardner, PhD, distinguished fellow at Harvard Law School's Center on the Legal Profession and faculty chair of the school's Accelerated Leadership Program and Sector Leadership Masterclass. She is well known for her view that:

> "Our toughest and highest-value challenges are becoming more VUCA – volatile, uncertain, complex, and ambiguous. These complex problems require people with different areas of expertise, experiences, and perspectives to integrate their knowledge to develop better solutions than anyone could produce on their own."[8]

Collaborative, continuous improvement cultures don't just "eat strategy for breakfast". I'll go on record with my statement that they are the best answer to every challenge or opportunity facing any business at any time.

Gaining buy-in for process improvement
There is no doubt that it is compelling and even inspiring to learn about who is employing process improvement and project management, and how and where those firms and law departments have been successful. People-focused activities in areas such as talent acquisition, integration, and cultivation, professional development, DEIA, women's initiatives, workplace wellness, working from home, work–life balance, time management, and practice management, while often siloed, are key components of strategy and culture for which leaders are responsible.

Returning to our theme of People, Process, Platform, one effective approach to gain buy in is to properly focus on the first P: People. W. Edwards Deming has many quotable sayings that emphasize the importance of process management, including, "A bad system will beat a good person every time".

For every business, success (or failure) depends on how the systems interact with other operations and duties. As such, it is critical to constantly optimize and improve processes. Even when you hire, align, and empower the best employees, you'll never maximize their talents and abilities with faulty systems. This extract sums it up:

> "Deming said that 90 percent of all problems were management's responsibility and workers were only responsible for ten percent of all problems. The root cause of most problems ultimately is the way the work is designed

within the production system. Most struggle to grasp this. The separation between actually doing the work and the design of the system for doing the work. In fact, most don't even know they are responsible for the systems the organization uses. That's why we end up with people watching machines do the work, with overly complex data input algorithms and with teams with no understanding of or connection to the customer. Have you ever seen a management team look at each other in bewilderment when asked who is responsible for driving improvement in one of the key systems?

"Organizations have many different systems – HR systems, Maintenance systems, Finance systems to name a few. What's the best way for Leadership teams to know which systems need to be strengthened? Go to Gemba and Go See and understand what's actually happening. As I did this with one executive he remarked, somewhat embarrassed, 'I can't believe we actually make people work like this'. As he said this though, he did take on the responsibility for changing the system."[9]

Most organizations have no idea what it costs to operate their process or how much people are struggling to perform despite the systems. One might argue that heroics are so prized in law that we create cultures and reward systems that reinforce this behavior.

Let's briefly examine the end-to-end lateral acquisition process, where the high-level steps include recruiting, hiring, pre-boarding, onboarding, and integration. How much effort is expended in just the first step, Recruiting? In one firm's lateral partner onboarding project, we examined time entries from the lawyers on the executive committee since the members of that team were integrally involved in executing the firm's growth by a lateral acquisition strategy. Using a simple calculation of billing rates x time entered, we (and they) were astonished to learn that their efforts alone amounted to over one million dollars in just the recruiting step. Since most lawyers do not capture all their time, this was a conservative estimate.

Correspondingly, we examined how long it took for the laterals to be "integrated", as indicated by their first full billable day (seven hours). The data easily showed what kind of return they were getting on that one-million-dollar investment and the news was not good. Data showed that, in a four-year period, it took laterals an average of 179 days to reach their first billable day. Simply put, laterals struggled with the new firm's processes. All that energy to acquire top-level talent, and the processes impeded their integration into the firm, dramatically impacting the firm's return on investment, frustrating new partners, and both directly and directly affecting their clients as well as other lateral prospects. This also impacted the legal and business professionals who performed tasks in the other steps and everyone in each practice group as well.

Another key point that helps make the case for Lean Six Sigma is to highlight that one of our goals in fundamentally changing our processes is to create even greater opportunities for lawyers to focus on the areas where they contribute the highest value, which are practicing law and applying strategic thinking to legal problems. This takes advantage of their experience and training by removing waste by reducing time spent on administrative tasks that irritate them and other non-value adding activities.

It is critical to show skeptics that, when we improve processes, lawyers will still have some autonomy, latitude, and flexibility. We never gratuitously standardize any part of a process or crudely suggest that improving efficiency is as simple as reducing headcount. The rigor of Lean Sigma demands that we not take the "bull in a china shop" approach to making changes and that we include our stakeholders as we progress through the phases of a process improvement project.

This is especially important to emphasize where business professionals who are not practicing lawyers are responsible for leading the charge.

Making the case with quick wins, positive experiences, and early success is important for beginning to build momentum and achieving "buy in" for doing this work or more of it. It is a truism that no organization has a second chance to do something right the first time. Selecting the right introduction, training, baseline, or demonstration project that will serve as your firm's own case study will always provide the most convincing evidence that "Lean Sigma works here".

Linking quality and performance

Lawyers, and rightfully so, care a great deal about quality, and often express concern that it will be sacrificed by making a process more efficient. They also worry that profitability will suffer. One of the first solid pieces of evidence linking quality and business results was groundbreaking research performed by PIMS (Profit Impact of Market Strategy).[10]

Over a period of years, PIMS amassed a large database documenting the strategies and financial results of more than 450 companies and nearly 3,000 business units to study the general relationships between strategy and company performance. Its purpose was not to prove a link between quality and profitability (or between any other particular business strategy and firm performance), but rather to discover those strategic principles most strongly related to performance. Among all the strategic principles distilled from the PIMS studies, one linkage between strategy and performance stood out above all the rest – quality.

A quality edge boosts performance in the short-term by allowing the firm to charge premium prices and in the long-term by enabling growth of the firm through both market expansion and gains in market share. PIMS found that businesses offering superior product/service quality are more profitable than those with inferior quality, based on two key measurements – return on sales and return on investment. In addition to these profitability and growth advantages, PIMS also revealed other benefits of superior perceived quality – "stronger customer loyalty, more repeat purchases, less vulnerability to price wars, and lower marketing costs".[11]

The link between quality and Lean Six Sigma in law lies in the application of Lean Sigma methodologies to improve legal services, enhance efficiency, and reduce errors. For lawyers, this could mean reducing time spent on repetitive tasks, minimizing unnecessary paperwork, and improving workflow efficiency. By identifying and eliminating activities that do not add value, legal professionals can deliver faster and more efficient services to clients. We can also improve quality by identifying and eliminating defects or errors in areas such as documentation, improving accuracy in case management, and ensuring consistent outcomes.

Practically speaking, this means creating processes that are not only streamlined but also produce high-quality results with fewer errors, such as improving client intake procedures or streamlining case management. By improving efficiency and reducing errors, law firms can enhance client satisfaction, leading to better client retention and more positive referrals, and achieving significant cost savings, such as less time and resources spent on correcting mistakes or managing inefficient workflows.

The quality argument is relatively easy to make with a basic business case and conservative estimates. Lean Six Sigma helps lawyers enhance the quality of their services by improving efficiency, reducing errors, and optimizing processes. This leads to better client outcomes, increased satisfaction, and more effective practice management.

In short, focusing on quality can help make a very compelling case for trying process improvement. Lean Sigma has provided particularly good quality case studies. This is due to the framework of process improvement and a focus on delivering bottom-line results.

Understanding changing client expectations

When we begin to learn about and engage in process improvement, we demonstrate our ability to speak our client's language. As Karen Dalton and John Dugga observed:

> *"While lawyers generally know their clients well, they are often surprised at how much their clients know about lean, six sigma, project management and even agile. Clients expect exceptional legal expertise, but what they are most interested in is how the firm is going to do their work. Clients are very interested and receptive to innovative value-added services that deliver results."*[12]

DuPont was one of the first law departments – but by no means the last – to act on the belief that legal professionals should bear some responsibility for their client's bottom-line success and that legal services, no less than other services, can improve through process analysis. They say process improvement is for lawyers who "are driven by a commitment to continuous improvement and who recognize that the complete lawyer brings more to the table than legal acumen".[13] We encourage every law firm that receives a request for proposal or outside counsel guidelines to read carefully. Efficiency, predictability, continuous improvement, and effective project management are major themes in every single one of those documents.

Convincing lawyers to embrace Lean Sigma and project management is no small undertaking. In fact, both the change management and the work of process improvement itself require vision, commitment, serious discipline, and proper allocation of resources. However, we must accept the fact that most lawyers, by training or nature (or both), seem to approach even the notion of any real change with a large dose of skepticism. As a rule, we tend to challenge things (especially new ideas) and base our thinking and decisions on precedent, rather than the possibilities and benefits that innovation may deliver to them.

Moreover, lawyers may initially resist the notion that their work can be reduced to a series of steps where predictability of activity and budgets are possible. It is important to have empathy and recognize that their concerns have some merit. Lean Sigma will not work for everything. At the same time, and especially if they are exposed to some of the concepts of Lean Sigma, lawyers are quick to recognize how many legal processes do have standardized components, such as completing forms or obtaining follow-up information. They are willing to extend that thinking to recognize that, when streamlined, a process improves both the work product produced and the service delivered to the client. In addition, the rising number of Lean Sigma successes is too significant to ignore. We have precedent at this point. The issue is no longer whether Lean Sigma should be considered; it is where and how to get started.

Law firms invest substantial effort in establishing their lawyers as thought leaders and experts. Clients expect them to know what they are doing, and that means being able to understand the process. From the client's perspective, it is inconsistent to be told that a firm has decades of deep experience in handling a particular kind of matter and then, in the next breath, have it explained that there is too much variation because every case or matter is so difficult that there is no way to predict how long something should take, what could happen at each step, and how much it will cost.

To be cost-effective, a task must be done by the lowest cost resource that is capable of performing it. Therefore, employing process improvement and project management becomes critical. Detailed knowledge of the effort required to carry out the work is required, recording time is very important, analyzing past engagements is key. Timekeeping is not just a core business process. It is the process that collects critically important data that is used to understand and improve so many other processes, both legal and business.

Without understanding who (meaning which function or role) is doing which tasks, when, and how long it took, it is nearly impossible to determine the actual cost of doing and delivering anything. How would any organization know how to staff something without this data? So often, we hear "We need more paralegals" or "We need associates" with absolutely no evidence to support the demand. Is this any way to run a practice or business? How is it possible to determine resource needs, costs, savings, opportunities, or profitability without this information?

With all that in mind, it would be difficult to reasonably argue the point that process efficiency and ongoing improvement in any professional services work is a bad thing. Yet for years the legal profession has managed business in a manner that creates disincentives to do so. The billable hour is one such distinguishing riptide. While we do not see the permanent demise of the billable hour ever coming to pass, other billing arrangements have worked successfully for quite some time now.

Chapter 7: The case for process improvement

Says Christopher Kelly, deputy chair of the Corporate Practice at Loeb & Loeb, a firm with more than 300 lawyers in Los Angeles, New York, Chicago, Nashville, Washington, DC, Beijing, and Hong Kong:

> *"Legal project management (LPM) has become absolutely critical to remain competitive in today's marketplace. It saves money, creates budget certainty, and makes clients more comfortable when they see exactly what their legal team is doing to become more efficient."*[14]

A legal department must be concerned with cost control – and that involves resource management. In a law firm, however, a primary objective is to be profitable. Bruce MacEwen, a recognized leader in the industry and the founder of Adam Smith, Esq., says:

> *"With the exception of a pandemic/lockdown-induced blip in 2021 and 2022, the indisputable message of the trend line is that law firms have been collecting about 90 cents on the dollar for well over a decade. This is not normal pricing behavior in a mature industry. Note – this is important, folks – that this is not data reflecting a single firm's experience, which could be explained through any number of factors idiosyncratic to that firm and its client relations; this is an industry-wide, chronic and systemic phenomenon."*[15]

Tim Corcoran, a former CEO, writes on his Business of Law Blog:

> *"Business clients are unhappy. Lawyers in the mid-size and big firms that serve us often do a terrible job of communicating. They fail to properly manage expectations by limiting the client's surprise. They tend to treat each matter as if it's unique and infinitely variable, yet at the same time expect us to believe their experience in a given field is meaningful. They believe in charging higher fees based on the length of time they've practiced, even when they are unable or unwilling to demonstrate this experience by using matter budgets or project plans.*
>
> *"And their fees are typically established irrespective of the value I place on the services rendered, and what alternatives exist for me to obtain these same services elsewhere, assuming that the seniority of the lawyer and the time necessary to deliver the work are the primary drivers of value. They claim that non-lawyers in a law firm, or worse, non-lawyers providing legal*

services outside the structure of a law firm, e.g., an LPO, must be incapable of providing quality legal services, even when these alternative providers can unassailably demonstrate higher quality at a lower cost."[16]

People and competitive advantages

The rate of change is not slowing down. It is an evergreen statement – if your processes are not changing as fast as the environment is changing, as former General Electric CEO Jack Welch would say, "the end is in sight".

The changes in the business environment create ever greater requirements for higher process capabilities and higher process efficiencies. We have extremely talented and capable people working in law in all sorts of positions. However, all too often, they are working with processes that do not allow them to function at their highest and best levels. Instead, legal and business professionals in law firms are sometimes coping with processes that are horribly broken. At the Legal Lean Sigma Institute, we routinely suggest that when you put talented people up against a broken process, the process will always win.

So, talent acquisition and retention, competitors, technology, employees, regulations, and, most importantly, clients are all part of the driving forces that are creating widening performance gaps in the processes in law firms. Because our processes are not capable, errors are made and waste occurs. Then, we spend time addressing those mistakes, making corrections, pacifying people and recovering. As a result, it is difficult for anyone to have the time to improve anything. We call this being stuck in the "fire-fighting doom loop".

For law firms, the two most compelling drivers for process improvement are clients and the competition (other firms and legal service providers). We leverage the realizations associated with those drivers to convince law firms of the importance of pulling the car over and finally fixing the engine rather than continuing to drive or attempting to repair it as we speed down the highway. Process improvement is an excellent way to get out of this fire-fighting doom loop.

Clients expect efficient processes

When a firm has law department clients, it should speak the language of business and that includes being at least conversant in Lean Sigma. Put positively, when people are knowledgeable and use the language and tools of Lean and Six Sigma, talking about efficiency becomes part of the reason to hire a lawyer or firm. The competitive advantages continue as well because the processes used and the conversations related to each project are the cornerstones of how people collaborate and work as a team. Without Lean Sigma, the difficulty of all that increases as the work, services, and number and depth of relationships between firm and client grows and becomes more complex.

We always suggest a firm reads and reviews what clients are expecting in their requests for proposals, outside counsel guidelines, and their survey results. Here are just a few examples from RFPs:

- Please address how you will accomplish greater efficiencies. For example, do you employ project management techniques, Six Sigma or Lean?
- How and why should Company A have confidence that your firm will handle matters efficiently and in a cost-effective manner without sacrificing quality?
- What changes could we as a company or law department implement to make your work for us more cost-efficient?
- Company A seeks reliable, financially stable Law Firms that can meet stringent cost, quality, and service requirements. A team will evaluate each proposal based on various criteria, including, but not limited to… processes generating operational efficiencies.

When competing these days, using flowery language and smoke and mirrors to respond to specific questions about how your firm is approaching efficiency and employing Lean and Six Sigma will not only be unresponsive, but could potentially harm your firm's position and reputation. Show you know what you're doing because you have a process for it. Corporate clients are wise to "theatre of innovation" and legal operations and procurement professionals expect real answers.

The *2024 ACC Chief Legal Officers Survey*[17] provides insights into the evolving role of the chief legal officer (CLO) and how legal departments are positioning themselves to help organizations most effectively adapt to the broader business environment. The report is based on responses from 669 CLOs from organizations spanning 20 industries and 31 countries.

There are several key findings in the survey that are worth considering and discussing at any strategy or practice management meeting. How do you respond to these?

- CLOs and legal departments continue to face intense pressure to do

more with less. Forty-two percent of departments received a mandate to cut legal costs and 58 percent experienced major rate hikes by their law firms.
- CLOs rank operational efficiency as their top strategic initiative. Forty percent of CLOs rank operational efficiency as their law department's top strategic initiative for the coming year, followed by the "right-sourcing" of legal services (15 percent), and talent management/retention (ten percent).
- CLOs want their staff to develop greater business acumen. Sixty-three percent of CLOs say they are seeking to develop greater business acumen among the lawyers in their department, followed by communication skills (51 percent), and executive presence (45 percent).
- The majority of CLOs experienced an increase in workload over the past year. Fifty-nine percent of CLOs say their workload has increased over the past year and just three percent say their workload has decreased.

These days, there is an increasing need to get legal procurement's attention. Dr Silvia Hodges Silverstein,[18] whose research and work in procurement has set the standard in this area, has contributed some of her work to chapter 11 of this book. She says of the above survey:

"Procurement is now involved in the purchasing of legal services and it's quickly becoming the 'new normal'. Larger corporations in particular engage procurement, not only for sourcing low-end, routine, or commoditized legal services, but increasingly for higher-stakes legal work as well. But that doesn't mean that law firms or in-house legal and procurement teams are well equipped to deal with this new landscape and to make these new relationships successful.

"Legal procurement analyzes many things that might not have been given a lot of attention in the legal profession before. Industry benchmarking analysis is conducted by 71 percent of respondents in the survey, followed by rate increase analysis and invoice audits (67 percent each). Half of the respondents forecast budgets, followed by alternative fee arrangement analysis and key performance indicator analysis.

"Procurement also embraces legal spend management (75 percent) and e-billing (71 percent). Contract database for legal, matter management and in-house e-discovery are used by 40 to 50 percent of respondents in the survey. Firms' project management and process improvement capabilities

are increasingly important: 48 percent of respondents in the survey deemed them 'very important', another 16 percent as 'important'."

Even clients and organizations that don't work with requests for proposals (RFPs) and information that asks for descriptions of process improvement or process management programs are being asked in some way, shape, or form about efficiency measures. Efficiency matters to them and so does our response.

To be clear, today's clients not only expect their legal departments and law firms to understand and employ process improvement methodologies in their own work, but also to provide recommendations as to how they can help the client with *their* processes. This requires that the lawyers and business professionals in law firms – whether they are client-facing or not – are able to identify and propose ideas for improvements.

The pressure to deliver value

A research report commissioned by Allen & Overy described how general counsel are responding to external and internal pressures to change the way legal work is delivered:

"Eighty-six percent of the respondents to our latest survey say they are under pressure to deliver more value to their business for less cost. Many legal teams now face increased workloads with headcount and budgets that are cut or frozen. This pressure is forcing legal teams to explore more fundamental change."[19]

The general counsel of "one multinational conglomerate" cited in the above report put the situation for law firms quite simply:

"The firms that sit around and think they are going to be able to just continue doing what they have done for the last 100 years are going to become redundant... The model of the provision of legal services is being challenged now more than ever. Law firms have to constantly think about how they are going to innovate and evolve."[20]

As the report notes, *"Not all law firms will be able to rise to this challenge, but it is clear that failure to do so carries the risk of not keeping pace with changing client expectations"*. These changing expectations include the requirement that firms provide a "one stop shop" for legal services (39 percent of interviewees), whilst 53 percent of respondents said they *"find it challenging to coordinate different types of legal service providers efficiently"*. Taking heed of the research, the firm reported, *"We are deploying technology, business process and project management to combine traditional law firm services and new legal services into hybrid legal solutions."*[21]

Uptake of Lean Six Sigma in law firms

David Skinner, a certified Lean Six Sigma Sensei with many years of experience of practicing in law firms, suggests:

> *"It may be that firms in the UK and Australia are slightly ahead of the curve because they've already adapted business structures that are more conducive to a business-like approach. Let's face it: a huge partnership is hard to manage. If you have to get 900 partners in ten different cities in six countries around the world on board, it's going to take you a while. Smaller firms are more agile and more able to adapt and that's where we see a huge uptake."*[22]

Given the success already achieved by many (client) companies as well as law firms who had by now implemented Lean Six Sigma and reported great results, I was astonished that more had not yet utilized the methodology. Things began to change very soon, however.

By September 2008, Seyfarth Shaw, with its emphasis on branding the firm based on experience and results, became a driving force behind change at firms competing against them for clients.

When Altman Weil released its 2014 survey, the contrast to the 2008 responses was dramatic.

> *"More than 90 percent of firm leaders have said they believe there is a permanent market shift requiring greater efficiency in the delivery of legal services.*
> - *In the area of efficient legal service delivery, 54 percent of the large firm group was pursuing change, compared to 34 percent of the smaller firms*
> - *43 percent of firms offer PM training.*
> - *Only 30 percent of law firms have taken on the really challenging task of re-engineering work processes."*[23]

Compare this with the 2020 report:

> *"For years, large majorities of managing partners have agreed in theory on the need to improve practice efficiencies in the face of intense competition, ongoing commoditization of legal work, price pressures, and encroachments of non-law-firm competitors.*
>
> *"Yet, as reported in the 2020 survey, only 22 percent of firms have attempted to systematically reengineer their work processes and only 31 percent have provided ongoing project management training and support to their attorneys.*
>
> *"Among the firms that are trying to make progress in those areas, most have not yet seen their efforts translate into significantly improved firm performance.*
>
> *"These two tactics are merely examples – the same is true for most of the tactics mentioned in the survey. We encourage you to study the What Works charts in detail as you order your leadership priorities. This year's survey asked managing partners to rate their firms' progress toward maturity in key areas of the law firm business model. The results show that, overall, firms have a long way to go. A majority of firms characterized their current progress as zero or early-stage development in the areas of pricing, staffing and efficiency."*[24]

Why is this part of "The case for process improvement" chapter? Because the firms that figure out how to do this work well and incorporate it into their strategy and organizational development plans will win. Big time. One top takeaway is that efficiency tactics are only effective if they are executed well and aligned with strategy. It may be evident to some, but since the Legal Lean Sigma Institute does a lot of training, we have seen first-hand that simply providing skill development and training is not enough. It needs to be connected to an overarching goal and it requires just a few "next steps" and follow up. Just because people have a chance to learn about something does not mean they will use the information. Context and goals, when offered by leaders, give the training purpose and meaning.

Moreover, developing rewards and other systems that foster a culture of continuous improvement and allow it to take root are needed. An untended garden does not magically produce crops from a scattering of seeds. It takes planning and care. Our response to the process improvement version of this metaphor is to develop the process architecture to plan what we want to

Efficiency tactics: What works

This chart combines findings from the two prior questions. Each bar shows the percentage of law firms using the tactic. Data points on the line show the percentage of those firms using each tactic that report it has delivered a significant improvement in performance.

Comparison of Use and Results:

Tactic	% using tactics	% experiencing significant improvement in performance
Using non-law-firm vendors	21.7%	37.1%
Using technology tools to replace human resources	53.6%	37.2%
Formal knowledge management program	22.3%	42.9%
Systematic reengineering of work processes	22.3%	45.9%
Ongoing project management training and support	31.3%	46.9%
Employing a project management director	15.7%	60.0%
Rewarding efficiency and profitability in compensation decisions	45.8%	66.2%

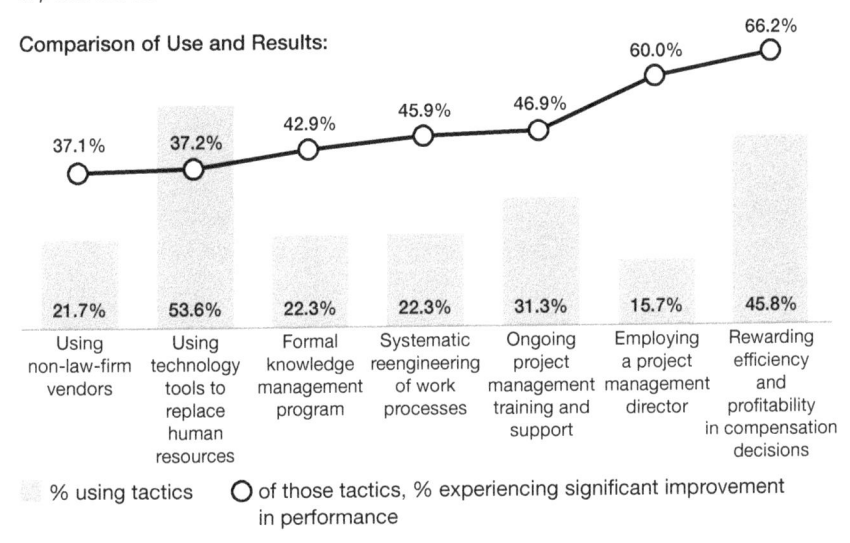

Figure 15: Efficiency tactics – what works. Source: 2020 Law Firms in Transition, Altman Weil.[25]

grow, when to put seeds in the ground, ensure we have the nutrients and attention they need to flourish, and enjoy a bountiful harvest that is well-sequenced and satisfying.

By now, I hope you are convinced (or at least starting to be persuaded) that Lean Sigma helps us to determine the best way to carry out a certain kind of work to achieve efficiency, excellent quality of work and service, high probability of successful outcomes, and predictability.

As I've suggested, though it is simple, process improvement is not easy. In fact, process improvement is hard work – to succeed, initial projects must be recognized priorities. Prioritization means that a project is resourced for rapid progress, supported by experienced Lean Six Sigma practitioners, and provided management attention on a regular basis. One way to make the case for process improvement to decision-makers is to gather data to show that the current process has plenty of waste and opportunity, discuss the benefits to the clients and firm of improving the process, and find an interested and supportive sponsor.[26]

References

1. www.ey.com/en_us/insights/law/the-general-counsel-imperative-how-does-contracting-complexity-hide-clear-profitability
2. www.gartner.com/en/insights/strategic-planning/legal-strategy-template
3. www.dlex.org/
4. www.forbes.com/sites/markcohen1/2021/11/22/the-inevitability-of-legal-industry-change-really/
5. Adam Smith Esq., *The Enabling Economy: The Essay*, 26 August 2013: www.adamsmithesq.com/2013/08/the-enabling-economy-the-essay/?single.
6. Campbell, R. W., "Rethinking Regulation and Innovation in the US Legal Services Market", *New York University Journal of Law & Business*, vol. 9, no. 1, Fall 2012: www.nyujlb.org/wp-content/uploads/nyb_9-1-1_scissored.7-76.pdf.
7. *Ibid.*
8. https://smartcollaborationaccelerator.com/
9. http://blog.leansystems.org/2013/09/dr-w-edwards-deming-people-work-in.html
10. Ryan, J. "Making the Case for Economic Quality, a White Paper for The American Society for Quality (ASQ)": http://asq.org/economic-case.
11. *Ibid.*
12. Dalton, K. and Dugga, J. "Lean and agile: How legal project management can transform client services", *Managing Partner* online, 25 March 2013.
13. Sager, T. L., and Winkelman, S. L., "Six Sigma: Positioning for Competitive Advantage", ACCA Docket 19 (No. 1), 2001.
14. www.loeb.com/en/newsevents/news/2014/09/case-study-in-legal-project-management
15. https://adamsmithesq.com/2024/05/if-supply-grows-faster-than-demand/
16. Corcoran, T. B. "Bar Associations: Protecting Consumers or the Status Quo?" blog post, Corcoran Law Biz Blog, 2 July 2014: www.law.com/sites/jdsupra/2014/07/09/bar-associations-protecting-consumers-or-the-status-quo/?slreturn=20140622111226.
17. www.acc.com/sites/default/files/2024-01/ACC_2024_Chief_Legal_Officers_Survey_Key_Findings.pdf
18. Silverstein, S.H. "Get legal procurement's attention" blog post, 19 May 2014.
19. Allen & Overy Global Survey, Unbundling a market: The appetite for new legal services models, May 2014: www.allenovery.com/SiteCollectionDocuments/global-survey-lsm.pdf.
20. *Ibid.*
21. *Ibid.*
22. Skinner, D. and Skinner, K., "Who says there's no messing with lawyers?" Process Excellence Network, 9 March, 2013: www.processexcellencenetwork.com/lean-six-sigma-business-transformation/articles/who-says-there-s-no-messing-with-lawyers.
23. Altman Weil Inc., "2014 Law Firms in Transition An Altman Weil Flash Survey: www.altmanweil.com/dir_docs/resource/f68236ab-d51f-4d81-8172-96e8d47387e3_document.pdf.

24 www.altmanweil.com/wp-content/uploads/2022/05/Law-Firms-in-Transition-2020-An-Executive-Summary-.pdf
25 *Ibid.*
26 In his report *The Legal Process Improvement Toolkit* (Ark Group, 2012), Mark Bull provides a 12 tool starter kit outlining the primary methodologies for delivering process improvement within your firm. These include how to build a simple process map of your organization; identify critical legal business processes; use models to assess process maturity; use Six Sigma to improve the quality of your process outputs; analyze the potential causes and effects of process problems; deliver process efficiencies using lean principles; capture and use VOC (voice of the client) data; and implement LPI as a fundamental component of a successful legal project management program.

Chapter 8:
P+ EcoSystem, assessments, and change management

"Without change there is no innovation, creativity, or incentive for improvement. Those who initiate change will have a better opportunity to manage the change that is inevitable."
William Pollard

Assessing organizational readiness for change is crucial because it helps ensure that any program or selected initiative is successful by understanding and addressing the organization's current capacity and willingness to embrace the change. There are several key reasons why this assessment is important. First, identifying the level and sources of support and potential obstacles allows for proactive planning and mitigation strategies. It also helps in designing appropriate communication and engagement strategies to secure necessary support and minimize resistance.

Evaluating resources and capacity helps us determine if the organization has the necessary resources (time, money, personnel) to successfully implement the envisioned change. This evaluation informs the design of effective change strategies. Understanding the organization's readiness level allows us to customize change strategies, training programs, and support mechanisms to address specific gaps. This enhances the effectiveness of the change process, increases success rates, and improves morale and engagement.

Knowing where we are facilitates a smooth transition to where we want to go with minimized disruption. A thorough readiness assessment helps in planning for a phased implementation, managing potential troubles, and ensuring that the transition is as seamless as possible. Moreover, benchmarking our current state is imperative for measuring, adjusting, tracking progress, and being able to show and tell our "before" and "after".

There are various mechanisms for assessing organizational readiness for change. Surveys and interviews are commonly used in law; however, they may not be developed or administered in a way that allows us to gather insights from employees, managers, and leaders to understand their perceptions, concerns, and readiness for change. We observe a lot of bias in how questions are framed and in how responses are reported.

Our goals are to assess whether the existing culture supports change or if there are cultural barriers that need to be addressed to determine if the organization has the necessary skills, tools, resources, support, and commitment to implement the change. It seems we skip this inquiry quite a lot in law, rather than taking a more planful approach in determining which change efforts are most likely to succeed. Most organizations do not even review the successes and challenges of previous change efforts to learn from past experiences.

The P+ Ecosystem, Continuum, and Scorecard
While we typically eschew "consultant speak", we did yield when it came to naming the assessment tools we developed to achieve those assessment goals. Because process improvement work involves change, and continuous improvement work involves constant change, and because the legal world is unique (it really is different to anything or anywhere else), Tim Corcoran and I conceived the P+ Ecosystem, Continuum, and Scorecard.

The P+ Ecosystem (see Figure 16) is a model that shows the interconnectedness of various elements in our organizations. Those are the Ps. There are other Ps, such as positioning, and other elements, so what is represented is not intended to represent the entire universe of things to consider. It is a starting point. It is intended to serve as a tool that helps us understand that, as soon as we begin to improve our processes, the other Ps will be triggered at some point, some more quickly than others. As planful change agents, we want to be thoughtful and prepared as to the change management aspects of our work.

Leaders, decision makers, and any program steering committee must consider the impact of process improvement work across the organization, so the P+ Ecosystem and scorecard are extremely useful tools. Their responsibilities are highly strategic and include providing oversight, direction, and support for process improvement projects to ensure they align with organizational goals and achieve desired outcomes. Presenting plans of work in the context of the P+ Ecosystem assures others, especially high impact, high influence stakeholders, that the requisite thought has gone into what has been proposed.

The P+ Scorecard (see Figure 17) was designed to learn about how leaders, project teams, steering committees, and stakeholders scored an organization's current state in each of the following "P" areas: Process improvement,

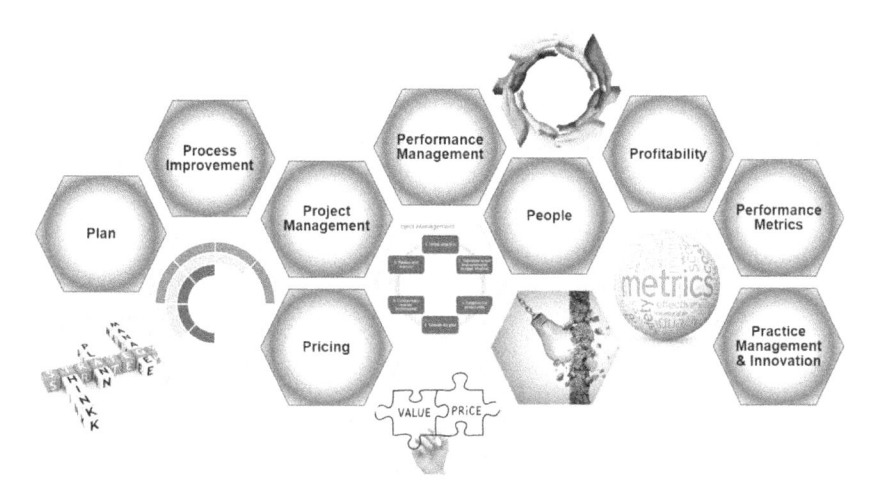

Figure 16: The P+ EcoSystem. A model invented by Corcoran Consulting Group and the Legal Lean Sigma Institute.

Project management, Pricing, Profitability, People, Performance management, Performance metrics, Practice management and innovation, and Planning.

An excellent exercise is to ask leaders such as an executive committee to complete a P+ Scorecard on their own – see Figure 17. Then, we see how closely aligned we are in our evaluation. Gaps give us areas for deep thinking and important conversations and similarities offer opportunities for confirmation. This tool can be used to gauge organizational readiness and maturity for process or continuous improvement as well as change programs, strategic thinking and planning, and organizational development work as a whole.

What's in each P?

Process improvement
- Agreed upon method for selecting and prioritizing projects.
- Established project approval process.
- Skill development – certifications, team leader, steering committee, project support, catalysts.
- Moving from opportunistic to a systematic approach.
- Understand the effort required to do and deliver our work.
- Developing competitive advantages.
- Strategic, funded, continuous improvement program.

P+ scorecard™	1 Clear competitive advantage	2 Some notable successes, improvements underway	3 Few successes, no plan to address	4 Clearly holds us back
Process improvement *We do the right things, the right way, the first time, every time*				
Project Management *We manage expectations and minimize surprises internally and externally*				
Pricing and Profitability *We know the costs and market value of our services*				
People *Our lawyers and staff are fully aligned with our strategy*				
Performance Management *We drive and reward behaviors that lead to long-term health of the organization*				
Performance Metrics *We establish, track, and share key performance indicators to improve performance*				
Practice Management Innovation *We're proactive in re-engineering our work*				

Figure 17: The P+ Scorecard. Source: Legal Lean Sigma Institute LLC.

Project management
- Incorporate voice of the client – those you have, those you want.
- Establish a formal process of PM.
- Enhance skills, roles.
- Agree on nomenclature.
- Build toolkit.

People
- What contributions and behaviors do we value?
- What do we reward?
- Accountability measures.
- Strategic recruiting or opportunistic?
- How do we measure "lowest cost resource capable of doing the work?"
- Staffing protocol.
- Aligned and empowered?

Pricing
- What's our cost of delivery? Our competitors?
- What's the market appetite?
- Time entry discipline, policy, hygiene.
- KPIs – write offs/write downs.
- Decision support training.

Profitability
- How do we measure profit?
  - Short or long?
  - Firm or PG?
  - Matter or timekeeper?
  - Isolated or integrated?
  - Allocations?
  - Good for partner or good for the firm?
- RULES: Realization, utilization, leverage, expenses, speed of collections.

Performance management
- What is the "highest and best use" of a leader/manager/partner/owner?
- Leading or lagging indicators?
- Establish and manage to expectations.
- Different paths to valued contributor.

- Open feedback loop?
- Compensation and non-monetary incentives.

Performance metrics
- KPIs established, communicated, monitored?
- New metrics: profit, efficiency, retention, penetration, value collaboration, leverage, fiscal hygiene.
- Technology tools.
- Decision support training.

Practice management and innovation
- Opportunistic, systematic or automatic improvements?
- Continuous improvement culture.
- Management skills vs honorary roles.
- Automation, technology, outsourcing, walk away.
- Productization of offerings.

Once we reach consensus as to how an organization scores in the P+ areas, we can document the team's assessment of where it currently is on the P+ Continuum (see Figure 18). This gives us a realistic benchmark of where we are, helps us identify strategic Specific, Measurable, Actionable, Realist, and Timebound (SMART) goals for our work, and shows the distance we must travel to reach our goals. When we get there, we can use the same tool to show our "before" and "after".

The P+ Continuum™

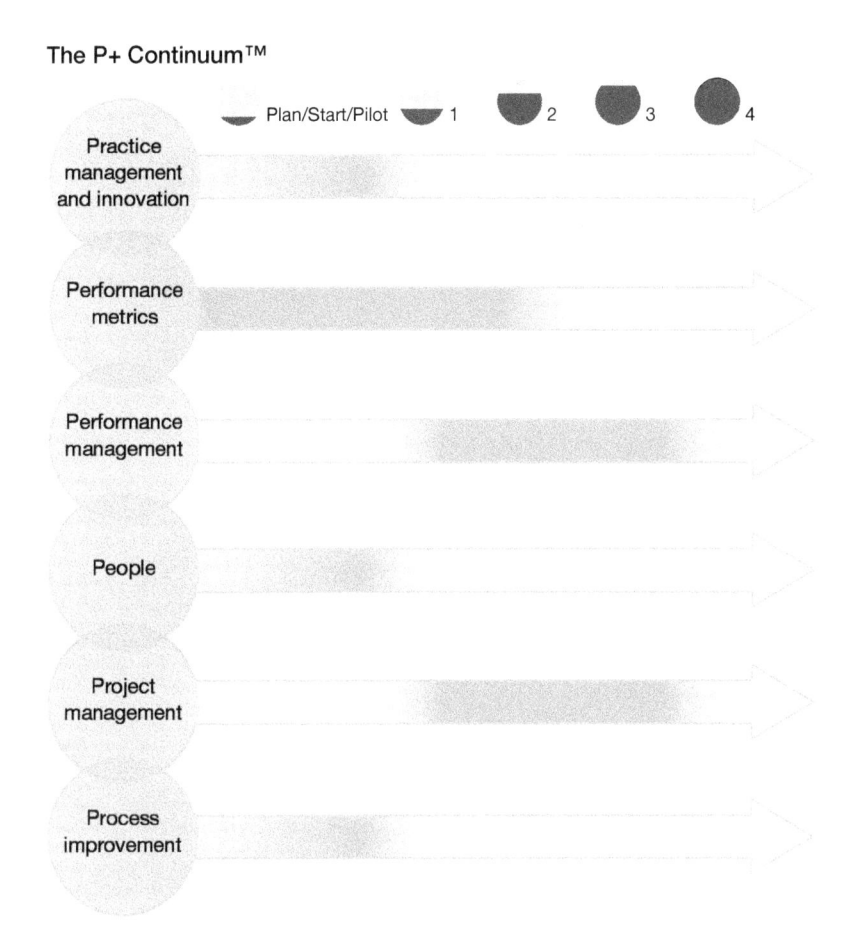

Figure 18: The P+ Continuum. Source: Legal Lean Sigma Institute LLC.

Assessing operational excellence

Assessing operational excellence involves evaluating how well an organization's processes and practices align with best practices and industry standards for efficiency, effectiveness, and continuous improvement. We look at performance across multiple dimensions, including KPIs, processes, organizational culture, technology, and best practices.

By systematically analyzing these areas, organizations can identify strengths, uncover opportunities for improvement, and implement strategies to achieve and sustain high levels of operational performance.

In law, we have found that it can take some time between an initial inquiry about an engagement and a decision, but once we have one, there is nearly

Chapter 8: P+ EcoSystem, assessments, and change management

always a strong desire to move quickly. For that reason, we have developed an operation excellence (known as OpEx, see Figure 19) assessment process that is designed for our specific purposes.

Legal Lean Sigma® OpEx assessment process

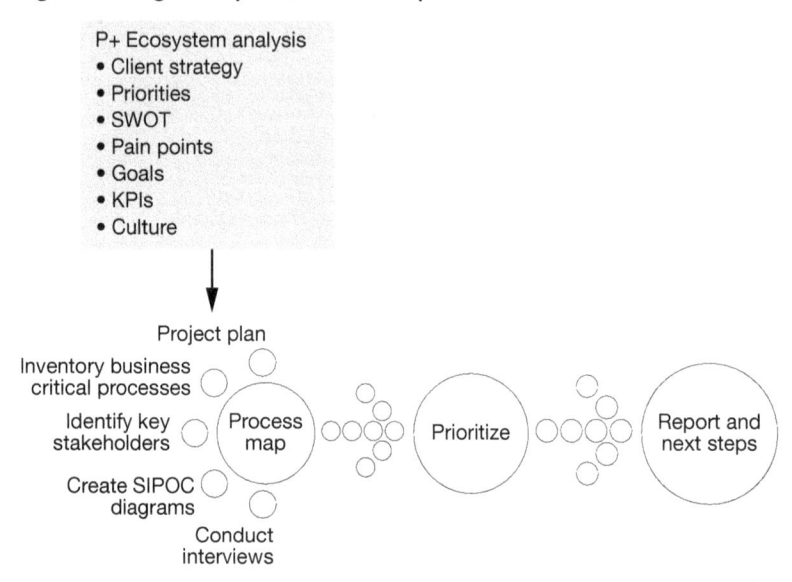

P+ Ecosystem analysis
- Client strategy
- Priorities
- SWOT
- Pain points
- Goals
- KPIs
- Culture

Project plan
Inventory business critical processes
Identify key stakeholders
Create SIPOC diagrams
Conduct interviews

Process map → Prioritize → Report and next steps

Figure 19: The OpEx Assessment Process. Source: Legal Lean Sigma Institute LLC.

To conduct the assessment process, we meet with leaders to discuss expectations, ensure clarity and alignment on what will happen before, during, and after the assessment, and develop the project plan. Then, we appropriately communicate the reason for the assessment, ask for cooperation, and ensure safety – for example, we might reassure people that what we are doing is not an exercise in headcount reduction.

Next, we inventory and summarize business-critical processes, documenting the process, its objective, and the process owner. We also identify the process stakeholders, using the RACI model, which brings structure and clarity to describing the roles that stakeholders play within a project. RACI is an acronym:
- *Responsible:* People or stakeholders who do the work. They must complete the task or objective or make the decision.
- *Accountable:* Person or stakeholder who is the "owner" of the work.

- *Consulted:* People or stakeholders who need to give input before the work can be done and signed-off on.
- *Informed:* People or stakeholders who need to be kept "in the picture".

We also measure the duration of the process or use some other relevant metric to benchmark the current state. This is done for a variety of reasons, from understanding how well senior management is aware of what is going on at the Gemba to measuring success when the process is improved in the future to a specified target condition.

Then, we meet and interview process owners and the workers within each of the business-critical processes. This gives us the information we need to create a SIPOC (suppliers – inputs – process – outputs – clients/customers) diagram for each business-critical process. Working with small groups, we teach and use tools, high level process maps (usually Block diagrams) are developed, and we prioritize issues and opportunities. After meeting with members from the leadership team and adding their perspectives and experiences, we generate a report and present our findings and recommended next steps and recommendations to leadership.

No matter what tool is used, assessing organizational readiness for change is a critical step in the change management process. It helps identify potential challenges, gauge support, evaluate resources, design effective strategies, and increase the chances of successful implementation. By understanding the organization's readiness, you can better prepare for and manage the change, ensuring a more effective and smoother transition.

What is change management?

Change management is a planned and purposeful event. It is a process that is undertaken at the beginning of the work that allows us to anticipate resistance and employ a variety of strategies and tools to achieve our goals. Because the legal landscape is different, overcoming obstacles and stakeholder engagement are addressed in targeted ways to gain buy in, build in flexibility and learning to allow for practice and change, and increase organization readiness, flexibility, and adaptability.

The stakeholder power-interest grid is especially useful in planning for change. This effectively helps us prepare for morale issues that always present themselves when we are dealing with human emotions and help people prepare for "the new way". By planning, we minimize the depth of any performance and productivity decline during change, accelerate and maximize performance during and following the change, and increase stakeholder utilization of and proficiency in the new way. In other words, we minimize the learning curve and speed to adoption of the new way and therefore increase the likelihood of benefits realization.

The five critical questions for addressing change
Cathy Etz's framework for addressing change, known as the "Five Critical Questions," provides a structured approach to managing change effectively by focusing on key aspects that influence the success of any change initiative.

By asking these questions, organizations can better understand the need for change, define the desired outcomes, identify impacted stakeholders, plan the implementation process, and provide necessary support, leading to a more successful change initiative.

1. *Why is this change necessary?* Clarify the rationale behind the change and ensure that the need for it is well understood. Answer what specific problems or opportunities does this change address, how does the change align with the organization's strategic goals, and identify the potential risks of not implementing the change.
2. *What will be different as a result of this change?* Define the outcomes and benefits of the change, making it clear what will be achieved. Answer what are the expected results or improvements from this change, how will the new situation differ from the current one, and what new processes, behaviors, or systems will be introduced.
3. *Who will be impacted by this change?* Identify all stakeholders and understand how they will be affected by the change. Answer which individuals or groups will experience the change directly or indirectly, what are their roles, how will their responsibilities shift, and how will their daily activities and workflows be affected?
4. *How will the change be implemented?* Outline the practical steps for executing the change and managing the transition. Answer what is the detailed plan for implementing the change, what resources (time, budget, personnel) are needed, what are the key milestones, and what is the timeline for implementation.
5. *What support will be provided to those affected by the change?* Ensure that individuals impacted by the change receive the necessary support and resources to adapt successfully. Answer what training, resources, or tools will be provided to help with the transition, how will feedback

be gathered and addressed, and what mechanisms will be in place to support individuals through the change.

Change management models

Since we do not believe in a one-size or one-model-fits-all approach, every change management plan and program should be tailored depending upon the organization's needs.

The change management models we employ and teach are ADKAR, Kotter's, Kubler-Ross, Lewin's, and McKinsey's 7S. While there are similarities, some are better suited to individuals than to organizations.

Regardless, applying change management in a legal environment involves guiding law firms or legal departments through transitions to ensure that changes are implemented effectively and embraced. Whether the change involves restructuring workflows, shifting firm culture, or adopting new technology, the principles of change management can help in navigating these transitions smoothly.

We will always suggest using a structured approach to applying change management in a legal setting (of course, it's a process, a series of repeatable, describable steps).

First, define the change (as in the first step in DMAIC and DMADV). This includes identifying the need and setting objectives. Next, plan the change, using project management basics and tools such as a project charter. Outline how the change will be implemented. This should include timelines, milestones, and resource allocation. Identify all stakeholders (e.g., partners, associates, support staff, clients) and understand their concerns and expectations. Also, evaluate potential risks and challenges associated with the change and develop mitigation strategies.

Then, create a communication plan for how you will communicate the change to different stakeholders. This should include the what, why, how, and when of the change, keeping the stakeholder power-interest results in mind, and should involve various communication methods such as meetings, emails, and intranet updates to ensure that the message reaches everyone. We encourage the greatest possible level of transparency – articulate both the benefits and potential challenges of the change to build trust and reduce resistance.

As we have seen, the methodologies we use involve testing and piloting to test the change on a smaller scale before full implementation. Training and support must be developed, built, and improved to make sure people understand how to adapt to the new processes or tools, and we have help available during the transition. We will track progress using key performance indicators (KPIs) and other metrics to monitor the implementation and effectiveness of the change, regularly collect feedback to identify any issues or areas for improvement, and adjust as needed to ensure that the change is successfully integrated.

This cycle should seem familiar. That is because it follows PDCA – Plan, Do, Check, Act. Change management also requires reinforcement, however, which is like the Control phase of DMAIC. This is where we celebrate successes and milestones to reinforce positive behaviors and outcomes, confirm that the change is embedded into the firm's culture and practices to sustain long-term benefits, and encourage a culture of continuous improvement where feedback is regularly sought and used to make further enhancements.

ADKAR Model
The ADKAR Model, developed by Prosci, focuses on individual change and helps manage the people side of change.

Components:
1. *Awareness.* Create awareness of the need for change.
2. *Desire.* Foster a desire to participate and support the change.
3. *Knowledge.* Provide knowledge on how to change.
4. *Ability.* Ensure individuals have the ability to implement new skills or behaviors.
5. *Reinforcement.* Reinforce and sustain the change.

ADKAR is an effective model to use for process improvement project work as it lines up neatly with the DMAIC and DMADV phases. Because it is effective for gaining individual buy-in and managing the personal side of change, it is one we use frequently in law, especially law firms, where partner buy-in is so important.

Kotter's eight-step change model
John Kotter's model is widely used and focuses on creating a sense of urgency and guiding organizations through change. It's particularly useful in environments that need to build momentum and sustain change.

Steps:
1. *Create a sense of urgency.* Highlight the need for change and the risks of not changing.

2. *Form a powerful coalition.* Assemble a team of leaders and stakeholders to drive the change.
3. *Create a vision for change.* Develop a clear vision and strategy for the change.
4. *Communicate the vision.* Ensure all members understand and support the vision.
5. *Empower action.* Remove obstacles and encourage risk-taking and problem-solving.
6. *Generate short-term wins.* Achieve and celebrate quick wins to build momentum.
7. *Consolidate gains.* Use early successes to drive more change.
8. *Anchor the changes.* Integrate the changes into the organization's culture.

Choose this model where there are major changes requiring broad buy-in and a structured approach.

Kübler-Ross
The Kübler-Ross Change Curve, initially developed to describe the emotional stages people go through when facing personal loss, can be adapted to manage organizational change in a law firm.
Stages:
1. *Denial.* The initial reaction where employees may not accept the reality of the change.
2. *Anger.* Frustration and resistance towards the change.
3. *Bargaining.* Seeking ways to delay or modify the change.
4. *Depression.* Feelings of helplessness or pessimism about the change.
5. *Acceptance.* Embracing and adapting to the new way.

This model is well suited for addressing the emotional responses of employees during transitions, such as implementing new technologies, restructuring teams, or changing processes.

Lewin's Change Management Model
Kurt Lewin's model is a classic framework that focuses on the process of change and is often appreciated for its simplicity.
  Steps:
  1. *Unfreeze.* Prepare the organization for change by creating awareness and addressing resistance.
  2. *Change.* Implement the change, making the necessary adjustments.
  3. *Refreeze.* Solidify the new practices and ensure they are adopted as the new norm.

This is an excellent choice for fundamental changes with a need for a clear, simple process.

McKinsey 7-S Framework
This model focuses on aligning seven elements within an organization – Strategy, Structure, Systems, Shared values, Skills, Style, and Staff.
  Steps:
  1. *Identify the changes.* Determine which of the seven elements need to be adjusted.
  2. *Align elements.* Ensure all elements are aligned and support the desired change.
  3. *Implement and monitor.* Make the changes and monitor alignment.

Consider this framework for comprehensive changes that require alignment across multiple organizational elements.

Choosing the best model involves careful consideration of several key elements. First, we will assess the nature of the change. Major system implementations or process overhauls might benefit from Kotter's model, while more incremental changes might fit well with ADKAR. We will also consider culture. A department, firm, or office with a collaborative culture might find the McKinsey 7-S Framework effective, while a department or firm needing to address personal resistance may prefer ADKAR or Kübler-Ross. Finally, scope and scale matter, a lot. For firm-wide transformations, Kotter's model provides a structured approach, whereas Lewin's model might be suitable for simpler, more focused changes.

Integrating change management and Lean Six Sigma
In a July 2023 article on the "Relationship Between Lean Six Sigma and Change management", Tahir Abbas writes:
"Lean Six Sigma and change management are two complementary methodologies that, when integrated, create a powerful synergy to drive organizational success. Both approaches share common goals, such as improving efficiency, reducing waste, and enhancing overall performance. By identifying areas of overlap, organizations can leverage the strengths of both methodologies to achieve better results in their improvement initiatives.

"For example, both Lean Six Sigma and change management emphasize the importance of data-driven decision-making and engaging employees throughout the process. The integration of Lean Six Sigma's analytical tools with change management's focus on communication and stakeholder engagement ensures that improvements are not only effective but also sustainable in the long run.

"Lean Six Sigma offers a structured and systematic approach to process improvement, which can be seamlessly integrated into change management initiatives. The DMAIC (Define, Measure, Analyze, Improve, Control) framework provides a step-by-step guide for problem-solving and continuous improvement, making it an ideal foundation for managing change.[1]

Change strategies
An excellent way to prepare people and organize for change is by following the People, Process, Platform sequence, carefully considering the effects on the P+ Ecosystem™ and using a project plan that is based on a change management model and includes change strategies.

Each of the five change strategies starts with a clearly articulated vision. Consider accelerators such as whether there is a sense of urgency that requires us to be alert and agile or whether we have a guiding coalition – change agents who want to lead and will help others do the same.

- *Directive strategy.* The leader / manager uses authority to imposes change with little or no involvement of other people.
- *Expert strategy.* Usually involves expertise to manage and solve technical problems that result from the change.
- *Negotiating strategy.* Leader / manager shows willingness to negotiate and bargain in order to effect change with timely adjustments and concessions.

- *Educative strategy.* When the leader / manager plans to change people's values and beliefs.
- *Participative strategy.* When the manager stresses the full involvement of all of those involved and affected by the anticipated changes.

Incidentally, these strategies are not mutually exclusive. It is not uncommon to use two, three, or even all five on larger, more complicated changes, which is almost always the case in law.

A change program framework considers three points along the continuum from opportunistic to systematic and then automatic improvements.

Opportunistic: Implementation of quality programs focused on skills and training

- Employees use tools as they see fit.
- Results in opportunistic improvements – sometimes valuable, but uneven across the organization.

Objectives:
- Rapidly create a step change in the capability of a process or a few processes to demonstrate the concept.
- Develop organizational skills and experience with change as the first step in a more systematic change program.

Elements:
- Way of finding and selecting improvement ideas.
- Reliable methodologies to deliver results (e.g. Kaizens, project management).
- Tools and skills.
- Project support infrastructure – sponsorship, resource allocation, project monitoring.

Systematic: Improving processes to their maximum potential with a structured approach

- All key processes eventually need to be included.
- A wide range of quality and lean tools need to be deployed in an appropriate sequence.

Objectives:
- Comprehensively redesign the processes of a business, to make them as capable and efficient as possible and transform the performance of the business.
- Build the capacity for ongoing change.

Elements:
- Process perspective.
- Clear need and goals for change.
- Assessment process to create change plan.
- Change skills and tools.
- Improvement culture.
- Knowledge-building.
- Benefits capture.
- Change infrastructure.

Automatic: The ultimate improvement capability
- Processes with good objectives, measurements, and change skills and ownership within the process.
- Processes "automatically" diagnose and improve themselves.

Objective:
- Build deep capacity for ongoing improvement in a large business system.
- Process performance and efficiency increase faster than stakeholder expectations.

No matter where you are on the continuum, begin.

Reference
1. https://changemanagementinsight.com/lean-six-sigma-and-change-management/

Chapter 9:
Getting started and structuring for success

While every organization's experience is different and there are many different routes that can be taken, the first recommended step in getting started and structuring a process improvement program is to assess your organization. Ultimately, this will help leaders determine whether to begin with training, workshop, project work, or organizational development.

When starting to think about how to approach doing process improvement work, first we will want to explore thoroughly and consider all the elements of the P+ Ecosystem. We want to be methodical in deciding the capabilities that should be built in those (and maybe other) areas to achieve the organizational mission and vision. It is critical to be realistic about your leadership, capacity for change, and interest in innovation. Also, ensure you have a stunningly clear understanding of the strategic goals and that they are not just SMART, but super SMART and understood by all.

When getting started on developing a process or continuous improvement program, we usually begin with a co-design discussion that explores readiness, culture, and strategy. Once we understand where we are and where we are going, we design a program and develop a plan that establishes a cadence of activities. Usually, we look at what is possible to do with the existing structures, policies, tools, and "wish lists" so that we are pursuing the path of least resistance.

We also listen to the stakeholders talk about what is going well and what can be improved. By focusing on the current state and figuring out what we have to work with and on, we learn the answers to the five critical change management questions covered in chapter eight. It's somewhat analogous to a certain reality show where designers are given specifications from homeowners that outline what needs to change for them to love their current home or to move to a new one. The designer's challenge is to come up with a design that addresses as much of the "must have" and "nice to have list" as they can – and finish the renovation within scope, meaning the time and budget allowed. The realtor's challenge is to find a new home that is so much better that it is worth moving. This tension of using the building blocks we have now as a starting point and "building a better mousetrap" is always present. In our metaphor, our processes are the building blocks.

My strong recommendation to every organization is to begin by establishing a formal method to select, prioritize, and resource projects. It is important to design and develop a process (as well as templates, policies, training, etc.) for people to surface ideas and manage a pipeline of potential improvement projects. It should be clear to everyone how the organization will agree on the processes that could most benefit from PI and PM and who will be responsible for contributing proposals as well as picking, managing, overseeing, and participating in projects, workshops, and other activities.

It is well worth the investment to develop a comprehensive scorecard that compares processes across all key dimensions; we typically use a weighted decision matrix for this. Another option is to carry out a baseline assessment. It is a less comprehensive but still systematic methodology. In the early stages of a process improvement program, projects are commonly selected based on purely practical considerations, and there is nothing wrong with that, though of course it is important to align them with strategic objectives.

Because law firms are comprised of a variety of practices that may have different drivers for efficiency, innovation, and collaboration, it is wise to expend the effort to understand what those are, at least for the groups that are strategic priorities. Regardless of the setting, we want to direct our efforts and resources to areas where we can start with the willing, our areas of strength, and where we can build on existing initiatives and programs.

All organizations should understand and consider the driving and restraining forces in their own organization that will either support a Lean Sigma project or initiative or work against it. More specifically, one of the biggest challenges to undertaking process improvement work in law lies in the lack of availability, accessibility, or quality of resources and good data. This is one of the reasons some firms are undertaking projects related to improving their timekeeping processes.

Without reliable and complete data, it is difficult (if not impossible) to tell how much effort it takes to do and deliver any particular work. This impacts a firm's ability to make important business decisions, including those related to strategy, pricing, staffing, infrastructure, and more.

It takes years to develop breadth and depth of skills and formal models. A plan that establishes key milestones, training goals, and a cadence of projects, as with all projects, helps ensure success. To the greatest extent possible, we want to be intentional about how we use knowledge, experience, artifacts and graphically analyzed data from one project to support another. This will contribute greatly to building the culture of continuous improvement.

Develop skills and learn a common language

A primary goal of any certification course or workshop is to simultaneously learn about tools and terms while getting improvement work drafted or done on selected processes. I believe strongly in a combined process improvement and project management course that is tailored specifically to each group.

A second goal is to engage people in a manner that facilitates team building and that enables positive and productive contributions from stakeholders (and is also fun!). In other words, the key stakeholders learn together and are part of conceiving, designing, planning, piloting, and implementing optimized ways of doing and delivering specific kinds of workflows. The result is that we have improvements in the People, Process, Platform sequence we always observe.

The Legal Lean Sigma Institute courses are thoughtfully designed with adult experiential learning (and legal professionals in particular) in mind. They include lectures, exercises, simulations, videos, discussions, group work, and demonstrations covering key process improvement methodologies (Lean, Six Sigma), tools, and concepts, with many examples and case studies from law firms and legal departments. We explore the key concepts and tools of process improvement and project management and look at how they are employed specifically in legal. With an introduction to Lean, Six Sigma, waterfall and agile methodologies, attendees get ideas about what efficiency really means and how to start doing things differently right away.

We have found that, when participants use their own processes and learn about Lean and Six Sigma in that context, our approach is far more effective for learning and making high-level decisions about the challenges and opportunities than are programs where tools and methodologies are taught in the abstract.

At this point, we have taught our courses to thousands of lawyers and business professionals in the legal space and successfully delivered dozens of projects that have returned tens of millions of dollars. Some of our clients have included internal or external clients or partners in their training programs, which offers additional advantages and benefits. Invariably, attendees find that being able to speak the language of process improvement with each other and with clients is a game changer that fundamentally and forever changes the way they view, value, think, and talk about the way we do and deliver our work. There is motivation plus competitive advantage in getting a cadre of practitioners certified (see Figure 20) and many of our clients proudly promote their new status as a certified White or Yellow Belt via various outlets.

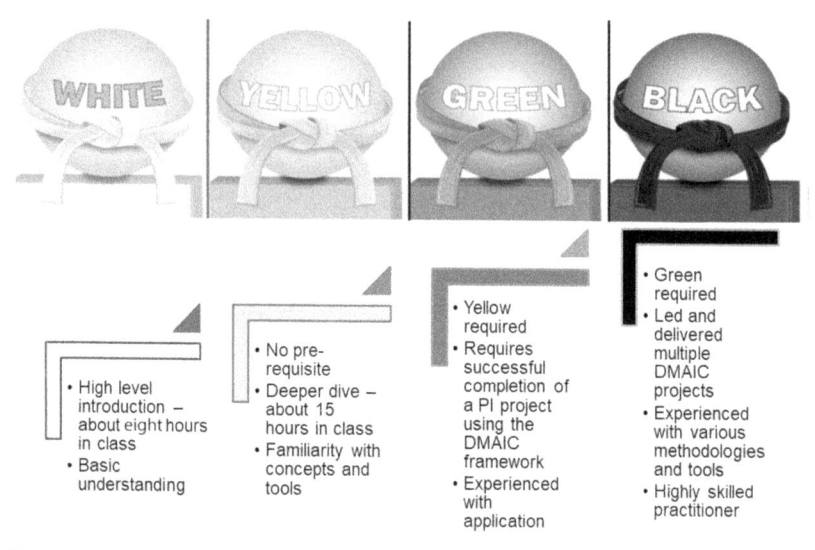

Figure 20: Legal Lean Sigma certification requirements. Legal Lean Sigma Institute LLC.

This common language and understanding of frameworks like DMAIC obviously enable teams to have the ability to think about, more clearly articulate and communicate, and reach consensus on the best next steps. This is true irrespective of whether we are exploring how to proceed within a department or organization or if we are collaborating with clients or other stakeholders.

The terminology and mindset of process improvement can fundamentally change how we approach challenges, make decisions, and drive change in meaningful ways. It emphasizes that the language is not only a tool for communication but also a transformative way of thinking and acting. As W. Edwards Deming once said:

> *"The most important thing is to understand the system. The system consists of people, equipment, and processes. The language of improvement must be a language that helps people understand how to improve the system."*

Process architecture – a systematic approach

A process architecture is a visual, hierarchical model of the processes of an organization. It is a critical blueprint that guides decision-makers and a framework that defines the structure and organization of processes within an organization. It provides a comprehensive view of how processes are designed, how they interact with each other, and how they align with organizational goals and strategies.

The process architecture shows how our processes relate to each other and to the overall organizational objectives. This starts with our core processes (client intake, case management, legal research, and document management) that are essential to delivering value to clients and achieving strategic goals. Then, we include more detailed sub-processes that support core processes and contribute to their effectiveness and specific activities within sub-processes that are carried out to complete the overall process.

We use process maps such as flowcharts, value stream maps, and swim lane diagrams to visualize our processes, their interactions, and their flow. Process inputs and outputs are documented to show what is required for a process to function (inputs, such as resources, information, or materials) and what is produced by the process (outputs, including work product, services, or results generated by the process). Process roles and responsibilities are included so that we can see who is responsible for executing, managing, and overseeing each process, from owners, managers, and participants.

Naturally, the architecture contains measurements of the effectiveness and efficiency of processes. Examples are Key Performance Indicators (KPIs) and metrics that allow us to assess how well a process is performing against its objectives and that provide insights into specific aspects of process performance, such as cycle time or error rates. It also looks at process dependencies, the relationships between processes where the output of one process serves as the input for another, and information flow, which is how data and information are shared between processes to ensure seamless operation.

Having a process architecture improves clarity and understanding and helps us design efficient processes and identify opportunities for improvement and optimization. It also ensures that processes are aligned with strategic objectives and contribute effectively to achieving goals. Finally, it provides a structured approach to managing changes in processes, making it easier to implement improvements and adapt to new requirements while enhancing overall performance.

Building a Lean Six Sigma program for a law department, office, or firm begins with designing the structure so that it supports clearly defined goals and the program charter. Defining objectives and scope, as with any project, requires we have a shared understanding of the problem / opportunity, have considered the business case, and have set specific, measurable goals that make it clear what we want to achieve with Lean Six Sigma. We also want to specify which areas of the organization will and will not be included.

To ensure our program gets the right attention and support, we must gain buy-in and secure commitment from senior leadership to champion the program. This is crucial for resources, buy-in, and aligning the program with enterprise, departmental, practice group, and team goals. Our Lean Six Sigma Team will include champions, who will be experienced professionals to lead the program, such as a Lean Six Sigma champion or a project manager, and a cross-functional, diverse team with members from various areas of the firm, office, or department.

We must also have a plan to communicate the purpose, benefits, and progress of the program to all stakeholders. Training and education must also be included – Lean Six Sigma training to team members and staff that includes Lean and Six Sigma methodologies, tools, and techniques is a must, and certification courses should be considered for everyone, but especially Yellow, Green, or Black Belt for key team members. An operational assessment will be helpful in inventorying and prioritizing processes that should receive attention. Also, we will want to gather data on current performance metrics such as case resolution times, error rates, or client satisfaction scores.

This approach requires a longer-term investment that takes time to deliver benefits – but it offers significant returns.

In 2002, Orrick, Herrington & Sutcliffe LLP migrated its back-office work to a low-cost "global operations center" in Wheeling, West Virginia. Although back-office migration is not a new concept, Orrick was the first large, US-based law firm to so thoroughly embrace the concept; Orrick grew from 70 professionals in 2002 – mostly IT, accounting, and operations – to 300 employees – including 47 career associate attorneys – by 2013.[1]

Current data shows that Orrick, Herrington & Sutcliffe LLP has approximately 1,500 to 1,800 lawyers and a total headcount of about 2,500 to 3,000 employees. This includes legal professionals as well as support staff.

> "A differentiation strategy involves boldly going where no firm has gone before – and where no or few firms are willing or able to go."[2]

In a corporate setting, one of the best-known systematic process improvement success stories is that of the General Electric Company, which made Six Sigma a foundation of GE strategy and a fundamental element of the company's business approach under its former chairman Jack Welch. GE's Six Sigma initiative began in 1995 with 200 projects delivering little to no financial benefit to the company, and then expanded within two years to 6,000 projects delivering $320 million in productivity gains and profits. By 1999, GE was publicly claiming $2 billion in annual benefits, and in 2001 the company reported that 500,000 Six Sigma projects had been completed since the start of the initiative.

There are many excellent examples that help to explain why a systematic approach is so powerful. One of the first things we ask a law firm to do is to look at what their clients are doing – that is central to being "client focused". Their continuous improvement programs should both inspire and shed light on the internal expectations of legal departments. It suggests why corporate clients of law firms are concerned with the kinds of waste and variation (and basic disconnects) that often exist with regard to their outside counsel.

Examples:
- AlliedSignal, for example, is also known for its successes with Six Sigma, which the company reports has saved it $1.5bn since 1991.
- Ford Motor Company started its Six Sigma effort in 2000 and, in 2003, stated that it had saved $1bn through waste elimination, experiencing record improvement in its "Things Gone Wrong" initiative. A year later, the figure had doubled due, primarily, to waste reduction and process improvements, rather than through cost avoidance.
- Samsung Electronics Company, which also launched a Six Sigma initiative in 2000, projected "cumulative financial benefits of $1.5bn through the end of 2002. These benefits include cost savings and increased profits from sales and new product development. Its Six Sigma projects also are credited with an average of 50 percent reduction in defects."[3]

A Lean Six Sigma structure provides a systematic approach for implementing and managing Lean Six Sigma initiatives within an organization. The components include governance and leadership, program management, roles and responsibilities, methodologies and tools, project selection and prioritization, training and skill development, metrics and measurement, change management and communication, continuous improvement, and documentation and standardization.

Each element requires thoughtful planning and implementation. However, with this structured approach, any legal organization can effectively integrate Lean Six Sigma principles into their operations. This drives continuous improvement and achieves better efficiency and quality outcomes.

Process improvement program steering committee
Establishing a governing body to provide leadership and strategic oversight also contributes to a successful program. The program steering committee has a different function to a project steering committee. Members typically include senior leaders to provide strategic direction and high-level support, process improvement experts, project managers from teams to provide updates and insights on project progress, and key stakeholders from different departments or areas who are impacted by the process improvements.

The committee's responsibilities are to determine which process improvement projects should be prioritized based on their potential impact, resources required, and alignment with strategic goals. This includes reviewing and approving project proposals, budgets, and timelines and ensuring that the project has all the resources it needs from participants and support to budget and technology. They will also track the allocation and utilization of resources to prevent overuse or misallocation. By way of example, many organizations do not yet have a knowledge management or data analyst function, so process improvement teams turn to members of the finance team for data gathering and analysis. If projects are planned without considering how we would strain that resource, we will have unnecessarily put our entire program at risk.

Ensuring effective communication between the steering committee, project teams, and other stakeholders is another important responsibility that includes keeping key stakeholders informed about project progress, outcomes, and any changes to the scope or direction. This requires the ability to monitor the progress of process improvement projects against established milestones and performance indicators and assess the effectiveness, outcomes, and impact of completed projects, ensuring that they meet the intended goals and deliver expected benefits.

The members of the committee are important ambassadors for the program as they promote best practices in process improvement and encourage the adoption of innovative approaches. Periodically, they should review and assess the overall process improvement program and its effectiveness, offering feedback on what is going well and what should be improved.

The process improvement program steering committee plays a vital role in ensuring that process improvement initiatives are successfully executed and aligned with organizational goals. By selecting the right combination of members, our organization increases the likelihood of a highly successful program because they, in turn will make intelligent decisions about the other elements.

In a *Harvard Business Review* article, author and former Konosuke Matsushita Professor of Leadership at Harvard Business School John P. Kotter points out that:

"In the more successful cases... the change process goes through a series of phases that, in total, usually require a considerable length of time. Skipping steps creates only the illusion of speed and never produces a satisfying result."[4]

In our steering committee workshops, we work with firms to design systematic change programs that guide a firm along the continuum from opportunistic to systematic improvements, where processes are stabilized and scalable and more connected and the firm achieves key performance measures relevant to key objectives. Our objectives behind a systematic change program include comprehensively redesigning the processes of a business to make them as capable and efficient as possible and to transform the performance of the business, building capacity for ongoing change.

The objectives of this kind of systematic approach are eventually to transform culture and the way the entire firm carries out its work, and to build lasting competitive advantage through processes that deliver the maximum value in high-quality legal services to clients at the lowest cost. To take this approach, the firm must believe that improvement is required (i.e. there is a compelling case for change) and must understand what improvements are needed and why. Furthermore, the goals for the change must be clear and credible; in other words, we must have measurable targets.

By taking a systematic approach, working with the DMAIC framework, following the process of process improvement, managing each process improvement project involving key processes of the organization well, and eventually building a culture of continuous improvement, law firms can create a "win-win-win" for business management, the legal department, and outside counsel.

Understanding corporate budgeting and the importance of predictability is of key importance. The financial links between excellent processes that are managed well – regardless of billing method – and profitability suggest that it is critical to take an approach that spans across an organization in order to achieve the win-win-win.

Ensuring effective communication between the steering committee, project teams, and other stakeholders is another important responsibility that includes keeping key stakeholders informed about project progress, outcomes, and any changes to the scope or direction. By definition, this requires the ability to monitor the progress of process improvement projects against established milestones and performance indicators and assess the effectiveness, outcomes, and impact of completed projects, ensuring that they meet the intended goals and deliver expected benefits.

The members of the committee are important ambassadors for the program as they promote best practices in process improvement and encourage the adoption of innovative approaches. Periodically, they should review and assess the overall process improvement program and its effectiveness, offering feedback on what is going well and what should be improved.

The process improvement program steering committee plays a vital role in ensuring that process improvement initiatives are successfully executed and aligned with organizational goals. The members should be thoughtfully selected. By selecting the right combination of members, our organization increases the likelihood of a highly successful program.

Demonstration projects

While process design or redesign might be too much to tackle for a first project, a quick win or even a process improvement would certainly get things off to a strong start.

Cisco offers an interesting approach to determining where to invest resources that gives us guidance about how to invest resources:
- *Core/mission-critical:*
    - Activities that contribute to competitive advantage.
    - If performed poorly, pose immediate risk.
    - Handled primarily with in-house resources.
- *Core/non-mission-critical:*
    - Activities contribute to competitive advantage.

- If handled poorly, would not pose a risk.
- Handled using internal legal staff and self-service tools and processes.
- *Context/mission-critical:*
  - Activities are necessary but not tied to competitive advantage.
  - If performed poorly, pose a risk to the organization.
  - Many of these activities are handled using outside resources.
- *Context/non-mission critical:*
  - Activities are necessary.
  - Present limited risk if performed poorly.
  - Most of these activities are outsourced.

Implementing a simple solution to a known issue, also called a "Just Do It" type of project, demonstrates that fixes can be quick and painless. This must be limited to one practice area or department. Also, we must know the root cause so that we can solve it right away. Kaizen or Legal WorkOut are also excellent choices for reducing defects, cycle, time, or costs. Again, it is best to start with something that is a well-known issue. By employing an approach like DMAIC or PDCA, we can let the frameworks help us uncover the root cause and enable us to solve it.

Align with clients

To get immediate traction with any process improvement program, we will make it client-focused because they usually offer the most compelling reasons to act and can create a sense of urgency like no other driver.

We start by determining the client's needs and values. Then, we discover the critical success factors for fulfilling those needs, tie those factors to the organizational objectives, and set the measures of success for them. Next, we identify the key processes that contribute to those measures of success. Finally, we determine the most important metrics for those processes; ideally, they will be leading, not lagging, indicators.

Tim Corcoran says:

"If you want to improve your law practice, your business, your customer service posture, then you need to ask two simple questions, and ask them regularly: What are we doing well and What can we improve? It's critical to know explicitly and specifically what clients value, why they value it, and that they want us to continue doing it."[5]

Corcoran goes on to state:

"If you don't know explicitly what your clients value about your service and if you don't know explicitly what they wish you would do better, then all the charts and graphs and analysis are just so much statistical noise... Sustainable profitability comes from client satisfaction; client satisfaction comes from continuous improvement; continuous improvement happens when we regularly ask our clients what we do well and what we can improve. It's that simple... there is no better job security than channeling the voice of the customer, and this isn't hard to do."

Though it is over 20 years old, this advice[6] from Dupont GC and a partner at one of his primary outside counsel firms remains relevant to this day:

- Identify processes, e.g. how the organization stores litigation case files, purchases deposition transcripts, or compiles company records for production in lawsuits.
- Start with paper processes, which often lend themselves to standardized process improvements, and often yield quick victories.
- Map the process – mundane though it sounds, mapping often yields dramatic results by highlighting the process as it really exists.
- Apply information technology – IT fixes often bubble up early.
- Leverage the learning – multiply the benefits by leveraging project learning to similar processes and functions.
- Be a forum for pent-up grievances – pet peeves are often the stuff of superb process improvement projects.

This demonstrates that originality of ideas is not required to be successful in using process improvement to align with clients to get started. We can learn what law departments have accomplished with their outside counsel and emulate them. There are now decades of collaboration case studies published by the Association of Corporate Counsel[7] to review and use as blueprints. Carpe diem! Law departments – don't be shy and sit by while the music is playing – tell your firms you want to dance. If they don't invite you, consider whether there isn't a better option. Law firms – don't wait for your clients to demand or ask for things. Be proactive!

Use precedent – learn from others

The Hunoval Law Firm
This firm has one of the most outstanding examples of cutting cycle times on highly productionized process work. Hunoval Law was able to reduce the number of days to process mortgage enforcement actions (specifically the Notice of Hearing) from 70 down to eight. The net result was $4m savings in 2012 through efficiencies and error reductions.

Based in Charlotte, North Carolina, the foreclosure firm was one of five finalists for the "Best Process Improvement Project" at the 15th annual PEX awards, along with Capital One and Pitney Bowes (the winner). Hunoval, a firm set up from scratch in 2009, was nominated for its implementation of Lean Six Sigma principles in a legal environment.

In March 2014, the *American Bar Association Journal* reported on The Hunoval Firm, relaying that it believes in investing in deep skill development "by sending staff to training based on real projects being developed for the firm" and expects "a full 70 percent to be trained by the end of 2014". The *ABA Journal* article also mentioned that the firm's "first project addressed the overly long process for a notice of hearing and achieved the impressive 88 percent timeline improvement."[8]

"I knew that we would attain real operational benefits – increased efficiencies and reduction in errors – and it would help us run a better, more efficient law firm management," says Matt Hunoval.[9] But, he adds, there were also a lot of unexpected benefits, including workforce engagement and marketing.

According to Hunoval:

"This is not about a change in how we practice law. It's about law practice management, improving the business side – an idea that is changing how law firms can be run."

What is more, these are changes that appeal directly to how clients run their own businesses:

"When they hear us speaking that same language, I can see the lightbulb moment where the client or potential client says, "Oh my god, here's a lawyer who actually gets it."[10]

Valorem Law Group / Elevate Next

Valorem describes itself as a revolutionary law firm made up of "large firm refugees" who are committed to killing the billable hour. In her 2012 article, "Five Firms Take Bold Approaches",[11] part of a series of four related articles that appeared in the *ABA Law Practice magazine*, Susan Saltonstall Duncan reported on firms that made a decision to do things differently from the very start.

In her interview with Pat Lamb of Valorem Law Group, which is widely regarded as a firm that led the "new normal" movement, Duncan reported:

> *"In 2008, when Patrick Lamb and three partners thought about starting a new kind of law firm focused on clients and value, they knew that a critical framework would be in pricing their services in a radically different way than their predecessor BigLaw firms (and most law firms) did. When they started setting fixed prices for their trial and litigation services, they realized that they needed to focus on the cost of providing those services – or they would never be profitable. Things would now have to be done faster, more efficiently and better than before."*

One of the cornerstones of Valorem's business model is that project management and process improvement are essential. Duncan elaborated:

> *"From the outset, lawyers took typical cases and produced process maps to delineate each step in the process. For example, before lawyers start to do any discovery on a case, they talk to the client first to establish an approach that is consistent with the client's desired outcome. The focus is on a full case assessment first, which dictates the fee, but more importantly, the value proposition and the winning strategy. The Valorem Toolbox provides tools for trial, budgeting, fee estimating and decision trees."*

Client David Graham of DSW explains the process:

> *"First we sit down and discuss the business case and objective. At every turn, we determine whether and how an approach would deliver value to the business. Throughout the three years up to trial on a recent case, at each juncture we wrote down all the tasks and pieces that would be involved in the next chunk of work, evaluated the objectives, then priced it accordingly."*[12]

Larger ships are more difficult and take longer to change direction. But there is plenty of evidence that making this sort of change is not just possible, it is critical.

Valorem Law Group *"operates in a family-like setting. Ideas and new approaches are welcomed and expected through biweekly 'collab-o-storms' with all lawyers and staff,"* says founder Pat Lamb.[13] In fact, the firm shows use of a registered trademark in Collab-O-Storm, suggesting that their approach and name for it really is unique.

In 2018, the innovative founders of Valorem Law Group, Patrick Lamb and Nicole Auerbach, created a new law firm called ElevateNext.[14] It was designed to work alongside law company Elevate to help customers significantly reduce legal spend, where ElevateNext performs all "attorney-required" work for clients using the Valorem model, and "attorney-not-required" work would be provided by Elevate.

The ElevateNext venture was a direct response to a growing trend in the legal market. Many law departments, especially Fortune 500 companies, now turn to law companies like Elevate for all aspects of legal work – except those few restricted activities that must be practiced by licensed lawyers.

Both Elevate and Valorem have a history of positive disruption in an industry notoriously resistant to change. Said Patrick Lamb in a press release: [15]

"The current ethical rules that prohibit non-lawyers from investing in or owning a law firm have created a void in the marketplace when it comes to providing clients with sophisticated legal representation backed by cutting edge technology and legal process management. Traditional law firms have not filled that growing void, leaving clients to inefficiently use multiple service providers to meet their needs. ElevateNext provides the first real alternative."

"Customers regularly ask Elevate to provide integrated practice of law and business of law capabilities," says Liam Brown, the pioneering founder of Elevate. *"We are excited to partner with Nicole, Pat and the Valorem team to now be able to offer that through ElevateNext."*

Auerbach adds, *"We created Valorem Law Group more than a decade ago because clients told us they needed an alternative to the billable hour model. Now we have created ElevateNext so clients can leverage the strengths of the well-established law company, Elevate, along with its technology, process engineers, technical experts, subject matter experts and consultants, combined with the type of legal representation that is the foundation of the Valorem model. Giving clients access to all this through ElevateNext will provide them savings and efficiencies."*

Some law firms and legal departments begin their process improvement initiatives very simply. Others are deliberate and strategic, where they investigate, consider, and then opt to begin with a conscious decision to make process improvement a cornerstone of their strategy. Obviously, the latter decision is a radically different approach, and a larger level of investment will be needed.

Some organizations may prefer to start out by dipping their toes in the water, developing some skills first, exploring which processes are in greatest need of improvement, and then deciding how and where to dive into process improvement.

The point is that there is no one right way to start. The only wrong answer is to not do it at all.

References

1. https://scholarsbank.uoregon.edu/xmlui/bitstream/handle/1794/18896/Callier.pdf?sequence=1&isAllowed=y
2. *Ibid.*
3. Ryan, J. "Making the Case for Economic Quality, a White Paper for The American Society for Quality (ASQ)": https://qualitymanagementinstitute.com/ebarchive/JohnRyanMakingtheEconomicCaseForQuality.pdf
4. Kotter, J.P. "Leading Change: Why Transformation Efforts Fail", Harvard Business Review, January 2007: http://hbr.org/2007/01/leading-change-why-transformation-efforts-fail/ar/1.
5. Corcoran, T. B. "The 2 Critical Questions that Lead to Continuous Improvement", 17 December 2012: www.corcoranlawbizblog.com/2012/12/the-2-critical-questions.
6. Six Sigma: Positioning for Competitive Advantage, Thomas L. Sager and Scott L. Winkelman, ACCA Docket 19 (No. 1), 2001, pp. 18-27.
7. www.acc.com/resource-library
8. Carter, T., Foreclosure firm goes statistical to improve speed and quality, *American Bar Association Journal* online: www.abajournal.com/magazine/article/foreclosure_firm_goes_statistical_to_improve_speed_and_quality.
9. PEX, "CEO of Hunoval Law Firm: Lean Six Sigma was a 'lightbulb moment'": www.processexcellencenetwork.com/lean-six-sigma-business-transformation/articles/six-sigma-in-law-interview-with-matt-hunoval
10. Carter, T., Foreclosure firm goes statistical to improve speed and quality, *American Bar Association Journal* online: www.abajournal.com/magazine/article/foreclosure_firm_goes_statistical_to_improve_speed_and_quality

11 Duncan, S. S. "5 Firms Take Bold Approaches" ABA Law Practice magazine, volume 38, No. 6, November/December 2012: https://rainmakingoasis.com/wp-content/uploads/2019/04/5-Law-Firms-Take-Bold-Approaches.pdf
12 *Ibid.*
13 *Ibid.*
14 https://elevatenextlaw.com
15 https://elevate.law/news/elevate-and-new-law-firm-elevatenext-join-forces/

Chapter 10:
Seizing opportunistic approaches for improvements

Since every process can be improved and it's a "target rich environment", this chapter is intended to spark ideas about how to seize specific kinds of opportunities to employ Lean Sigma early on or at any point.

It is known that "the competition" is using process improvement to their advantage. In and of itself, that suggests everyone in law should consider how to keep up or at least use the notion of a rising tide lifts all boats to take an opportunistic approach to this work. In short, we have a choice – we can operate as we always have and continue to experience performance gaps, or we can act and improve.

Each person, team, department, and organization has unique reasons and imperatives for improving the way work is done and delivered as well as managed and priced. Tap into those first, follow the steps in your selected framework, and you'll get a return on investment. As Dr W. Edwards Deming once said, "People work in the system that management created". It is all too easy to ask about the who and not about the why; most people are surprised by how productive it can be to ask workers: What is going well? What can be improved?

Most of the time, people try their best (often, heroically) to work efficiently, but the thing that prevents them from performing to their highest potential is the system. When you give workers the power to help change the system, you will have done impactful work that very quickly becomes "the way we do things here". You will have a culture of inclusion, innovation, and improvement, and you certainly will make the case that process improvement works in your environment.

At any point, there are so many opportunities to improve our processes. One effective way to decide what we will work on is to get people to contribute their ideas about all the potential projects and improvement ideas. Then, we discuss how impactful and difficult each one would be and place them in the appropriate quadrant of an Impact-Ease Matrix. This helps us select, prioritize, and plan a cadence of projects. Some teams will mix shorter and simple with longer, more complex projects; others choose to only undertake fast-fix type projects. Every situation is different, which is why there is no one right way to do this work. That said, there is nothing like seizing whatever opportunities exist to try new approaches, learn, establish a foundation, and make the case for process improvement.

In law, there are some general areas that present opportunities for improvement. The easiest and most productive ways we have seen to begin are to address pain points, take advantage of a current situation (such as a crisis), and work on areas that people have already agreed are priorities.

Pain points

I often say that process improvement is an excellent forum for pent up grievances. It is also an excellent way to channel ideas that people have about how to make things better and give some structure to how we assess, select, and implement those contributions.

If people are complaining, it's usually not because they are whiners, but because they are grappling with a process that does not serve them well. Thus, there is a golden opportunity for improvement that starts by encouraging people to share the pain points they are experiencing, and then address them.

It's rather simple, but it's perhaps the most opportunistic way to employ process improvement. Also, to avoid randomly trying things and seeing what works, Lean Six Sigma offers a structured and data-driven approach to address pain points in a way that engages the key stakeholders at the outset and then eliminates waste, reduces variability, and improves process efficiency in ways that are directly and immediately impactful.

Pain points will stem from inefficiencies such as wasted time, underutilized talent or wrong / not enough resources, or effort (Lean) or the variability in processes that leads to inconsistent results, defects, and customer dissatisfaction (Six Sigma). Typical complaints involve poor communication, well-intentioned but siloed efforts, and a general lack of alignment between teams or departments. Another area that produces significant pain is the lack of standardization that leads to inconsistent outcomes, miscommunication, and reliance on "tribal knowledge" – information known only by a few employees. These things can (and often do) cause frustration and inefficiencies.

In law, the employee experience may be getting more attention, and rightfully so, but the client has always been the most important VIP. As such, grievances related to their satisfaction or quality of work product or service are likely candidates for focused attention. That is true whether it is a direct, overt complaint or a more subtle suggestion, such as write-down or write-off requests. The tools of process improvement can be used to map out the client experience, identify touchpoints where pain occurs, and streamline the journey for a smoother, even frictionless, more positive experience.

Ideally, we will have mechanisms in place to listen for and really hear the voice of the customer on an ongoing basis and a way to capture, analyze and use that information. By this, I mean something besides client feedback interviews or surveys, especially where positively biased questions are used to validate a purchase decision. In this context, I refer to continually gathering feedback and integrating it into process improvements to ensure that client expectations are consistently met or exceeded. One measure that is tried and true is to look at what clients will and will not pay for, what they will and will not accept, and to see what that range looks like.

Reducing bottlenecks and frustration while increasing employee engagement and utilization can start with a "quick fix". Start by standardizing work and establishing documented and repeatable processes. These kinds of solutions provide stability, consistency, and reliability in execution and helps get people "off the hamster wheel". One of the tools that we employ with great success early on is the RACI matrix. This is used to clearly define roles – "lanes" – and exactly who is Responsible, Accountable, Consulted, and Informed for each process. This prevents confusion, missed handoffs, miscommunication, gaps, and overlaps.

Another very easy and quick way to address pain points is to establish file naming and email subject line conventions. Too few teams use this tactic to full effect and it really does address a lot of pain points, especially those related to finding things in emails and searching for files in any document management system.

Whether it's a "low hanging fruit" pick or something more complicated, the Lean Sigma approach is excellent for identifying pain points and constraints through understanding value in the eyes of the client as well as the real problem. Gemba walks, where managers or leaders visit the front lines of where work happens to observe processes, are easy and excellent ways to gather input from employees and identify improvement opportunities directly from the people doing the work. We involve employees whenever possible to foster ownership, morale, and engagement while harnessing their expertise to resolve pain points. Without them, we cannot collect the data that helps us measure and analyze process performance.

With their help, we can look for the root cause, which also leads to sustained improvements.

We use VoC to gather feedback directly from clients or stakeholders to pinpoint areas of dissatisfaction and map the current processes to visualize pain points such as delays, redundancies, excessive steps, or bottlenecks. Then we focus on the most significant issues by employing the Pareto Principle and identifying the 20 percent of problems causing 80 percent of inefficiencies or defects.

We also employ various tools to dive deeper into pain points and understand their underlying causes. Rather than address the symptoms and get caught in a fire-fighting doom loop, we engage in root cause analysis by using the Five Whys technique and try to understand the possible causes of a problem into categories such as people, methods, machines, materials, environment, measurement (a variation of the 6M methodology). Tools such as a Failure Modes and Effects Analysis (FMEA) zero in on potential failure points within a process to determine where issues are likely to arise. This thinking and information helps to maximize our chances of success.

Another thing to consider is that addressing pain points does not necessarily require dramatic shifts to be effective. Incremental improvements to processes can remove waste and inefficiencies in ways that immediately relieve constraints and improve experiences of the workers. That said, we will need to monitor and sustain improvements, otherwise they may degrade over time and lead to recurring issues.

Don't let a good crisis go to waste

The idea of process improvement received increased attention in the legal industry in the wake of the pandemic, which obviously was a global driver for efficiency.

Frederick J. Esposito, Jr, MBA, CLM, is a senior consultant and faculty member of the Legal Lean Sigma Institute as well as COO of the regional law firm Rivkin Radler (a case study of which is included in chapter 5). He has more than 25 years of law and accounting firm experience, is an author and speaker specializing in financial and organizational management, process improvement, and project management, and has managed and worked in a consulting capacity with several domestic and international law firms. He is a Certified Green Belt in Legal Lean Sigma with a Project Leader designation and a Black Belt candidate.

In a series of interviews with Thomson Reuters,[1] he discussed how law firms are approaching process improvement in the post-pandemic environments. When asked about the effect of the pandemic on the interest in process improvement and why it is so important now, Fred stated:

> "The pandemic offered many industries, legal among them, both an imperative and a pause in which to consider and change (out of sheer necessity) how they were doing business and what could be done better. This had its benefits in terms of pushing firms to look at how they perform and deliver legal services, and I think that in turn has brought process improvement to forefront.
>
> "Process improvement helps us work as a cross-functional, diverse team. We lift the hood and see how and why the engine runs the way it does. In this way, the use of process improvement provides law firms an opportunity to examine how they currently perform their legal services."

Obviously, this involves a change in mindset as well as operations. Fred suggests that people should:

> "Think of improvement as the relationship between urgency and innovation. We can help people to see the reason for necessary improvement and the path to how it will get done. Working with clients on their process improvements, I've seen that many times it is people – the staff, the associates, and of course, the partners – who are coping with a broken process and often, while well-intentioned, contributing to the problematic efficiency issues. Helping people work as a higher functioning team is at the heart of transformation work for us."

People first – talent, DEIA, and generational challenges

Focusing on people first is always an excellent choice, whether your organization is just starting out or has a more sophisticated program. In my view, law overuses sticks and underutilizes carrots. There is a general failure to tap into what motivates people and create a culture of continuous improvement. All too often, we see a too heavy reliance on policy development with typically uneven application as the mechanism for managing people. What a missed opportunity to align and empower employees!

In the case of using process improvement opportunistically, we can use the "talent war" as a driving force for change. It impacts every kind of organization and applies to both legal and business professionals. In law, we are accustomed to news of lateral acquisitions making headlines. More recently, we have seen high-profile C-Suite executives making moves and getting the same kind of attention, particularly as more enterprises become increasingly sophisticated in employing business systems.

From pre-hire to alumni status, every employer benefits from focusing on critical "talent" processes such as recruiting, pre-boarding, onboarding, integration, offboarding, compensation, performance management, succession work, training, professional development, and staffing. More clients now are interested in "employee journey mapping" – just like customer/client journey mapping, only from the unique perspective of the prospective and hired employees.

One of the best examples of addressing a root cause in the talent area – the lack of diverse students in the pipeline – is Kean Miller's Connection.[2] To increase the number of diverse law students, the firm has successfully run a law school preparatory program for eligible college students. Attorneys from Kean Miller, along with others, provide an intense overview of the law school experience. The goal is to "connect" students with information helpful to their decision to attend law school and become an attorney. The RoI? The firm hires law school graduates who participate in the Connection program.

For every business driver, there are corresponding imperatives to improve the processes that are needed to support the people and activities in which they engage.

A 2024 survey[3] conducted by Wells Fargo on Q1 law firm performance revealed significant growth in demand and billing rates, particularly noticeable among larger firms. This surge resulted in revenue gains that more than doubled compared to the same period the previous year. According to Wells Fargo's Legal Specialty Group, there was a notable 9.5 percent increase in revenue across Am Law 200 firms in Q1. This growth was propelled by heightened demand, supported by a resurgence in capital markets, substantial mergers and acquisitions activities, and continued momentum in countercyclical work.

Addressing talent opportunities requires a focus on *what* we do, the *way* we do things, and *who* is doing them. Somewhat obviously, using economic drivers and demand for services metrics are important for any organization – paying attention to the legal processes that are used to do and deliver the most critical legal work is vital. To hire top talent and then have them spin their wheels doing non-value add work seems like a terrible investment. In one law firm, we calculated the cost of lateral acquisitions. By looking at time captured by the members of the executive committee alone, we quickly determined that an average of over $1 million in effort was being spent on each lateral – and, of course, there were plenty of other costs associated with recruiting, hiring, and onboarding each one.

Another reason to apply Lean Sigma within the broad area of talent is to reduce or remove single points of failure and to become what I call "treasure hunters", meaning uncovering hidden best practices and catching people doing things right. More enterprises should expand succession planning and include those who possess unique knowledge about "how to get things done" because there can be no knowledge management if it is not captured in the first place. How much valuable information do we lose when people leave? Often, it's unknown. As such, Lean Sigma projects are highly effective in uncovering what our talent knows, where we have gaps, and helps insulate us from the reality that, eventually, for one reason or another, people leave their places of work.

Consider how your organization would handle the departure of an entire department or team. Is there a plan for that? What would it cost to replace the talent and knowledge that was lost? How disruptive would it be and on whom? How long would it take to regain lost ground? Who would need to be involved in the hiring and onboarding of replacements? How would you fill the gap in the interim?

In law, the "cherry picking" and movement of top legal talent is in the daily headlines. Once upon a time, this did not extend to the business side of the house, but times have changed. A rare group move of law firm professionals made headlines in 2022, when the marketing team at Cooley left for Fried, Frank, Harris, Shriver & Jacobson. They followed a chief marketing officer who made the move in the prior year.

> *"In all, the lateral group includes six marketing and communications professionals who transferred between the two law firms. One law firm marketing expert said law firms in general could start seeing more business professional group moves such as this one, describing the team departure as a 'harbinger of things to come' in the industry."*[4]

Employing Lean Sigma as a mechanism for insulation and managing risk associated with talent departures is one thing. Another involves using it to capture best practices from those who are either on (as a retention tactic) or new to the team. Many corporations and law firms have a growth strategy that involves combinations, office, practice, and lateral acquisitions. This presents significant opportunities for employing process improvement. Having a good process is as good an incentive for people to stay as it is for anyone considering or making a move.

Lateral movement by lawyers is a daily occurrence, though it has slowed down. Following a 31 percent decline in 2023, lateral law firm movement was expected to dip further in 2024, both at the partner and associate levels.[5] However, using data to delve into what is really happening in a highly specific and relevant manner is so important (which means, by definition, we have to collect and have that data in the first place).

Paul Hastings has been one of the more active in the lateral market, both in terms of general volume and high-profile hires over the past couple of years. Between 1 January 2022 and 14 May 2024, the firm saw 97 partner hires and 54 exits, according to third-party data obtained by Law.com, a net gain of 43 people.[6] Assuming bringing in "higher caliber" lawyers is a good thing, Paul Hastings seems to be playing the lateral game well. But while figures differ and firms are getting better about vetting, generally, about one-third (36 percent) of lateral equity partners don't work out, according to survey data from Citi.[7]

Leopard Solutions[8] succinctly and correctly stated:

"Data accuracy is an essential component of being able to forecast future outcomes. Without a sufficient understanding of past performance and variables, attempts at predictions are fundamentally flawed. Their analysis clearly shows there is a significant shift towards entry-level hiring surpassing lateral hiring within the industry."

Lean Six Sigma (LSS) and diversity, equity, inclusion, and accessibility (DEIA) are distinct concepts, but they complement each other in meaningful ways. For one thing, the way we do process improvement work supports DEIA. Lean Six Sigma projects are delivered by cross-functional, diverse teams. The methodology and frameworks require the use of data to make objective decisions. This often helps organizations identify inequities in their systems. Through data collection, gathering feedback from diverse employee groups, and analysis (e.g., surveys, process metrics), we reveal barriers they face. Organizations can identify disparities related to areas such as hiring, promotion, pay, or resource allocation for example. Moreover, we always observe the first Lean Sigma principle by emphasizing the Voice of the Customer /

Client (VoC), meaning the users of the process. We are always careful to include the Voice of the Employee (VoE) in this definition of "client" to ensure all employees and key stakeholders are heard.

A goal for our projects usually involves some element of improving it for "fairness". Tools like process mapping (e.g., SIPOC, value stream mapping) identify inefficiencies and redundancies. This approach can be applied to recruitment, employee evaluations, or team dynamics, ensuring processes are free from bias and are inclusive for all employees. Another objective is to eliminate waste (non-value-adding activities) and optimize resource usage. We would consider biases and unfair practices to be forms of "waste" that detract from employee potential.

Lean Six Sigma fosters a culture of accountability by using metrics and instituting process ownership. Leaders can apply methodologies to track DEIA metrics, such as diversity in leadership positions, equitable promotion rates, or the success of inclusive policies. This ensures accountability at every level of the organization and standardization for fairness, which reduces variability and ensures consistency in processes. Standardizing processes like hiring and performance evaluations helps eliminate subjective bias, ensuring that every employee is evaluated based on consistent, transparent criteria.

In addition, we are undergoing a sea change in culture and processes attributable to the well documented generational differences in the workplace. These differences, and how lawyers of different ages view such basic topics as to who should perform tasks, and how the work should get done and when, have been laid bare by the pandemic. They have also created the potential for conflict, which can be useful.

Most organizations need help in changing the attitude about conflict. We encourage constructive conflict because it pushes teams to be more than the sum of their parts. It is not useful to have a process improvement team where everyone agrees on everything all the time – this does not help us consider and address all the different stakeholder perspectives. Each team works with ground rules and a facilitator helps to guard against "group think".

Lean Sigma helps us tackle – head on – the "Five Dysfunctions of Teams",[9] including one that is so prevalent in law: false harmony. We prize collegiality and simultaneously avoid confrontation to such a degree that we seem to have environments that look – but do not feel and simply are not – harmonious. This means that people work together to get things done, but somehow feel like they're not supposed to talk about problems, obstacles, conflict, fears, or concerns. Lean Sigma responds to this by offering concepts, frameworks, and tools for teams to have true harmony, an environment that looks and feels harmonious and where people work well together while solving problems, removing obstacles, responding to conflict, learning from fears and concerns, and getting things done.

One of the sources of conflict comes from the co-existence of several generations in law. Each has distinctive characteristics:

- *Silent (1935-1942):* Cautious, believe in "working within the system," not risk takers, like to play it safe.
- *Boomers (1946-1964):* Idealistic and committed to work, they value loyalty and hierarchy in the workplace. They are individualistic; within a law firm, this often shows up as being less client team focused, sharing of clients, and origination. They tend to be short-term thinkers and planners, prioritize "doing good work", and make a distinction between service partners and "rainmakers". They are also not retiring or doing a good job with succession planning and implementation.
- *Generation X (1965-1980):* Known for their independence, entrepreneurial spirit, and pragmatism, they seek a balance between work and personal life. They are self-reliant and have a higher tolerance for risk; they are more willing to try new things and are also peer-focused and collaborative.
- *Millennials or Generation Y (1981-1996):* Mobile. Collaborative. Technologically proficient, they seek purpose in their work and value constant feedback.
- *Generation Z (born after 1997):* Digital natives, they aspire to diversity and inclusion, and prefer flexibility in their work schedules and locations.

In their excellent work in this area, Heather Morse and Jonathan R. Fitzgarrald[10] have highlighted the differences and motivators of each generation. The vast majority of managing partners in law firms are boomers – their charge includes constantly designing and building an inclusive workplace both for now and in the future. And, since the future always belongs to the next generation, the processes we design can be especially helpful in paving smoother transitions.

Their data overwhelmingly supports the need to pay attention to closing the gaps that exist and will cause issues without serious focus. Morse did an interesting study and discovered that:[11]

- Gen-Xers – some of whom are by now in their early 50s according to

the US definition – were still largely shut out of law firm management. They made up less than five percent of managing partners or their equivalent. Their clients? Younger.
- Of those presiding over the legal spend at Fortune 100 companies, roughly 20 percent were Gen-Xers, born between the mid-1960s and the mid-1980s. That jumped to 30 percent of in-house counsel at the more tech-heavy NASDAQ-listed companies.

Says Morse:

"When you saw the data in a table, visually, it was so impactful. You could see that the law firms were not shifting at the same rate as the client base. Whether it's general corporate America, represented by the Fortune 100, or the NASDAQ, which has a lot more tech companies that skew a little less risk averse, it was so prevalent. There's a disconnect between what's going on in law firm leadership versus what's going on in the client-base leadership. It really shifted our conversation."

At a time when corporate law firms are struggling under client cutbacks and increasingly scraping for work, Morse says what she saw persuaded her that the age divide should become part of a firm's basic client-facing strategies. *"Smart law firms out there are including age as one of the defining measures of diversity."*

Everyone benefits when we understand people. Empathizing enables us to better relate, communicate, lead, manage, and motivate, and effect transformative, sustainable changes.

The takeaway from this is that diversity is not just about gender or race; age is part of the equation, too. Know who you are working with; know what motivates them, makes them tick. It'll enable you to get done what needs doing, no matter the task at hand.[12]

Moreover, understanding generational and all differences is the key to implementing improvements that are sustainable. The more we understand how to leverage diversity of experience, personality types, communication styles, and generational differences, the more likely it is that we will harness the power of a true team and that our improvements will be adopted. The key isn't to only approach the execution and rollout challenges with "stern messages" and punishment (i.e., the beatings will continue until morale improves – which does not really motivate any generation!), but to thoughtfully, inclusively, and intentionally build reward and recognition systems that appeal to the primary motivators for each generation.[13]

Taking a broad view of the talent category, we can easily see it is causing a helpful swing from "old" to "new" thinking. This gives us momentum on which we can build. Instead of viewing employees as the biggest risks, prizing skill over behavior, and rigid working schedules, organizations are evolving, if only out of necessity. Now, employees are the biggest assets, behavior is at least valued in addition to skill (it is not enough to be technically proficient anymore), and working schedules are far more flexible. One of the most fundamental and tectonic shifts can be seen in the move from a fear of failure to something closer to "fail in a controlled environment and learn, then apply the lesson". This creates ripe conditions for trying new things, like Lean Sigma, and innovation generally. Law gets better in creative conditions and leaders will do well to make this a goal.

Our success in successfully navigating those shifts rests on having good processes to support people *and* a good process for picking the processes to work on *and* an inclusive approach to improving them *and* building in the right incentives and control mechanisms to sustain improvements. Lean Six Sigma can be a powerful tool to support talent, DEIA, and generational challenges. By identifying inefficiencies, eliminating bias, and using data-driven strategies to ensure processes evolve over time, our culture continuously becomes more fair, inclusive, and equitable.

Mergers and acquisitions

When two law firms / offices or company law departments merge, there are significant opportunities for process improvement. A merger presents unique opportunities to streamline operations, enhance efficiencies, and harmonize both the people and the best practices of both organizations. Typically, those opportunities exist prior to, during, and after a merger. Having a good process to surface, select, and deploy those "best practices" across teams and organizations is arguably the single most engaging and effective way to integrate the best of both worlds and establish new norms.

Some key process improvement areas include those related to legal workflows, core business processes such as time keeping, conflict checking, intake, billing, and onboarding of both employees and clients. In addition, marketing and communications, technology, finances, knowledge management, business / client development, and facilities are all high priority areas on which to focus when merging.

Each enterprise will have its own procedures for handling legal matters. Moreover, each practitioner or office is likely to have their own ways of doing and delivering work. Each is also likely to perform core business processes differently. We worked with one law firm that had grown so quickly that, in about a year, they were supporting a half dozen different time entry and billing systems alone. Standardizing workflows will not only improve efficiency but will provide some clarity and calm for those who are expected to carry out tasks.

One recommendation is to conduct an operational assessment to inventory the key legal and business processes, and then develop and document standard operating procedures (SOPs) for the most important workflows. A top contender for immediate focus by merging firms is intake overall and conflict checking specifically. With increases in the complexities and numbers of business and legal conflicts, this core process is more important than ever. It is an excellent idea to implement a robust, firm-wide conflict-checking system to ensure potential conflicts of interest are identified early and handled consistently. This reduces legal risk and improves compliance with ethical guidelines. We know of firms that lowered their malpractice policy insurance premiums by so much that it paid for the process improvement project – and then some.

Other areas that should receive early attention are human resources and staffing integration. If staffing models are not aligned and HR processes not integrated, it becomes significantly more challenging to operate processes related to staffing matters, recruitment, professional advancement, client development, training, onboarding, performance evaluations, etc. Working on these early can ensure an easier transition for employees from both organizations; this, in turn, benefits clients. By streamlining the new hire process for attorneys and support staff and harmonizing HR policies, benefits, and performance evaluation criteria, we offer a much better employee experience. As a result, we can expect higher levels of productivity and morale.

Client, case, and contract lifecycle management systems are also critical areas for attention. CLM alone is an area deserving its own book. There are untold numbers of reasons and opportunities to ensure consistent client intake, tracking, and communication across the newly merged team, department, office and/or firm. Harmonizing different case management systems can eliminate redundancies and ensure cases and projects are handled consistently. Useful tools can be implemented, such as a unified client relationship management (CRM) system and integrated case tracking tools, to ensure that all client and critical information is centralized and appropriately accessible.

Financial practices are also a highly impactful area for attention. Disparate billing practices and systems can cause confusion and inefficiency for both clients and staff. By standardizing invoicing practices, including capturing outside counsel guidelines and readiness for effective e-billing, we ensure a consistent approach to timekeeping, billing rates, and invoice generation. Integration of systems and automation tools will help reduce errors and delays in billing. This requires focused attention and proper allocation of resources.

Knowledge management systems can become fragmented where two organizations have different document management systems, precedents, and research tools. It will be vital to create a centralized knowledge repository where legal resources, templates, and best practices are accessible to all attorneys and staff. This reduces duplicate efforts and ensures that legal teams have access to the same information. Similarly, mergers often involve different IT systems, which leads to inefficiencies and communication breakdowns if not addressed. Consolidation of the IT infrastructure, such as document management systems, communication tools, and practice management software is required. Moreover, all employees must be trained on the new systems, support must be available on an ongoing basis, process ownership must be instituted, and inquiries into automating repetitive administrative tasks should be made.

Last, but certainly not least, effective client management, communication, and reporting are essential. Variations in how people communicate with either external or internal clients can cause confusion, delays, or dissatisfaction. Standardizing client communication protocols, including how and when clients are updated on case and project progress, billing and budget, and deliverables is an excellent candidate for early and priority attention. Moreover, we suggest instituting service standards to ensure consistent posture, delivery, and professionalism in all client-facing communications. For law firms, a merger provides opportunities to cross-sell services between the newly combined firm's practice areas. As such, develop a unified business development strategy and clear procedures for cross-selling. This includes identifying and prioritizing clients who will benefit from the broader range of services, having a firm policy on how originations are to be handled, and allocating and aligning resources to support the effort.

Because clients may feel uncertain about the merger, which can lead to churn if not managed properly, focusing on the transition and retention processes is yet another high priority area. Having processes in place for retention work, such as proactive communication plans to reassure clients of continuity in service, along with a clear transition plan for key client accounts will go a long way to reassuring everyone involved.

Since cost optimization is often realized by merging firms through the discovery of redundant expenses or resource imbalances, another valuable exercise is to identify overlapping expenses, such as office space, software licenses, or support staff, then streamline resource allocation to reduce overhead and ensure that resources are allocated based on overarching priorities.

In summary, a law firm or company merger provides a unique opportunity to evaluate and improve processes across client management, operations, and internal workflows. The work here does not necessarily involve fast fixes overall but rather represents how the situation itself can be a forcing function for process improvement, whether it is scoped as a larger or small project. It is true that starting with quick wins often generates enthusiasm (and resources and budget) for larger projects. By integrating systems and standardizing practices, a newly merged enterprise will most certainly be more efficient, client-focused, and competitive.

Capturing effort – time-keeping

Most of us in law are now focused on data, which we seem to have in abundance but not always the right kind and not necessarily of the quality we would like. For a law firm – and its clients – timekeeping data is so important. It is an essential ingredient needed for many other things.

Yet, most organizations do not effectively, accurately, or thoroughly capture effort. Thus, they cannot accurately determine the true cost of doing and delivering any particular kind of work. It therefore becomes guesswork as to what kind of staffing is required for projects, especially those with varying needs and value in the eyes of the client. How do we track capacity and use leading indicators (and predictive analytics) to inform when we should add a resource and at what level? So many are just winging it. This applies to everyone in law, not just law firms.

With unavailable metrics and less than stellar data to show the magnitude of a problem or opportunity, sometimes process improvement teams will use industry data. This also helps us to begin to build a business case for a project. One example of this kind of benchmarking for a timekeeping project is the Law Firm Timekeeping Survey co-sponsored by Smart WebParts and Adam Smith Esq. in 2010,[14] which was augmented by the Smart WebParts team by adding average hourly rates.[15] We still use this information to build our business cases today.

In this survey, it is established that untimely recording of billable time results in an under reporting of time by the timekeeper, known as "leakage".

Even those who record their time contemporaneously leak about 45 hours annually, and those who reconstruct their time leak more than double that amount of time at about 97 hours per year.

It seems obvious to point out, but it takes time to enter time, also known as opportunity cost. According to the survey, the difference between the amounts of time a timekeeper takes to enter time is dramatic, especially when we compare practices of time entry:

How often do you enter time?	*Total annual hours to enter time*
Daily	32.4
Weekly	48
Monthly	69.6

One team was able to build a business case for its timekeeping project based on the data from the survey, since firm data could not easily be acquired. We extrapolated, making conservative estimates as to how many of the firm's timekeepers entered time on a weekly or less frequent basis, then applying the average hourly rate of all timekeepers. We also looked at a sample that showed us when time was entered and the date the work was performed. This indicated that, with one notable exception, none of the firm's timekeepers were entering their time contemporaneously.

Case study – business case for timekeeping project

1. LEAKAGE – Industry data shows that untimely recording of billable time results in an under-reporting of time by the timekeeper

Timekeeper Behavior	Hours Leaked	Average Hourly Rate				Conservative estimate: 50 percent of firm's timekeepers enter time on a weekly or less frequent basis = $4.7M of lost revenue to the firm.
		300	400	500	600	
Contemporaneous	45	13,500	18,000	22,500	27,000	
Reconstructionist	97	29,100	38,800	48,500	58,200	

2. OPPORTUNITY COST – Industry data: it takes longer to record time when it is not done daily.

How often do you prepare your timsheets	Monthly hours	Annual hours	Average Hourly Rate				Firm's opportunity cost = $2.4M
			300	400	500	600	
Daily	2.7	32.4	$9,720	$12,960	$16,200	$19,440	
Weekly	4.0	48.0	$14,400	$19,200	$24,000	$28,800	
Monthly	5.6	69.6	$20,880	$27,840	$34,800	$41,760	

Business case: $4.7 + $2.4 = $7.1M

Figure 21: Business case for timekeeping project. Source: Legal Lean Sigma Institute LLC.

Using industry data and making conservative estimates enabled us to develop the business case for improving the firm's timekeeping practices, since we could easily show the undeniable magnitude of the problem and how it translated into real dollars – an estimated $7 million. Since law firms as a business are not the highest performers when it comes to profitability, we did not have a difficult job of convincing leaders that the project was worth doing and the firm would get a substantial return on investment, just for doing a better job of capturing time on work they had already won and were already doing. This same formula can be used to make the case for improving timekeeping at any size firm. See Figure 22.

Moreover, using data further facilitated the team's ability to calculate that, for every one percent improvement this firm made, it was worth $2 million to the firm's bottom line, without adding additional work or infrastructure.

Chapter 10: Seizing opportunistic approaches for improvements

With that information, the team set a project goal of a very modest and achievable five percent improvement, or $10 million, which was exceeded.

In addition to improving financial performance, a firm that begins with a timekeeping process is able to generate better data about effort that it can use in nearly every area of business or practice operations.

This point about the usefulness of firm data and what to do about it was articulated well in an ILTA white paper by Lann Wasson of Husch Blackwell LLP:[16]

Timekeeper Behavior	Hours Leaked	Average Hourly Rate			
		300	400	500	600
Contemporaneous	45	13,500	18,000	22,500	27,000
Reconstructionist	97	29,100	38,800	48,500	58,200

$450 per hour × 45 hours leaked = $20,250
× 100 timekeepers
LEAKAGE = $2,025.000

How often do you prepare your timesheets	Monthly hours	Annual hours	Average Hourly Rate			
			300	400	500	600
Daily	2.7	32.4	$9,720	$12,960	$16,200	$19,440
Weekly	4.0	48.0	$14,400	$19,200	$24,000	$28,800
Monthly	5.6	69.6	$20,880	$27,840	$34,800	$41,760

32 hours per year × $450 = 32 hours per year × $450
× 100 timekeepers
OPPORTUNITY COST = $1.440.000

Total: $3.465,000

Remember:
- Use conservative estimates
- Point out this is BEST case scenario based on contemporaneous/daily timekeeping

Figure 22: Show your math. Legal Lean Sigma Institute LLC.

"Lean, Six Sigma and the management approaches called by their names are fundamentally rooted in measurement, so it is common practice to observe the workplace and collect data either by conducting time studies or mining existing internal databases. Unlike some other service industries, law firms are technology-rich office environments where the intellectual, social and creative work is often invisible and impossible to capture in traditional ways.

"To determine whether data in the firm's time entry system could be incorporated into the value stream map, the practice group chair asked each lawyer in the pilot to identify a short list of matters from the last few years as a representative sample for comparison. Using a recent matter as a test case for analysis, the firm's financial reporting group compiled the data and graphed the results as a composition and distribution of time worked per role, per day.

"After several hours of discussion with the lead partner on the deal, we concluded that there was simply no way to extrapolate the cost of process segments, much less the individual process steps, based on the existing data points. The dynamics of corporate transactions, the practice of block billing and a lack of coding had resulted in a set of unstructured data that was of little use in defining a baseline. Furthermore, given the complexity of the transactions in the sample, the opportunity cost of attempting to restructure the time entries by manually parsing the data was simply too great.

"While the lack of useful hard data presented another challenge to the development of the value stream map, it also prompted a deeper discussion of the dynamics of information flow and of other more qualitative attributes of activities within each process segment. As a result of this dialogue, the team began evaluating the benefits of different forms of estimation and again reached consensus on a viable way to approximate values for cycle and lead times. Going forward, the team concluded that if lawyers started coding their time based on a defined set of project phases, data could be gleaned from the accounting system and layered onto the process map. Until then, the group would continue to focus on describing and understanding the dynamics of transactions from a Lean Six Sigma perspective in order to gain as much insight as possible."

Frederick J. Esposito, Jr., MBA, CLM uses a performance metrics dashboard as a powerful management tool. While most organizations in law measure various behaviors and business indicators of health and performance, the challenge is to identify the set of metrics that are critical to success and to create a dashboard to effectively manage the law department, firm, or office. It is vital to track key performance indicators (KPIs), metrics, and other key data points relevant to the department, firm, a practice group, or a specific process. With the power of data visualizations, dashboards simplify complex data sets to provide leaders and managers with "at a glance" awareness of current performance.

In addition to focusing on different types of KPIs most important to a legal organization and considering how they can be used in a performance metric dashboard to contribute to strategic initiatives, a Balanced Score Card approach can be used in developing dashboards that address financial, strategic, and operational performance, including client satisfaction. With the ability to interpret data so that it tells a story, we can more easily discover where we must leap into the breach and, better yet, proactively discover future potential.

When people trust the information and the process, they will support the response(s) to the opportunities that exist for improvement. As Esposito said:

> *"Change is a funny animal and I think that when people are put to the test, I do believe that the human spirit or the resilience of people, I don't think it should ever be underestimated, because I think people really will rise to the occasion."*[17]

Good benchmarking and key performance data plus the requisite skills and experience are keys to seizing opportunities when – not if – they arise. When an organization has infrastructure and a culture that facilitates the ability to channel anything from mild concern to major agita into a way to address them, it greatly improves the chances of turning what could have been a negative into an opportunity to generate incremental improvements at one end of the spectrum to groundbreaking innovative programs at the other – and everything in between. It also helps to engage and align the people so they are more positive and productive as we respond.

References
1. www.thomsonreuters.com/en-us/posts/legal/leveraging-process-improvementtaking-steps/
2. www.keanmillerconnection.com/

3   www.leopardsolutions.com/comparing-the-current-lateral-market-and-the-pre-pandemic-landscape/
4   www.law.com/americanlawyer/2022/10/13/marketing-team-exits-cooley-for-fried-frank-highlighting-competitive-landscape-for-business-pros/
5   www.law360.com/pulse/articles/1826464/law-firm-lateral-movement-expected-to-fall-again-in-2024
6   www.law.com/americanlawyer/2024/05/30/how-do-we-know-who-wins-the-war-for-talent/?slreturn=20240808120731
7   www.law.com/international-edition/2024/04/21/a-safe-bet-lateral-hiring-and-gambling-on-a-firms-future/
8   www.leopardsolutions.com/comparing-the-current-lateral-market-and-the-pre-pandemic-landscape/
9   Lencioni, Patrick, *The Five Dysfunctions of a Team: A Leadership Fable*, 2002, Random House.
10 www.linkedin.com/pulse/how-law-firms-can-navigate-generational-divide-jonathan-fitzgarrald/
11 www.lexpert.ca/archive/the-generation-divide-between-law-firms-and-clients/350468
12 www.jdsupra.com/legalnews/why-understanding-generational-differenc-30427/
13 www.legalwatercoolerblog.com/wp-content/uploads/sites/27/2014/04/generationalmarketing.pdf
14 Gerstein, T. "Recommendation for Law Firm Timekeeping Best Practices", Smart WebParts LLC, 2010; see www.smart-webparts.com/pdfs/timekeepingbestpractices.pdf.
15 Gerstein, T. "The Agony of Unbooked Time" blog post, Smart Time Time Keeping Blog, 31 August 2010; see http://blog.smart-webparts.com/page/13 .
16 Wasson, L., "An Unconventional Alliance: Lessons from a Lean Six Sigma Pilot", ITLA, June 2011. https://epubs.iltanet.org/i/34417-km/40?
17 www.bighand.com/en-us/resources/podcasts/we-are-seeing-process-improvement-on-steroids/

Chapter 11:
Process improvement, pricing, and procurement

There are tremendous challenges for law firms involved in reconnecting value to costs for legal services and meeting the demands of chief legal officers, general counsels, legal operations, and procurement professionals.

Pricing
One of the responses from law firms is to bring in pricing professionals – a role that has grown significantly in numbers and maturity since the first edition of this book was published. The exact number of law firms with pricing professionals varies significantly by location and firm size. However, the trend of hiring pricing professionals has been growing steadily. Larger firms and those focused on innovation in legal services are more likely to have dedicated pricing experts.

Reasons for the increase in pricing professionals in law firms include:
1. *Increased competition.* With the legal market becoming more competitive, firms must offer transparent and competitive pricing to attract, acquire, and retain clients.
2. *Client demand.* Clients seek value-based billing and alternative fee arrangements rather than or in addition to traditional hourly rates. Pricing professionals help firms develop and manage these models.
3. *Cost management.* Firms are looking to optimize their pricing strategies to balance profitability with client satisfaction. Pricing professionals analyze data to ensure that pricing structures are both competitive and sustainable.
4. *Data analytics.* The rise of data analytics in law firms has led to a greater focus on pricing strategies. Professionals in this field use data to forecast pricing trends and make informed decisions.
5. *Value proposition.* Firms are using pricing professionals to enhance their value proposition, ensuring that their pricing reflects the quality and uniqueness of their services.
6. *Regulatory changes.* Some jurisdictions have seen changes in regulations that impact how legal services are priced, prompting firms to employ experts who can navigate these complexities.

Overall, the presence of pricing professionals reflects the broader trend of legal services becoming more business-oriented and data-driven. According to Thomson Reuters' "Compensation for law firm pricing professionals at the start of 2023" report:[1]

> "Among the top five activities where lead pricing professionals spend their time, developing pricing options is, unsurprisingly, the top activity, with analysis and approval of pricing requests, evaluating historical client and matter performance, developing and embedding pricing systems, and negotiating directly with clients rounding out the top five.
>
> "Legal pricing had its advent coming out of the Great Recession. In the economic downturn brought on by the pandemic, pricing professionals played a key role in protecting law firms' paths to profitability and pricing integrity through strategies such as proactive offers for AFAs, strategic billing credit practices, and pricing training for lawyers. In the current market where clients are being pressured from all sides by forces ranging from inflation to their own boards, law firm pricing professionals seem poised to jump to the forefront once again. The importance of budgets for legal matters, effective scoping of work, and a potentially renewed interest in AFAs on the part of clients will all require experienced professionals to lead law firm efforts to protect and grow profitability in a challenging market."

We can determine the definition of value by considering different models, such as John Grant's value theory, and we can greatly improve our ability to develop AFAs and value-based billing with a new model for looking at, improving, and managing work – and the way it is delivered.

However, pricing directors and teams cannot achieve significant change when working in isolation. The entire firm has to be focused on the business, not the practice of law, to achieve real, sustainable improvements in profitability in an increasingly cost-squeezed market. Imagine how powerfully process maps can be used as tools for this purpose – and also to educate clients and prospects about what you do, how you do it, and why the budget looks the way it does. Then, project planning is possible. What client does not want to experience a well-run practice that has pricing under control while delivering value?

Amanda Mui, senior product value engineer at Litera articulates the situation perfectly:

> "Firms face the dual challenge of satisfying client demands for substantive value while also achieving their own profitability goals and maintaining equitable partner compensation. The question looms: How can firms redefine value beyond the confines of the billable rate cycle? The answer lies in a paradigm shift from a finance-centric approach to one rooted in human experience.
>
> "To achieve this, pricing departments should focus on being strategic partners, not only with their downstream partners in billing and collections but also with their Business Development workstreams. Together, they must create new metrics and lexicons for measuring value, stepping away from finance-driven paradigms and towards a framework that emphasizes client experience and outcomes over pure numbers. Such a transformation entails the creation of pricing models that incorporate novel criteria, distinct from the traditional billing rate, to articulate value to clients.
>
> "Additionally, law firms must align their internal benchmarks of value with this broader perspective. If the aim is to convince clients to not focus on the billable hour as their yardstick for value, then firms must also recalibrate their methods of quantifying worth, shifting the focus from sheer production or volume to performance elements like those applied to professional staff."[2]

At this point, there is also widespread recognition by the majority of those in the legal ecosystem of the need for change, innovation, and the availability of technology solutions to deliver accessible real-time information that can support far more effective pricing and profitability management. It is worth underscoring a critical point – as with anything else, without good processes, both the function and the roles of pricing and procurement cannot be optimized. A law firm investing in a smart idea but in random, disconnected, or silo fashion, by design, cannot yield the best results. Without a good process for preparation and approval and follow up of alternative fee arrangements or documenting it and measuring its success – using high quality timekeeping entries, of course – how would anyone know there has been a return on investment or that it is working as intended? Plan, do, check, act!

Obviously, AI and predictive analytics can be gamechangers for everyone. However, according to the 2023 LDO Survey,[3] when asked if "Law firms are leveraging technology to deliver legal services more effectively and efficiently", 68 percent disagreed – an increase from 51 percent in 2022. This raises several questions: Is this a lack of communication between clients and law firms? Do clients feel this way because they are mostly still on hourly billing arrangements? Or is there something else behind this? No matter the reason, firms' efforts are clearly not being appreciated by their clients. Amongst survey participants, the general consensus is that pricing models will evolve for work incorporating GenAI, with AFAs increasing, as more than 90 percent of firms believe they will increase AFAs for work augmented by GenAI.

Returning to our earlier theme of the art–science balance in process improvement, this observation about pricing also caught my interest:

"When legal pricing and project management executives were asked if measuring the value of legal services is more art than science, 25.8 percent strongly agree and 58.1 percent agree that it is more art… that raises many fascinating questions, particularly since firms are using metrics which is scientific in nature. Respondents say it's more art than science, but there is clearly some science. And when most people agree it's art, that becomes a problem when we need to capture and report on the ROI."

Fixed fees encourage greater efficiency
Using data as evidence, you might start with looking at pricing and the fee arrangements in your firm. According to Six Sigma Black Belt Micah Ascano:

"A simple way to think of how a process or legal service can be done with fewer billable hours is a flat fee or collared fee arrangement. Why? Because if we have a flat fee arrangement with a client and are more efficient with our work (not more sloppy or reduced quality), the amount of savings internally (money/time) turns into extra profit or additional capacity for more clients without reducing the current level of profits for partners.

"To start, a law firm should focus on accurate prediction of legal costs in order to establish a baseline for measurable process improvements. Then, once the return on investment of the process improvement has occurred, the firm can make a strategic decision on whether or not to share that measurable cost savings with the client."[4]

For law firms trying to deliver better value to clients, Lisa Damon of Seyfarth Shaw offers the following suggestions:
- Be willing to invest and commit to changing for the long haul.
- Ensure you have commitment from the top.
- Find client advocates who will help champion your cause.

- Accept small successes at first. Change comes slowly for many lawyers, and organizational change does not happen rapidly.[5]

One of the most important things we can do is to use our client's definitions of value and quality. Firms must look at their business from the client's perspective, not their own – this is evidenced in Lean Sigma Principle 1: Define value in the eyes of the client.

By understanding the situation, issue, case, matter, or transaction lifecycle from the client's needs and processes, we can discover what they are experiencing. When we have this knowledge, we can identify areas where we can add significant value or improvement from their perspective. We can also isolate activities that are not adding any value and determine whether we can reduce or even eliminate that waste entirely.

"I think most clients would be okay with the idea that firms [that] would learn how to be more efficient would take a little more in profit, as long as that profit isn't an increase in costs to the client, in exchange for the security of a flat fee for the business savvy client. Long term, once cost savings is calculable to the firm, that savings can then be passed on to the client. Again, what business client will balk that if the firm takes the risk with a flat fee, it should be rewarded with additional profit, barring a complete windfall, if it tries to learn how to be more efficient?"[6]

Firms have been creative about how they are responding to clients' needs for years now. One early example was Torys LLP, which opened a small "insourcing" office called Torys Legal Services Centre where the firm performs high-volume, recurring legal work such as reviewing contracts or performing due diligence on corporate deals for the firm's established corporate clients.

According to the press release, the Torys Legal Services Centre:

"Will be charged with developing new, more efficient ways of doing this kind of legal work that can then be rolled out across the rest of the firm, which has offices in Toronto, New York, Calgary and Montreal... The move comes as debate over new ways of doing business continue to ripple through the legal profession. The corporate clients that use the country's elite law firms are increasingly demanding they curb the spiraling costs that come with $800-an-hour senior partners, or provide more predictable legal bills with fixed fees or flat rates.

> *"Torys says its plan is unique in Canada, although British firm Allen & Overy opened a similar office in Belfast in 2011, where it also moved human resources and other support staff to cut costs... Mr Fowles, who articled at Torys in 1994, said the new office is simply a response to client demands: 'They want to know upfront what things are going to cost and we'll be able to tell them, and they will be able to rely on it.'"*[7]

As say Josh Kubicki and C. Wood:

> *"As there is a relationship between cost and price, there exists a relationship between process and cost. How a firm performs services impacts cost. Performance is indelibly tied to process/workflow. This is true even in the practice of law."*[8]

With internal and external pressures to be more efficient and a keen interest from partners in remaining profitable, it is certain that a specific role that is focused on process improvement will become another business function in a law firm that is the rule rather than the exception. The increased number of those responsible for process improvement, project management, and/or pricing suggests that this will occur sooner rather than later.

Procurement

Structured approaches to buying legal can be found all over the world. It is more than just large corporations that purchase legal services; governments in every corner of the planet contract with many providers, for instance, and they are scrutinized for resource management.

A good example to study is the Whole of Australian Government Legal Services Panel,[9] which is administered as a coordinated procurement arrangement. The Attorney-General's Department (AGD) through the Office of Legal Services Coordination (OLSC), has established a whole of Australian Government legal services panel (the Panel). The objectives of the Panel are:
- Optimising access to the right services;
- Achieving the best price for those services;
- Efficiency and reduction of red tape;
- Fairness and transparency for Legal Services Providers; and
- Facilitating access to key information for Agencies and Legal Services Providers.

The panel leverages the Commonwealth's purchasing power, increases price transparency, and creates efficiencies in the Commonwealth's engagement with external legal services providers (LSPs). All non-corporate Commonwealth entities, and other Commonwealth bodies that have opted-in, must purchase legal services consistently with the panel arrangements. It also has reporting templates, which create a level playing field, consistency, the first sign of quality, and a predictable experience with less undesirable variation for the participants.

LSPs are appointed to the panel under six broad areas of law, each with an associated schedule of rates:
1. Workplace, industrial relations and compensation.
2. Public law.
3. Corporate and commercial (general).
4. Corporate and commercial (specialist).
5. Property and environment.
6. Legal support services.

Interestingly, there are important exceptions and a great deal of flexibility built into the process, including pricing mechanisms:

> *15.1 An Agency may request that an LSP provide a quote using a particular pricing mechanism, so long as the maximum rate does not exceed the Panel Rate, except as outlined in clause 14.3.*
>
> *15.2 Pricing arrangements that Agencies may consider include, but are not limited to:*
>   *a. hourly rates, broken down per lawyer level;*
>   *b. daily rates;*
>   *c. hourly/daily secondment rate;*
>   *d. blended rate (i.e. one hourly rate that applies regardless of the level of the lawyer);*
>   *e. fixed price (i.e. agree up front on the total cost of the matter);*
>   *f. fixed cap (i.e. invoices for a matter cannot exceed a fixed amount);*
>   *g. milestone payments (i.e. with each milestone being capped or each milestone having a fixed price); or*
>   *h. a combination of any of the above pricing mechanisms.*[10]

Thriving when legal procurement is in the mix[11]
The increased involvement of procurement and legal operations in the purchasing of legal services is one of the side effects of a power shift to the

client. The message to law firms is get your cost house in order, improve your efficiency and processes, sharpen your pencil, and come out ready for legal operations and procurement. Also, keep it up.

Unless you sit across from corporate purchasing, procurement, sourcing, or supply managers in a pitch, procurement is an anonymous person who may be accused of everything from interfering with the lawyer–client relationship, having neither the knowledge nor ability to judge the quality of legal services, playing firms against each other and cherry-picking in order to get the lowest price, and unreasonably squeezing firms' margins. With the help of procurement, more and more companies have taken a more rigorous approach to selecting firms and ensuring that the relationship continues to deliver expected outcomes. Corporate purchasing has changed the way professional services are bought over the last few decades – engineering and architectural services since the late 1980s; marketing, public relations, and advertising services since the mid-late 1990s; accounting, auditing, and tax services since the early- to mid-2000s; and legal services in the last 15+ years.

Legal budgets are under cost scrutiny like any other part of an organization, since legal spend has become a significant line item that no CEO and CFO can ignore. Top management sees legal departments as cost centers and wants legal to be managed efficiently and effectively. They call on procurement to get the job done – spending less on suppliers can directly improve the bottom line. Procurement's mandate is traditionally based on the idea of cost control, getting external suppliers to reduce their prices, and preventing departments from unnecessary spending through managing what is purchased. Top management is very aware of the strategic benefits that can be achieved through the intelligent use of purchasing and supply management.

General counsel are no longer the only buyers of corporate legal services
Procurement takes a process-driven, business-to-business sourcing approach. This approach may collide with the traditional, relationship-driven selection by in-house counsel. Procurement adds process expertise and makes the selection more objective and transparent. Procurement professionals negotiate hard and facilitate the sourcing process. Procurement assists in-house lawyers with defining the scope of the project, selecting the right supplier, negotiating and structuring compensation, evaluating supplier performance, and leveraging business with preferred suppliers. Their involvement allows in-house lawyers to focus on what they do best –

the world of law, rather than having to deal with selecting the right legal service providers. And with in-house counsel's pay increasingly tied to legal spend management and staying within budget, procurement is now more often embraced by in-house counsel than it once was.

Controlling legal spend is frequently at the top of the priority list for many organizations. Since the early 2000s, when the Sarbanes-Oxley Act (SOX)[12] and other new financial regulations took effect in response to several large accounting scandals at Enron, WorldCom, and Tyco International, CFOs have come under greater scrutiny related to companies' internal financial controls.

Increased enforcement, potentially leading to significant financial penalties and possible criminal conviction, has made the C-suite more and more concerned about departmental compliance with these and other federal regulations. However, because legal teams are understandably more focused on practicing law than managing the business' finances, in-house lawyers are sometimes the last department to implement systemic financial controls. Herein lies a significant problem – legal departments are frequently unaware of how much they spend on legal services rendered by outside counsel. As a result, they may be unknowingly paying too much.

Businesses have been spending more for legal work performed by outside counsel. According to the Corporate Legal Operations Consortium's 2021 State of the Industry report,[13] spending on outside law firms almost doubled from the previous year, reaching $14.5 million in 2021 compared to $7.9 million in 2020.

Market intelligence research conducted by legal sourcing specialist Buying Legal Council[14] has concluded that company size (in terms of annual revenues) governs the calculation of legal spend:

For example: A Fortune 500 company with revenue between $4.1 billion and $25 billion spends an average of $173 million on outside legal services (between 0.6% and 4.2% of its revenue), while an organization earning between $501 million and $1.7 billion might spend $31 million (between 1.8% and 6.2% of its revenue) on third-party counsel.

Why involve procurement and CFOs in legal spend?
Company CFOs are known for being concerned with controlling legal costs, which appear to be taking a bigger bite out of company budgets each year. Yet, when called into question, in-house lawyers that want to improve their

departments can find it challenging to justify increasing expenses. However, legal departments can bridge this gap by turning legal process involvement into a value proposition that will resonate with even the most skeptical CFO.[15]

Master negotiators and bad cops

The involvement of procurement typically starts with the negotiation of master service agreements (MSA), management of the panel selection, or legal commodities such as e-discovery. This is sometimes done through so-called "reverse auctions". In a reverse auction, a client puts work out for bid, using specialized software or online. Multiple firms offer bids on the work and compete to offer the lowest price that meets the specifications of the bid. Standard practices also include billing guidelines and a robust invoice review process, as well as case management guidelines. The intelligent use of purchasing helps companies rein in rising legal costs by separating legal services into commoditized segments, including paralegal and research needs, and creating sourcing strategies for individual segments.

Legal procurement's main role is that of a "buyer" and "influencer". As buyers, legal procurement professionals are responsible for price and contract negotiation, as well as for the engagement letter, retainer, or framework agreement. Legal and procurement often assume "good cop" and "bad cop" roles – as in-house counsel, if you must deal with your counterparts every day, it is much better to have procurement people be the tough negotiators. It does not destroy in-house lawyers' working relationship with outside counsel. As influencers, they aim to affect the outcome of a decision with their opinion.

Opponents of legal procurement warn that the process-driven business approach collides with the traditional relationship-driven, trust-driven selection by in-house counsel. In the 2014 procurement study, some respondents commented on lawyers' warning that procurement's spend savings are illusions as they are not sustainable spend reductions. According to the comments in the study, procurement's approach was said to "ruin" the law firm-client relationship and jeopardize the quality of legal advice and outcome. Legal procurement consultant Winmill reported that an in-house lawyer accused his legal procurement colleague, who suggested and outlined a standard and simple procurement process, of "destroying the profession". Emotions run high in this arena.[16]

Another common role for legal procurement professionals is "gatekeeper" because they control the flow of information from the firm to the deciders. They are less likely to be "deciders" themselves – only rarely do they make the final decision regarding which firm to choose or have the ability to veto a decision that has been made. The general counsel and her designated lawyers still retain the right to shortlist firms. This has not changed. In some companies, senior executives, such as the CEO or the board, are also involved in shortlisting law firms.

The general counsel, and to a lesser degree, other in-house lawyers and in some cases legal operations, also have a final say in the selection of the company's legal service providers. CEOs and other management are typically not involved in the final decision. A CEO cares about the total cost and the win rate. She or he typically delegates specific choice to the general counsel or CLO.

Legal procurement professionals are rarely the "initiators" of sourcing legal service. It is typically the in-house lawyers suggesting that or which legal services are needed.

In line with their roles, legal procurement professionals are most likely to be involved in the negotiation and contract development phase and in the development of (purchasing) criteria, outside counsel guidelines, and strategy. Post-purchase evaluation of legal services providers and monitoring compliance with outside counsel guidelines has become an important part of their work. Legal procurement professionals are least likely to be involved in the selection phase of legal service providers.

Despite the widely held belief among lawyers that procurement officers normally buy widgets and are ill equipped to understand and buy legal services, about one fifth of legal procurement professionals have a legal background. The remaining majority of respondents in the studies held MBA degrees or bachelor degrees in business subjects.

From legal commodities to high-stakes work

Procurement is typically involved in purchasing routine services but has made progress in purchasing "bread and butter" legal services – those between high-stakes work and commodities. Procurement is increasingly involved in the purchasing of complex, high-value, high-stakes legal services. GlaxoSmithKline is a pioneer in this area. The pharmaceutical giant uses a procurement approach to all legal matters in excess of $250,000.[17] GSK's general counsel Dan Troy says that involving procurement paid off; in the nearly four years since GlaxoSmithKline looked to revamp the way it hires and pays for outside legal services, the pharmaceutical giant saved tens of millions of dollars in legal fees, according to a 2012 article in *The Legal Intelligencer*.[18]

The intelligent use of purchasing helps companies rein in rising legal costs by separating legal services into commoditized segments, including paralegal and research needs, and creating sourcing strategies for individual segments. Procurement is also involved in all types of legal services – litigation, transactional, and to a somewhat lesser degree, advisory work. It appears that no stones are left unturned. All types of matters have become subject to scrutiny.

Who pays sticker price?
Unless alternative fee arrangements are used, legal procurement professionals clearly expect discounts on law firm's rack rates. "You would not buy sticker price at the car dealer", a legal procurement professional at a Fortune 100 company pointed out. But just how much of a discount do they expect? In 2014, Dr Silvia Hodges Silverstein, vice president, strategic market development at Sky Analytics, undertook a groundbreaking study to understand just this point, which found:[19]

- Half of the respondents in the study expected a discount of over 20 percent.
- What's more, about a quarter of respondents expected a discount of over 25 percent.

However, if so much importance is placed upon the hourly rate discounts, legal procurement professionals should also monitor what other metrics this impacts. In other words, if I negotiate a steep discount, will that affect the level of experience on a matter, where the work is done, or the staffing efficiency? It is important to embrace analytics and look at total cost and see a more holistic picture of legal spend, rather than just focusing on discounts.

Legal procurement analyses so many things that might not have been given a lot of attention in the legal profession before:
- Industry benchmarking analysis (conducted by 71 percent of respondents).
- Rate increase analysis and invoice audits (67 percent each)
- Half of the respondents forecast budgets, followed by alternative fee arrangement analysis and key performance indicator analysis.
- Procurement also embraces legal spend management (75 percent) and e-billing (71 percent).
- Contract database for legal, matter management, and in-house e-discovery are used by 40-50 percent of respondents in the survey.

- Firms' project management and process improvement capabilities are increasingly important: 48 percent of respondents in the survey deemed them "very important", another 16 percent as "important".[20]

What are procurement's other tools? How do they manage to reach their goals? Billing guidelines are still the most common standard practices when sourcing legal services. A huge 81 percent of respondents said they use them in their organization. It is good procurement practice to make the organization's terms and conditions (T&C) be part of the minimum requirements upfront. T&Cs should get accepted before a request for proposal (RFP) is issued, together with a non-disclosure agreement (NDA). Attempts to deviate from the T&C typically count against the firm during the evaluation process. Also important are invoice review processes (70 percent). Case management and counsel selection and evaluation processes, as well as analysis, have also gained in importance.

RFPs – a tire-kicking exercise?

Many law firms are busy filling in requests for proposal (RFPs) issued or initiated by legal procurement. Is it worth their time? How often do new suppliers win business over the incumbent law firms in an RFP issued by their organization?

Law firms are advised to have a clear understanding of whether an RFP is a tire-kicking exercise or if the company is looking for alternatives to their current firms. Law firms need to carefully qualify opportunities and be clear of their go/no-go criteria to avoid wasting their time and resources. A misguided service mentality of marketing and business development would be to help partners with every RFP that lands on their desks. Not every RFP should receive the same level of attention. The firm needs to have a clear understanding of when they draw the line or when an "opportunity" presented is not one that they should be interested in. Only RFPs that are in line with the firm's strategy should be pursued. One might say that the "assess and qualify" step of the RFP process ought to be improved – or maybe, added!

It is worth speaking directly with the client to learn more about how procurement works in their organization, what influence procurement has, and how the two departments collaborate. It is important to start building a relationship with the client's legal procurement. As a key stakeholder with growing influence, most procurement officers are open to learning more about what services firms currently provide and those the firm may be able to provide in the future. They may be looking for ways to consolidate spend, or to increase spend with the goal of getting volume discounts. Law firms should be aware of procurement's goals, objectives, challenges, and strategies.

Strategies for law firms
The involvement of procurement and their way of comparing law firms requires a different approach from the firms themselves – they need to consider a different way than just thinking in terms of hourly rates and billing. Procurement professionals demand predictability and project and budget management, even more than most GCs. It is advisable to understand what the client values – in particular, which metrics the organizations uses when evaluating law firms. More and more companies are data- and metrics-driven, conduct detailed cost analysis, and plan and manage their organizations with sophisticated metrics and benchmarks, which influences their selection.

The chief procurement officer (CPO) of a large company shared that "if you know your business, you should know how long something takes and how much something should cost". He used to work in the nuclear energy sector, which in his opinion had many more unpredictable factors and was much more complex than your average litigation. Yet, the engineers were able to come up with a price. He thought that lawyers being unable – or unwilling – to put a price tag on a piece of work told him that they did not really know their business. He assumed that lawyers never bothered to analyze their business, because they did not have to.

Generally speaking, legal procurement professionals look for experience with similar matters or "closest to the pin". Has the firm done similar work for another client? Argued in front of this judge or court? Solved a similar issue? Procurement wants to be sure the law firm will hit the ground running. Many might have the general expertise, but which firm will not need to do extensive, expensive research to get up to speed? It is good practice to ask firms to present examples or case studies to demonstrate the ways in which they have solved similar problems and how they work with clients and other law firms. Firms can also win points with procurement if they can show industry experience as it also promises the efficiency procurement seeks. Finally, value for money and service excellence are important factors for procurement. Procurement wants to see efficiency. A robust project management approach helps do just that.

For procurement, there are a number of subjective factors that influence the decision to award work to a particular law firm. According to the 2014 survey mentioned above, the most important were:
- Responsiveness ("They are willing to help us to provide prompt service").
- Reliability ("They are able to perform the service dependably and accurately").
- Availability ("They are there when we need them").
- Chemistry ("We like working with them").
- Empathy ("They make an effort to know our company and its needs").
- Assurance ("They have the required skills and knowledge to perform the service").

Now consider what kinds of metrics we are tracking and reporting that speak to each of these factors. These subjective factors all ranked above previous relationships with specific lawyers. Contrast these with what lawyers typically place a lot of value on – peer recommendations and industry rankings – that have little importance for legal procurement professionals. The (lowest) price, which was one of the two least important factors in the 2012 study, on the other hand, has gained in importance. Clients appear to be less shy about their intent to save cost.

When assessing a firm's value adds, legal procurement saw great value in continued legal education (CLE) seminars and business-level training, as well as "hotline" access for quick questions or to discuss new matters. Other desired value-adds included:
- In-person visits of the client's office, plant, or facility to get to know their business;
- Participation on internal calls that provide insight into a specific business or practice area;
- Secondments;
- Provision or development of basic templates and forms;
- Conducting pre-matter planning sessions; and
- Share-points with real-time access to the company's documents.

With legal procurement influencing purchasing decisions, law firms are advised to understand how procurement works and to collaborate with them. While procurement may not be the final decision-maker, the findings of all three legal procurement studies clearly suggest that firms are well advised to work with procurement, understand what is important to them, and to create a capability to respond to procurement demands. In other words, firms need to have a good process for all of it. And it has to be real. This is no time to "fake it 'til you make it".

The time to invest in proposal preparation, project management and process improvement, analysis, and cost control is now.

References

1. www.thomsonreuters.com/en-us/posts/wp-content/uploads/sites/20/2023/01/Compensation-for-Pricing-Professionals-2023.pdf
2. https://blicksteingroup.com/wp-content/uploads/2024/08/4th_Annual_LPPM_Survey_Report-2.pdf
3. www.blicksteingroup.com/law-department-operations-survey
4. Ascano, M. "Statistics and the Flat Fee Part 1: The Theory", Small Firm Innovation blog post: www.smallfirminnovation.com/2013/04/statistics-and-the-flat-fee-part-1-the-theory.
5. Duncan, S. S. "Five Firms Take Bold Approaches", ABA Law Practice magazine, volume 38, No. 6, November/December 2012: www.americanbar.org/publications/law_practice_magazine/2012/november-december/5-firms-take-bold-approaches.html.
6. See n. 8, above.
7. Gray, J. "Bay Street law firm launches legal 'incubator' in Halifax", *The Globe and Mail*, 1 July 2014.
8. Kubicki, J., and Wood, C. "Business Design for Law Firms, Part 2", Commentary on Legal Transformation Institute online, 3 July 2014: http://legaltransformationinstitute.com/blog/2014/7/3/business-design-for-law-firms-part-2.
9. Whole of Australian Government Legal Services Panel: https://legalservicespanel.gov.au/
10. www.ag.gov.au/sites/default/files/2020-03/guidance-material-web.PDF
11. The author is grateful to Dr Silvia Hodges Silverstein for her insights into this section.
12. www.law.cornell.edu/wex/sarbanes-oxley_act
13. Corporate Legal Operations Consortium's 2021 State of the Industry report: www.prnewswire.com/news-releases/cloc-releases-annual-state-of-the-industry-reportthe-key-annual-benchmarking-report-for-law-and-legal-operations-301287148.html
14. www.buyinglegal.com/ABOUT
15. www.legalbillreview.com/blog/procurementlegalspendmanagement
16. https://scholarcommons.sc.edu/cgi/viewcontent.cgi?article=4174&context=sclr
17. See the case study co-authored by Silvia Hodges Silverstein and Heidi K. Gardner for an in-depth look into the company's approach. Gardner, Heidi K., and Silverstein, S.H. "GlaxoSmithKline: Sourcing Complex Professional Services." Harvard Business School Case 414-003, September 2013. (Revised June 2014.)

18 Passarella, G. "GlaxoSmithKline Saves Millions in Legal Fees With Value-Based Programs", *The Legal Intelligencer*, 9 July 2012: www.abajournal.com/news/article/glaxosmithkline_to_use_millions_saved_in_legal_fees_to_pay_3_billion_settle/
19 This data comes from a groundbreaking study conducted in Q1 2014 by Dr Silvia Hodges Silverstein, vice president, strategic market development of Sky Analytics, and lecturer in law, Columbia Law School & adjunct professor, Fordham Law School. Links to the survey programmed on Qualtrics were posted to LinkedIn (legal) procurement groups and sent to a list of legal procurement professionals by email. 40 percent of respondents had the title procurement/purchasing/sourcing. 32 percent had the title chief procurement/purchasing officer or director of procurement/purchasing/sourcing. The majority of respondents came from Fortune 100 and Fortune 1000 companies. Most respondents said that their company had involved procurement in the sourcing of legal services for three or more years.
20 *Ibid.*

Chapter 12:
Strategic, systematic, and structured approaches

Lean Sigma programs have a place on a continuum. They vary in scope, depth, and maturity as well as effectiveness and impact. While opportunistic improvements can be excellent places to begin employing Lean Sigma, the greatest benefits come from employing a strategic, systematic, structured approach whereby all key processes are included, and work is performed in furtherance of clear, strategic objectives.

When your organization is prepared to engage in process improvement strategically, the elements of strategic thinking are always useful for figuring out how we will decide our priorities. In other words, how will we decide which problems are the most important to solve? How will we know when we have succeeded?

These are two very basic questions. Yet, they are often overlooked entirely when they ought to be the starting point. In the rush to get a strategic "plan" teams seem to skip the strategic "thinking" step that is underrated, overlooked, and should be the precursor to decision making. Having the right questions is more important than coming up with answers that may not be all that useful or even accurate.

When I'm engaged for strategic thinking, I like to use a TOWS analysis. This is an extension of the classic SWOT analysis, used to help assess internal and external environments. While SWOT stands for Strengths, Weaknesses, Opportunities, and Threats, TOWS rearranges these elements to emphasize the strategic connections between them.

A SWOT analysis comprises:

1. *S (Strengths):* Internal attributes that are helpful to achieving the organization's objectives.
2. *W (Weaknesses):* Internal attributes that are harmful to achieving the organization's objectives.
3. *O (Opportunities):* External conditions that are helpful to achieving the organization's objectives.
4. *T (Threats):* External conditions that are harmful to achieving the organization's objectives.

In a TOWS analysis, we use these elements to create four types of strategies:
1. *SO (Strengths-Opportunities) Strategies:* Use strengths to capitalize on opportunities.
2. *WO (Weaknesses-Opportunities) Strategies:* Overcome weaknesses by leveraging opportunities.
3. *ST (Strengths-Threats) Strategies:* Use strengths to mitigate threats.
4. *WT (Weaknesses-Threats) Strategies:* Minimize weaknesses and avoid threats.

The TOWS analysis helps us articulate the imperative for taking a more systematic and sustained approach. It also surfaces and makes clear the reasons to invest in a process improvement program, and develop mechanisms for deciding which specific process improvement opportunities to seize. By focusing on how to match internal capabilities with external possibilities and challenges, we can more easily identify gaps in performance and the resources needed to engage in this work in a strategic and structured manner.

A firm or department that embraces a systematic approach employs a wide range of Lean and Six Sigma, as well as planning and management tools. It requires discipline to be methodical. By definition, "continuous improvement" is not something that ever ends. Also, building this kind of culture can neither be achieved overnight, nor is it a one-time event. However, projects will be undertaken in a planned cadence, properly supported, and delivered in an appropriate sequence to build and sustain a well-structured, efficient, and high-quality operational environment and program.

One effective approach is the Improvement Kata,[1] a framework for continuous improvement that was developed by Toyota. Improvement Kata is based on what is known as "the scientific method" and involves a series of steps taken to achieve goals by breaking down complex problems into manageable pieces, so it is especially translatable to legal environments. It is both a continuous improvement mindset and a set of practices with four primary steps supportive of strategy development:
- *Understand the direction and the challenge.* This involves identifying the desired outcomes, understanding the current state of the process, and setting a target condition.
- *Grasp the current condition.* This step involves analyzing the current state of the process and identifying the obstacles that are preventing the process from achieving the target condition.

- *Establish the next target condition.* This step involves setting a specific, measurable, achievable, relevant, and time-bound (SMART) target condition that moves the process closer to the desired outcomes.
- *Conduct experiments.* This step involves testing and implementing changes to the process that are designed to move the process closer to the target condition. The results of the experiments are then analyzed, and the process is refined and improved based on the findings.

This approach ensures that whatever we decide to build or tackle for improvement is aligned with the organization's goals and objectives, and that decisions and activities are based on data and facts. It also instills a culture of continuous learning and improvement by encouraging individuals and teams to experiment and try new things. It is intended to build a safe environment for learning and growth and fosters a culture of trust and collaboration, as individuals and teams work together to achieve common goals. Finally, it helps organizations stay ahead of the competition.

For many years, legal services seemed to be excused from the same requirements the business world had of products and other service businesses. It should be abundantly clear that this is no longer the case. There is nothing inherently different about most aspects of the practice of law that exempts anyone from being able to continuously improve, price, budget, manage projects, and apply the same kind of systematic approach to Lean Sigma in order to achieve the excellent results seen in a corporate setting.[2]

Learning from other industries

That sounds straightforward, but as someone who made a considerable investment in translating to legal and figuring out what works (and what does not), bridging the Lean Six Sigma concepts and tools that work in other industries to legal does require effort. Legal really is different, but inspiring and instructional examples from business are easy to find.

Many organizations, and law firms in particular, have grown through mergers, acquisitions, and combinations. Moreover, law firms have identified service as a key strategy for differentiation and law departments certainly are held accountable for meeting or exceeding service standards.

Looking at how other service companies have successfully navigated those waters gives us plenty to emulate. In an October 2003 *Harvard Business Review* article entitled "The Lean Service Machine",[3] Cynthia Karen Swank related how Jefferson Pilot Financial (JPF), a US financial services company, was able to apply lessons learned from manufacturing. After tripling in size due to four acquisitions, the company was exploring different kinds of growth and improvement strategies to meet marketplace demand for new products and services while making service a strategic priority and point of differentiation. The state of the industry should be quite familiar to law firms: other, specialized players offered "better, faster, cheaper" options.

Swank relates:

"To determine where improved service would have the greatest impact, Jefferson Pilot Financial undertook an in-depth analysis of the operations... The study unearthed considerable variation in the quality of existing services... It was clear that management could significantly increase revenue by improving operations. Indeed, the company estimated that it could increase the paid annualized premium for its Premier Partners by ten to 15 percent if it could issue all policies within three weeks of receiving the applications, offer periodic application status reports, simplify the submission process, and reduce errors to one percent."

Applying Lean production principles, JPF understood that the insurance policy process is a series of steps, from initial application to underwriting, or risk assessment, to policy issuance. As with any other process, every step should add value to the work in progress. The company appointed a "lean team" to reengineer the new business operations.

"The initiative has delivered impressive results. The company halved the average time from receipt of a Premier Partner application to issuance of a policy, reduced labor costs by 26 percent and trimmed the rate of reissues due to errors by 40 percent... These outcomes contributed to a remarkable 60 percent increase in new annualized life premiums in the company's core individual-life-insurance business in just two years. Similar results are being recorded in other departments as the company rolls out the new systems across the whole organization."[4]

These kinds of examples are relatively easier to translate to legal and business processes used in law. If we replace key terms in this case with legal examples, the applicability of Lean to law firm strategy becomes more obvious:

- After making four acquisitions that more than tripled its size, Law Firm

- A was searching for new ways to grow in a fiercely competitive business environment. Rising client expectations had led to a proliferation of service offerings by players in the market, as well as an increase in service delivery complexity and costs. At the same time, the specialized niche players touting lower costs and faster handling of legal services, such as document review, were forcing full-service law firms to improve service and speed of delivery while reducing costs (or at least making them predictable).
- To add an extra dose of reality, consider that the legal process outsourcing market value is anticipated to reach $45.4bn in 2028,[5] with a predicted compound annual growth rate of 26.7 percent, 41 percent of law firms use blockchain for transactional legal services, and there are 731,340 lawyers employed in the US alone.
- The executive committee of Law Firm A recognized that the firm needed to differentiate itself in the eyes of its clients, prospects, and referral sources. Law Firm A identified superior service as a key ingredient of that strategy.
- It was clear that the firm could significantly increase revenue by improving operations. Indeed, the firm estimated that it could increase the profits per partner by ten to 15 percent if it could speed up the delivery of legal work to the most utilized services of its key clients within three weeks of receiving the request for work, offer periodic status and budget reports, simplify the intake process, and reduce errors to one percent.

Early adopters

Early adopters create blueprints and breadcrumbs for others to follow. While every individual's and each organization's journey is unique, they do share some common aspects:
- Lean Six Sigma early adopters focused on applying Lean Six Sigma principle to improve various legal processes. Often, they seized opportunities and selected low hanging fruit that was ripe for picking, such as case management, contract review, and document handling.
- They invested in training and certifications in Lean Six Sigma methodologies for staff to build internal expertise, so that everyone spoke a common language.
- Pilot projects were used to test and refine Lean Six Sigma approaches before rolling them out more broadly across their organizations.

- The emphasis was on fostering a culture of continuous improvement and data-driven decision-making within their legal and business teams.
- There was leadership commitment.

DuPont

Within a short time of starting my career as a practicing lawyer, I was surprised and dismayed by the pervasive, extensive inefficiencies I experienced within my law department, the organization as a whole, and within and between our outside counsel. In looking for the panacea, I came across the early reports of consolidation and other efforts underway at DuPont. This is how one of the earliest "influencers" informed my thinking, gave me language to describe what I was observing, and a way to solve for it.

Thomas Sager served as the senior vice president and general counsel of DuPont, and he is an icon well known for his leadership in advancing innovation, efficiency, and diversity in corporate legal departments. During his tenure at DuPont, Sager was a key figure in the DuPont Legal Model, which became a widely recognized framework for transforming how corporate legal departments operate through efficiency, cost control, collaboration, and diversity. The model has been adopted by many companies worldwide.

Introduced in the early 1990s by DuPont's legal department under the leadership of Sager and others, the Dupont Legal Model challenged traditional approaches to managing legal work, particularly the billable-hour model, and emphasized using process improvement and a more strategic, business-focused way to manage operations and handle legal matters. DuPont's legal department remains one of the best-known examples in the legal industry of using Lean Six Sigma to reduce inefficiencies. As a result, its work in process improvement has helped many forward-thinking members of law departments to elevate the efficiency and effectiveness of their departments.

DuPont adopted Six Sigma in 1999, applying it across various business units, including legal. Sager served as a Six Sigma Champion, helping the department focus on improving workflows, reducing defects in legal processes, and creating more predictable legal budgets. Because of this, DuPont Legal reduced outside counsel costs, improved case management, fostered stronger relationships with external law firms, and used data-driven insights to structure alternative fee arrangements.

Sager was strategic and highly collaborative, involving his outside counsel in his process improvement initiatives. As a manufacturing company, Sager said, DuPont placed a premium on efficiency and productivity, and was sensitive to productivity among internal practices and its supply chain. This included legal services. They were not to be treated differently.

Through a combination of panel convergence, alternative staffing, and process improvement, DuPont developed a new approach to early case assessment, document management, and discovery to achieve millions in cost savings. Sharing knowledge and best practices was encouraged by law firms with each other and with DuPont's in-house team. These exchanges helped to create efficiencies across the legal ecosystem and encouraged innovation.

The DuPont Primary Law Firm Network – a collection of select law firms working with DuPont – was designed to facilitate collaboration and continuous improvement. Participants were judged by the contributions as well.

DuPont's convergence process managed outside legal fees by reducing the number of preferred law firms. It also provided clarity around how to evaluate firms and demystified how firms could be chosen for a panel.

This also served as a forcing function for law firms and corporate law departments to improve the quality, cost, and efficiency of legal services. The model is grounded in strategic partnering and collaboration, where the overarching goals are to build relationships for the long-term, so resources are reused, rather than recreated or learned, in preparation for each subsequent legal matter.

The premise was that fewer law firms meant that a company would be able to save on expenses, reduce cycle time, and more easily manage and use leverage in negotiating fees and conditions. It also meant that staffing and budgeting forecast accuracy would improve and that they would no longer pay switching costs.

To achieve its goals, the model contains incentives and offers alternative fee structures that distribute risks and rewards and further the financial success of all parties. The process is continuously improved and refined through the use of performance metrics – a series of standards for evaluating program compliance, efficiency, and best practices.

When DuPont conceived its legal model, it used 350 law firms and 150 outside vendors who provided expert analysis, jury consultant services, document management, etc. to handle its legal projects worldwide. From 1992 to 1996, the company studied its use of legal services and reduced these numbers to 34 law firms and four vendors, saving millions of dollars in the process.

DuPont reported[6] that
- Legal service expenses were reduced by 39 percent from 1994 to 1997.
- Litigation savings amounted to over $30 million in the last four years of the program.
- Cycle time dropped from 39 to 22 months in two years and the docket was cut in half.
- Legal staff requirements could be forecast accurately.
- Purchasing power was leveraged.
- More women and minorities were employed in the PLF and supplier firms.
- True partnering was achieved – work was performed so seamlessly that outsiders had trouble distinguishing between DuPont's outside attorneys and in-house counsel.

The DuPont Legal Model moved away from the traditional billable hour system, which was inefficient and incentivized longer work hours rather than being focused on results. Instead, DuPont negotiated alternative fee arrangements (AFAs) with its outside counsel. These included fixed fees, success-based fees, and other value-driven pricing mechanisms. AFAs promoted cost predictability and encouraged law firms to focus on outcomes rather than the time spent on a matter.

This also encouraged more effective staffing of projects, for example, using skilled paralegals rather than associates to handle specific tasks.

DuPont's model utilizes and rewards talented individuals. In turn, this increases their job satisfaction, adds to employee retention, and ultimately affects the company's bottom line. From the firm's point of view, fostering a relationship with the client at all levels will build loyalty and lead to repeat assignments.

In fact, the model encouraged a truly collaborative approach between DuPont's in-house legal team and its outside counsel. This included sharing risks and rewards, collaborating on strategies, and working together as a cohesive team. Law firms were expected to function as business partners rather than mere service providers, aligning their incentives with DuPont's business objectives. Sager regularly collaborated with outside counsel on publishing articles as well. Regular meetings, feedback, and shared goals were part of this approach; each primary law firm was expected to fully adhere to the model and was held accountable.

The DuPont Legal Model emphasized the use of metrics and data analytics to track performance and control costs. By closely monitoring the time, resources, and outcomes associated with legal matters, DuPont was able to better manage its legal spend and ensure that outside counsel was delivering value and adhering to the rigor and discipline of the legal model. This data-driven approach also allowed DuPont to make informed decisions about where to allocate resources and how to structure legal strategies.

Annual benchmark surveys were completed by firms and data about the firm's success in achieving objectives, ability to save the company money, effectiveness in partnering with the company and members of the legal network, commitment to leveraging technology, promotion of diversity, and acceptance of alternative fee arrangements. Legal spend, settlements, and recovery amounts were also tracked as well as staffing in terms of partner-to-associate-to-paralegal ratio. Key performance indicators included measures of performance capability and efficiency, such as the time it took to bring matters to closure. Firms were also evaluated based on their use of technology to reduce costs and increase efficiency. This included investing in legal technology, such as document management systems, e-discovery tools, and litigation management software, which helped streamline legal processes and reduce costs.

DuPont required its outside law firms to demonstrate a commitment to diversity, both in their staffing of DuPont matters and in their overall firm practices. Law firms that did not show adequate progress in promoting women and minorities within their ranks risked losing DuPont's business.

This initiative helped reshape the legal landscape and increase the representation of underrepresented groups in the profession. The DuPont Legal Model has had such a positive impact on the recruitment, hiring, and retention of minorities and women by DuPont's legal department and its primary law firms that it is a model for every corporate law department committed to a diverse workforce.

As a result, Tom Sager is known for being a strong advocate for diversity in the law and he played a pivotal role in promoting diversity within DuPont's legal department too. His commitment to diversity earned Sager widespread recognition, and the Thomas L. Sager Award[7] was established by the Minority Corporate Counsel Association (MCCA) in his honor. The award is given to law firms that demonstrate a commitment to improving diversity in the legal profession.

It would be many years before I would actually meet him, but Tom Sager opened my eyes to what efficiency really meant in the 1990s. In the introduction to the first edition of this book, Sager said:

"In 1999, under the leadership of CEO and chairman Chad Holliday, DuPont embarked upon its Six Sigma journey, which was designed to eliminate costs, drive efficiency, and accelerate the company's transformation. It was clearly understood by all corporate officers in attendance at this kick off that no business, staff function, or region was exempt. This was a business imperative – one that could arguably determine the company's future. While our initial focus was upon cost reduction, the power of Six Sigma was, as we subsequently learned, more than that. Shortly thereafter, I was tapped to assume the role of Six Sigma champion for Legal.

"While Six Sigma was initially met with skepticism in some quarters, legal leadership had gained considerable credibility over the previous eight years in leading a law firm and supplier convergence process and in the implementation of the DuPont Legal Model, which emphasized the importance of applying business discipline and data in our representation of DuPont. In short, we were able to recognize early on that process improvement matters and that, if it was embraced by legal, it could provide us with a means to contribute to the company's transformation. So, we began to implement function-wide Six Sigma with no practice group, profession, or region exempted.

"As an aside, several years into the initiative at a subsequent corporate officers meeting, our outside speaker, Jeff Immelt, who was among two others vying to succeed Jack Welch as CEO of General Electric, spoke to the group about the power of Six Sigma. At this point, GE was 'all in' and was driving this initiative throughout the corporation with typical Jack Welch intensity. Immelt spoke with great persuasion and intensity about the impact of Six Sigma upon GE. And as if that wasn't compelling enough, he stated to the officers in attendance, 'And even the lawyers can do it!' That was all that I needed as further provocation. From that point forward, we drove process improvement at all levels of the organization and with our network of providers with great resolve.

"The impact upon our culture through the implementation of Six Sigma has been incredibly forceful and telling. Under the broad heading of process improvement, our professionals have developed and honed their leadership, communication, and collaboration skills – and, most significantly, their bottom-line focus. The program has evolved to embrace certainly Six Sigma, Lean Six Sigma, and project management – all of which serve to drive process improvement. Collectively, these tools have served to enable Legal to speak the language of the business, drive efficiency, and deliver superior results by any metric or criterion one might choose."[8]

The DuPont Legal Model became a groundbreaking framework for corporate legal departments, providing significant benefits to DuPont, including considerable reductions in its legal spend, legal services that were more closely aligned with the company's overall business goals, enhanced diversity and inclusion internally and amongst its PLFs. It set a new standard for legal operations management and demonstrated that legal departments could operate as strategic business units, contributing directly to a company's overall success.

After retiring from DuPont, Sager continued to be involved in the legal community. He has taken on roles such as partner at Ballard Spahr LLP, where he has focused on advising companies on legal strategy and innovation. His legacy as a key figure in modern legal management is certain – what should also be known is that he was quick and generous with his support of the first edition of this book and my earliest work. I will always be grateful to him for that example as well, which I find is prevalent amongst process improvement leaders and practitioners.

Equitable
In 2019, Equitable's head of legal operations laid out a strategy for an aggressive five-year modernization strategy with the primary goal of transitioning the company's law department into a modern, innovative, proactive, streamlined, and highly efficient organization through:
- Stabilization of existing infrastructure and elimination of risk.
- Replacing inefficient or ineffective legacy technology.
- Reducing and reinvesting third party spend.
- Process efficiency and reduction of manual hours.
- Operational centralization of all vendors, projects, and technology.
- Enforcement of Equitable's diversity policies for procurement.

This technology modernization project yielded several cost-saving results, including reduced outside counsel expenses by five percent, reduced time of invoice review by 25 percent for invoices over $5,000, reduced time of invoice review by 100 percent for invoices under $5,000 (~2,400 hours annually), 100 percent offshore reduction, increased speed to payment by 20 percent, and ensuring five percent quick pay discount applied to invoices. Several other additional beneficial outcomes beyond the cost were also realized.[9]

Enstar Group

Enstar's legal department was recognized as an ACC Value Champion in 2023[10] for building a legal operations function from the ground up to "positively impact and serve staff, but to also solidify the team's role as a value-driven department and strategic partner to the business". Accordingly, the team also focused on collaboration, alignment, and innovation.

The department designed a legal ops function that strategically aligned priorities and programs with existing enterprise technology; promoted cross-functional collaboration; and introduced new technology. General Counsel Audrey Bowen Taranto focused the team's efforts on business-supporting initiatives and projects that were achievable, timesaving, and that would continuously create value for the company.

Instead of having lawyers respond to emails, the department leveraged technology already in use to create a chatbot that answers questions about Enstar's many group entities. The chatbot provides users with basic entity information such as officer and director names, authorized signatory lists, jurisdiction of incorporation and license, and organizational documents.

Said the Association of Corporate Counsel when announcing the award:

"Creating the chatbot is an example of a small solution that resulted in a big time save for the legal department. The win, including saving an estimated 500 hours of lawyer time and improving accuracy of responses to frequently asked entity questions, was achievable without a significant investment of resources and money. Getting buy-in to change a process or two is one thing – convincing them to invest in a long-term solution that can include technology, people, or a partnering with an outside firm, is another. Luckily, Enstar Legal had data to support their asks... and leverage tools [they] already have.

"Additional improvements achieved by Enstar Legal include implementing a new AI optimized contract review process (with time savings estimated at 1,000 hours or five percent of internal spend); continuing to identify ways to deploy chatbots and other types of self-help tools that will free up attorney time to focus on strategy; and e-billing system enhancements and an outside counsel management program, which saved the company over seven percent on outside counsel spend and allowed them to collect enough data to begin piloting a value-based pricing program."[11]

Law firms

Two of the most recognized early adopter law firms are Morgan Lewis, which published the first example of a firm using Six Sigma in the 1970s, and Seyfarth Shaw LLP, which developed the SeyfarthLean program. Case studies on these companies and others follow.

Morgan Lewis

Typically, opportunistic approaches occur because one person, usually a leader in a particular practice area or business function, determines that process improvement is worth trying. Morgan Lewis' use of Six Sigma was the earliest and most specific case studies I could find when I began to build the first Legal Lean Sigma Institute's programs and certification courses and then again when researching and writing the first and second editions of this book. The firm continues to use Lean Sigma and Design Thinking to innovate and improve today.

Applying process improvement to a specific service that is viewed as commodity work is not new, but Morgan Lewis was at the forefront with Six Sigma in application to its mortgage loan services, touting "Up to 25 percent reduction in time charges, dramatically enhanced quality". According to a case study by Richard J. Sabat,[12] Six Sigma Green Belt at Morgan Lewis, the firm began applying Six Sigma to its loan services starting in 1974 and was then employed institutionally in 1988 with FDIC/RTC. As a testament to continuous improvement, the process was retooled in 1997 with Total Quality Management, and then again with Six Sigma in 2000-2003.

Sabat's case study provides excellent data on the approach used and the results achieved, including the fact that the firm was able to realize up to a 25 percent reduction in time charges and dramatically enhanced quality in mortgage loan services. While this type of reduction might not have been the most desirable result for a firm charging by the hour, it certainly is appealing to any client who is looking for the best, lowest cost solution, and to any firm performing the work for a fixed or capped fee.

Causes of defects (considered waste in Lean terms) were identified as:
- Transaction data input;
- Intermittent data flow;
- Inefficient data communication to entire team;
- No data quality control; and
- Lack of standard forms and poor quality forms (the precedent docu-

ments contained defects and there was a lack of baseline and/or quality control).

Additionally, the Socratic associate training method employed by the firm reportedly resulted in a lack of written transaction practices and written standard operating procedures. Finally, time pressure and disorganization were also identified as causes.

Using the data gathered in the Measure phase of the DMAIC framework, and the work performed in the Analyze phase, Morgan Lewis developed its improvement ideas, which included human behavior items such as client protocols and standard practices and procedures. It also focused on what Sabat refers to as the "physics of the transaction", meaning data input and integrity, standard forms, and standard communication. Interestingly, document preparation software was part of its solution.

The charts included in the case study[13] show compelling "before", "early Six Sigma", and "later Six Sigma" graphical results, indicating that the firm did not just improve the process once; it committed to continuous improvement and realized better results each time it improved how it performed and delivered work in this area.

More recently, Morgan Lewis' e-data group employed Lean Sigma. With ever more legal services being deemed "commodity" type work, and the use of fixed fees and value-based billing on the rise, we know that there is increasing pressure for firms to be highly efficient. Those who are strategic and structured increase their points of differentiation and develop signature approaches. Firms are investing in process improvement and reaping the rewards. Stephanie A. "Tess" Blair, a now retired partner and former Chair of Morgan Lewis's eData Practice, related to the author:

> "I first became interested in using Lean and Six Sigma in my practice group after earning my Legal Lean Sigma Yellow Belt certification while obtaining a Masters in Law Firm Management at The George Washington University. In short order, I determined my goal: to have everyone in my group trained and certified in Legal Lean Sigma. First, I arranged for private delivery of the same Yellow Belt certification course to a core group in the eData practice. Potential projects were used for the exercises and workshop elements of the program. Then, some of those certified Yellow Belts were trained to support the Legal Lean Sigma Institute instructors so they could serve as facilitators at one day, White Belt certification courses in seven offices. This

approach allowed us to train nearly everyone in our practice – over 100 in number – in seven offices very quickly. This not only provided everyone with a common vocabulary but supported a critical shift in thinking about how we work with clients and do our work both with them and each other."

The draft work done in the Yellow and White Belt Certification courses helped with assessing the impact and difficulty of each potential project. Following the skill development of the entire practice group, two cross-functional teams were carefully selected and formed. A Kaizen approach was preferred, so the process improvement projects were tightly scoped. The teams went through Kaizen training together and then worked independently, moving through the DMAIC phases in an accelerated, workshop fashion.

The project work was set up so that the teams worked at the same time, with two different expert consultants in separate rooms at the same office. Everyone met at the end of each day to present their work and observe each other's gate reviews with the steering committee. This exponentially increased the learning and communication around both projects. It also enhanced understanding about how the same process improvement tool, such as a project charter, measurement plan, process map, or a fishbone diagram, could be applied to two different processes with such different outcomes. Continues Blair:

"One creative member of the team came up with the idea of calling our work area 'Kaizenville', which indicates that while the work was performed with the utmost seriousness, the teams also really enjoyed being immersed in the process of process improvement. We engaged in one of the process improvement projects to facilitate our ability to estimate the cost of an activity. This was the first time we attempted to use the DMAIC methodology and the tools and Legal Lean Sigma to help us get a better handle on how we approached pricing, budgeting, and planning a project, as well as competitive assessment and improvement identification."

The estimating project team began by highlighting the issues around the e-Data group, which had a great deal of data, but not all the right information needed to understand the variability in processes, and the way they are operated across the group. Says Blair:

"Ultimately, we wound up possessing significantly greater abilities to quantify what factors MOST drive the cost of an activity and HOW they drive the

cost. And, from a management perspective, it was critical to develop a methodology that can be applied to all or almost all key activities plus determine a way to update the estimates a couple of times a year to capture what we've learned. We want to be the best at this and that means we have to continuously improve."

Morgan Lewis's eData practice was just getting started, serving as a host firm for a Legal Lean Sigma Institute's open enrollment certification course in 2013, and also layering on project management skill development. In 2014, the eData group engaged the Legal Lean Sigma Institute to deliver another privately delivered Yellow Belt certification course. But this one was different. It was the first one that was specifically tailored to include clients.

At each table, a Morgan Lewis client and client team spent two days working together. Each team used a selected process for the duration of the certification course to use in their table work. This allowed them to both learn how to apply tools and concepts using a relevant example and simultaneously discuss areas where both the firm and the client could work together to improve the process.

Morgan Lewis's successful approach is a model for how other law firms can develop skills and use the educational experience to learn and begin working with clients. As Blair puts it:

"Inviting our clients to join us in our pursuit of continuous process improvement by training together on Lean Sigma has been a unique way to enhance already great relationships with key clients. Sharing a common process language and commitment to continuous process improvement aligns us with our clients in a way no other outreach can."

The education continued, with nearly every person in the group certified in Legal Lean Sigma process improvement and project management. The group also modeled superior succession planning and execution when Tess Blair passed the torch to Scott A. Milner, who said, *"I can share that all things process improvement is still an important effort of ours. We continue to focus on driving innovation and disruption using a variety of LLS and design thinking principles."*

The practice group takes a highly integrated and collaborative approach to every aspect of its work, as is evidenced by the case study on its website:[14]

The explosion of electronic data in every aspect of business and law has created ongoing risks and challenges in litigation, information governance, regulatory compliance, and corporate transactions – from financing and M&A to simple contract negotiations. Our eData practice leverages the proliferation of data to reveal new insights and offer eDiscovery solutions to optimize the way legal services are delivered.

Our technology portfolio and deep bench of technologists, engineers, and data scientists take command of data to serve our clients. At the same time, we are practicing lawyers who remain trusted advisers with the know-how to guide litigation and business strategy and handle their execution of that strategy – in court and on paper.

Morgan Lewis was a pioneer in establishing a dedicated "data practice" in 2004, and we have been innovating the practice and serving as thought leaders ever since. We are an industry leader in effective eDiscovery that leverages robust technology including artificial intelligence (AI) to deliver high-quality, defensible, cost-effective solutions. Clients benefit from our ability to practice law while understanding the ever-evolving technological landscape. Our eData lawyers are intimate with the newest technologies and how courts and agencies are handling novel eDiscovery issues – including AI, and emerging technologies like collaboration platforms, short messages, hyperlinks, and ephemeral messaging.

We seamlessly combine the legal, technical, and process know-how of our firm's 2,200 lawyers and legal professionals with the right processes and technology. Morgan Lewis clients get the assurance of working alongside a trusted global firm in the top ten of the AmLaw 100 with all of the benefits of an innovative alternative legal services provider.

Milner highlights its recent Hackathon as *"an incredible example of our team coming together to look for ways to improve practice".*

The goal of the Hackathon was to foster innovation, collaboration, and rapid ideation, creating a dynamic environment where eData team members with diverse skills in programming, design, legal, technology, and project management can generate high value, actionable products/product ideas that will automate, increase efficiencies, reduce risk and, ideally, generate revenue for the benefit of the overall practice group.

In three 90-minute sessions attended by 65 people with different roles and functions, 63 ideas and pain points were surfaced with 17 "quick wins" identified. The top-rated ideas included:

- *Custodian interview* – an app to allow for direct entry of custodian interview data points, aggregate for all custodians, clients and matters and allow for easy access, searching, and analysis.
- *Estimate generator* – estimate generation wizard with templates that will aggregate and track all eData estimates.
- *Auto privilege log* – to automate name normalization and the creation of privilege log legends.
- *Bates identifier* – a search tool allowing for Bates number searching from a list that will also identify Bates numbers from within a document range.
- *eData "inbox"* – an application that allows end users to get 24/7 access to quick answers utilizing chat bot style conversational AI trained on all eData training resources. All outreach is logged for follow up with human resources.

In the month following the Hackathon sessions, a build or buy decision took place with the selection of final applications for development and third-party vendors, along with identification of applications for internal development. The next month, third party development started with a four-month window given for completion of the development of the selected applications. Implementation, ongoing reporting, and support was expected a month afterward.

This team is dedicated to continuous improvement. It has leadership support, and it shows. Morgan Lewis's eData group has garnered well deserved recognition and impressive awards, including winning the E-Discovery Technology and Innovation category at the 2024 *Legalweek* Leaders in Tech Law Awards with its eData Tech Stack. In talking about the importance of innovation in the legal industry in a *Legalweek* interview, Milner said:

> "By seeking out innovations to speed up important but time-consuming processes, keeping up with ways in which tech applications are being used, and constantly sharpening our skills, we show our commitment to meeting, or even exceeding, clients' expectations. Our clients have real-world needs and harnessing the right tools helps us as a firm meet those needs."[15]

Most recently, the group was shortlisted in the Best Use of Technology (featuring eData's OffComm Detector) category for the 2024 American Lawyer Industry Awards, which recognize outstanding achievements and contributions made by individuals, law firms, and legal departments across various practice areas and specialties.

In a statement, *The American Lawyer* said, "It was the most crowded and competitive year for entries, and making the finalist cut was tough and an achievement in and of itself."[16]

Members of the team graciously shared their innovation experiences and insights by participating in many events and programs, publishing, and guest lecturing at innovative schools, such as Suffolk Law.

Seyfarth Shaw LLP
Inspired by Lean manufacturing techniques and Six Sigma (which had been successfully applied in industries like manufacturing and healthcare), Seyfarth Shaw sought to introduce these principles into its practice to provide more value to clients. This effort led to the formalization of SeyfarthLean[17] in 2006. SeyfarthLean was built on three main pillars:
- *Process improvement* – emphasizing streamlined workflows to eliminate inefficiencies.
- *Project management* – implementing detailed planning, communication, and management of legal matters.
- *Client collaboration* – tailoring services to better meet client needs and offering transparent pricing models such as alternative fee arrangements (AFAs).

With several key leaders at the firm playing crucial roles in its creation and implementation, the development of SeyfarthLean was a collaborative effort. Two leaders led the way – chairman and managing partner, Stephen J. Poor, who served in that role for 15 years, and partner Lisa Damon.

Poor led the firm's shift toward innovation in legal service delivery. A prominent figure in the legal industry, during his tenure, he led the firm through a period of significant transformation and growth. This included the introduction of SeyfarthLean, which became one of the most notable innovations in legal service delivery, focusing on process improvement, efficiency, and client value. His leadership in adopting Lean Six Sigma methodologies made Seyfarth Shaw a recognized leader in legal innovation. The approach was groundbreaking in an industry traditionally resistant to change and helped establish Seyfarth as a trailblazer in the legal world.

After stepping down as chairman in 2016, Poor continued to be actively involved in the firm's strategic initiatives. He took on the role of chair emeritus and worked closely with the firm's leadership to ensure the continued evolution of SeyfarthLean and the firm's innovative approach to legal services.

Lisa Damon is known for her key role in the creation and implementation of SeyfarthLean. As one of the early adopters of this innovative approach to legal services, she helped lead the firm's effort to transform how legal work is done and position Seyfarth as a pioneer in the legal industry's shift towards more efficient and client-focused service delivery. As a champion of innovation in legal services, Damon has been instrumental in shaping how law firms use project management, process improvement, and technology in practical ways to better serve clients.

She has been at the forefront of initiatives to leverage technology, data analytics, and alternative fee arrangements to create more value for clients and provide greater transparency and predictability in legal services. Damon continues to be a driving force behind Seyfarth Shaw's commitment to innovative legal service delivery, and her work has made a lasting impact on how law firms approach client relationships and operational efficiency.

Together, these leaders, along with other partners and team members at Seyfarth Shaw, contributed to developing and refining SeyfarthLean, making it one of the most innovative and client-focused legal service models in the industry.

In her article, *The rise of Lean and Six Sigma for improving legal service*,[18] Connie Crosby, Crosby Group Consulting & Houser Henry & Syron LLP, highlights the journeys of early adopters (including myself) and how they started applying process improvement to law. One of those people is Ken Grady, who became a Lean law evangelist at Seyfarth Shaw LLP and adjunct law school professor. After moving from a law firm to HON, a furniture manufacturer that was implementing process improvement across the organization, he started "playing around with the ideas of Lean" for his law department.

Interestingly, writes Crosby:

"Grady moved from law to take over one of HON's manufacturing plants. He was sent to Japan to be trained at Shingijutsu Co. Ltd, a consulting company created by former engineers from Toyota, to learn the Toyota Production System Lean method. He worked with his sensei, or mentors, on the shop floor, doing Kaizen activities and events. Back at HON, he became immersed in Lean on the shop floor. Five years later, he went back into law as general counsel with Wolverine. Grady started working on these methods with Seyfarth while he was still GC at Wolverine. In 2013, he retired from practice and joined Seyfarth to head Seyfarth Lean."

To integrate the SeyfarthLean approach, the firm trained its attorneys and staff on Lean Six Sigma principles, creating a culture that embraced continuous improvement, transparency, and innovation. SeyfarthLean required a shift in mindset from focusing solely on billable hours to concentrating on delivering measurable value to clients.

SeyfarthLean evolved by incorporating legal technology solutions like document automation, artificial intelligence, and data analytics into its framework. This integration allowed Seyfarth to further enhance efficiency, predict outcomes, and provide insights to clients in real time.

SeyfarthLean became and continues to be a model for other law firms looking to improve service delivery. Many firms began adopting similar frameworks, while Seyfarth Shaw continued to refine its model, demonstrating a commitment to staying at the forefront of innovation in legal services.

It may also be the best known and first firm to go to market with a firmwide process improvement initiative. By 2009, Seyfarth Shaw had completed more than 75 projects, branded "SeyfarthLean", and reported that "total fees on certain legal projects reengineered through Six Sigma have been reduced from 13 percent to up to 50 percent".[19]

The firm reported that:

"Seyfarth Shaw set out to see if there was a better way to drive value for our clients than the traditional model of delivering legal services. What we heard from our clients was the same then as it is now – a need for the efficient delivery of legal services, lower costs, budget predictability, quality work and value for fees. Urged by clients who had successfully implemented Six Sigma and Lean Six Sigma in their organizations, we invested in the approach to see if it might help us better meet our clients' needs.

"The solution developed by Seyfarth was to work with experts to create a tailored version of Lean Six Sigma that could be implemented without the challenges presented by the strict Six Sigma and Lean approaches. We chose what we believe was best from both approaches for the legal industry and applied them to how we deliver legal services. Improved collaboration, communication, and efficiency are key objectives in adopting the process-driven methodologies that constitute this approach. With SeyfarthLean, we continually strive to perfect how we work with our clients and every day find new ways to improve the way we provide services."[20]

Chapter 12: Strategic, systematic, and structured approaches

Throughout the 2010s, SeyfarthLean gained widespread recognition for its success in improving legal service delivery. The firm demonstrated significant client satisfaction through cost control, efficiency, and more predictable outcomes. Seyfarth became one of the first large law firms to receive accolades for its focus on innovation. In 2011, the International Legal Technology Association recognized the firm twice with the Innovative Law Firm of the Year award and Innovative Project of the Year award. The following year, Seyfarth received the College of Law Practice Management's InnovAction Award.

The marketing opportunities that a focus on process improvement generates are significant. Even the Seyfarth Shaw branded name "SeyfarthLean" became well known and was used in conversations about law practice management. This is an excellent example of developing a serious competitive advantage and generating a high-visibility campaign around a specific approach to using Lean Six Sigma and project management to drive value for clients. This was a firm that embraced the idea of being first, rather than waiting to see who else would follow, thereby raising the bar for all law firms.

The firm's messaging and marketing of its accomplishments continues to be effective. With a strategically designed and executed program, it developed deep skills and delivered results. As such, it had compelling stories and data to include in its award applications, branding, marketing, communications, and business development efforts. Also, it was way ahead of the market, so it became – and remains – known for its leadership and for educating its clients as well as legal and business professionals in law about the power of process improvement. One might argue that the name Seyfarth Lean itself is associated with efficiency.

The firm's strategy of demonstrating practical applications opened minds, eyes, hearts, and opportunities – and not just for the "easy pickings" either. For example, litigation is often an area in which, initially, it is more difficult to imagine how process improvement can be helpful. Two case studies that were published by Lisa Damon of Seyfarth Shaw in January 2014 are instructive in this regard.[21]

The first involved a retailer facing an increased number of personal injury lawsuits relating to store conditions. Obviously, there were unique facts that led to each plaintiff's injury, however, the facts about the stores were relatively consistent.

> "At the inception of the process improvement program, the retailer faced more than 100 lawsuits... A combination of process improvement and

project management, with the use of an AFA, helped the retailer manage its defense costs. The integrated approach reduced the volume of lawsuits pending in the portfolio from approximately 100 at any given time to less than ten. The average cost per lawsuit also dropped from approximately $50,000 to less than $10,000. Overall, the retailer lowered its projected uninsured risk exposure from $5 million to $100,000."[22]

The second case study included in Damon's article involved managing a litigation portfolio of a large US defense contractor with multiple business units across the country. The client identified greater consistency in practices, quality of outcomes and efficiency as success targets for the legal team and sought one law firm to handle its high volume of litigation and counseling needs. Again, process improvement was key to meeting the client's objectives and delivering value.

With input and support from the in-house lawyers, the firm:
- Conducted extensive "voice of the client" interviews with corporate and division counsel to identify issues and potential root causes at the portfolio and matter levels.
- Developed a standard trial process map to assess each case for its potential to go to trial on the front end and throughout the case.
- Launched a new trial approach that triaged cases and staffing based on potential risk, with a flat fee AFA.

The overall strategy led to improved outcomes and provided the client with greater predictability of its legal expenses. It created cost savings of 30 percent on an average per-matter basis for single-plaintiff employment litigation, based on a five-year track record of nearly 180 matters.[23]

Clifford Chance

An example of one of the world's largest firms that made process improvement a cornerstone of its strategic endeavors, Clifford Chance trained all its lawyers in continuous improvement. Within a short time, it had delivered process improvement projects in various areas of the firm.

In January 2014, the firm announced that it had published a white paper on the use of Continuous Improvement, stating that, *"Clifford Chance is at the forefront of the deployment of Continuous Improvement techniques in the legal sector".*[24]

The paper discusses the firm's *"experiences over the past five years of* applying this methodology within an elite law firm; the benefits experienced by our clients and by the firm; and our views on how Continuous Improvement will be used by lawyers in the future."

The firm highlights case studies[25] on the use of Lean Six Sigma at Clifford Chance, including document review flow in litigation.

It reports:

"We were able to increase the flow of documents through the review team – which comprised both paralegals and junior lawyers – by giving them more efficient access to the experienced lawyers working on the matter. Queries from the review team were dealt with on a daily basis, therefore reducing the number of documents tagged incorrectly. Feedback is immediate, giving the reviewers a clearer understanding of the documents and related issues. The introduction of a statistical 'sample size calculator' also enabled the team to decide, on a mathematical basis, the optimum number of documents to be checked for quality assurance purposes."

A second process improvement case study focuses on how the firm has made bound volumes easier, cheaper, and faster in transactions:

"The new process has reduced the cost of producing a bound volume by approximately 60 percent and has reduced the time taken to dispatch a bound volume following the end of a transaction by up to 80 percent."

Another discusses how the firm has changed the way the client operates:

"It is easy for private practice lawyers to believe that inefficiencies are inherent to a transaction, because the process is believed to reflect client needs. This was the case when we started a project reviewing a particular type of asset disposal we work on regularly for one of our clients. During the analysis, we identified a number of opportunities for improvement, including some changes that the client needed to make. We took our analysis and recommendations to the client and they were amenable to the proposed changes, including a suggestion that a different team at their end should be involved in some aspects of the transaction. Having implemented changes on both sides, these asset disposals are much smoother – and cheaper – for everyone involved."

With the release of this white paper,[26] the firm cemented its place as a pioneer in applying continuous improvement methodologies to its legal services. Clifford Chance has completed an impressive array of initiatives with continuous improvement, including launching a firm-wide continuous improvement program aimed at enhancing the quality and efficiency of legal services. This program is built around the principles of Lean and continuous improvement, emphasizing process optimization, client service enhancement, and cost reduction.

The program involves identifying key legal workflows and using process mapping tools to find inefficiencies, redundancies, and areas for improvement; implementing legal project management techniques to ensure that matters are delivered on time, on budget, and according to client expectations; and providing regular training to lawyers and support staff on Lean methodologies and continuous improvement practices. This ensures that the principles are embedded across the firm and applied consistently.

It also established Continuous Improvement teams that are responsible for identifying and implementing process improvements across the firm. These teams work closely with legal professionals and support staff to understand their daily workflows, identify pain points, and develop solutions that eliminate waste, reduce errors, and save time. These teams also focus on client-specific solutions and cross-department collaboration. This way, processes get customized for individual clients based on their unique needs and preferences, ensuring greater alignment with their business objectives. Collaboration between different departments (e.g., legal, finance, technology) is part of the role and this is the "glue" that helps the firm integrally apply continuous improvement practices across all functions of the firm.

Clifford Chance has continued to apply Lean Six Sigma principles to various areas of legal work, particularly focusing on transactional processes like M&A and litigation support. It has streamlined document review and due diligence processes, reduced inefficiencies in the management of large-scale transactions and projects, and improved the accuracy and speed of legal work through better workflow optimization.

The firm has integrated continuous improvement with legal technology to further enhance efficiency. This includes automated document generation and contract review tools, which speed up routine tasks and reduce the need for manual intervention, AI and machine learning tools to improve document discovery and analysis in litigation and large transactions, and collaboration platforms to facilitate communication and knowledge sharing between teams and with clients, making the management of legal projects more transparent and efficient and repositories of best practices accessible.

Its Best Delivery Hub helps disseminate continuous improvement ideas and practical tools across its global offices, ensuring that the same high standards are applied consistently, regardless of jurisdiction or legal practice area.

Clifford Chance's efforts in continuous improvement have not only improved its internal processes but also positioned the firm as a thought leader in legal innovation. The firm regularly participates in industry conferences and contributes to publications on the benefits of Lean Six Sigma and continuous improvement in law firms.

Husch Blackwell

In his whitepaper, "An Unconventional Alliance: Lessons from a Lean Six Sigma Pilot",[27] Lann Wasson of Husch Blackwell LLP reflects:

> *"A complex mergers and acquisitions practice is an unlikely place to start a Lean Six Sigma pilot in a large law firm. Conventional wisdom would suggest that these methodologies from the manufacturing sector would more likely fit the operational side of the firm, as well as the more repetitive matters in commoditized practice areas. So in April 2010, when the chair of Husch Blackwell's mergers and acquisitions practice invited me to participate in a pilot to assist lawyers in using Lean Six Sigma on acquisitions, I knew that there would be many hours of work and challenges ahead for the whole team.*
>
> *"The genesis of the pilot started months earlier as lawyers in the firm began investigating different approaches to matter management, alternative fee pricing and a greater degree of leverage. While it was tempting to simply fine-tune existing approaches in an effort to control costs, these lawyers recognized that a new approach was needed to address the root causes of deal expense and client frustration. By identifying ways to achieve client goals more efficiently and effectively, the partners aimed to differentiate their services to ultimately give their clients a marketplace advantage and the firm greater market share.*
>
> *"Of the range of project management and process improvement methods available, the chair selected Lean Six Sigma as the pilot's frame of reference because these methodologies resonated with a cross section of the business community, including success in service sectors such as health care and banking. Furthermore, the tenets of Lean and Six Sigma, such as*

listening to clients, continuous improvement, process thinking and measurement, distinguished these approaches from others commonly used within the legal industry and promised to challenge status quo assumptions. Since the partners worked with different types of clients – from private equity investors to strategic buyers – the team needed an approach like Lean Six Sigma, which would allow them to develop their capability to collaborate with a client to design a framework that could improve its approach to deal management."

Today, the firm has more than 20 offices across the United States, including the *Link virtual office*, which "houses" 200+ lawyers working from the location that is best for them. The firm has decades of innovation, case studies, and success metrics that demonstrate its commitment to continuous improvement and desire to *"repeatedly put our clients in front of business trends and industry challenges through technology, monitoring systems, and a strong network of relationships"*.

During a corporate merger, a spike in the nationwide litigation portfolio strained client resources. To restore balance, Husch Blackwell introduced an innovative proprietary algorithm and outside counsel billing suite. Process implementation decreased risk and spend while optimizing compliance, reporting quality, and allocation of resources to strengthen defences. While the number of litigation matters increased by 35 percent, decreases were seen in time spent per matter (39 percent), law firm partner time (20-30 percent), average spend (30 percent), legal fees (ten percent), and active cases (53 percent).[28]

For many years, legal services seemed to be excused from the same requirements the business world had of products and other service businesses. It should be abundantly clear that this is no longer the case. There is nothing inherently different about most aspects of either the practice or business of law that exempts anyone from expectations of efficiency. Smart legal and business professionals are expected to be able to continuously improve, price, budget, manage projects, and apply the same kind of systematic approach to Lean Sigma as any other business to achieve the excellent results seen in a corporate setting.

Levenfeld Pearlstein (LP)
Somewhat obviously, a data-based approach to strategic thinking and decision making is the best way to achieve clarity and consensus. However, most

organizations collect too much data they don't use, that is not accurate, in the right wrong format, or the wrong amount. Taking a strategic approach means building out the function and tools to harness the knowledge of the people and the data produced by processes. Fortunately, more organizations are realizing how critical it is to have this information and enable people and systems to talk to each other. Consequently, they are investing in additional roles, resources, and responsibilities in the form of knowledge and innovation professionals, data scientists and stewards, and so forth.

Rebecca Holdredge, JD, is a knowledge management expert and a visiting scholar at the Legal Lean Sigma Institute. She maintains that there are specific tools and technologies that can be integrated into this infrastructure, called a knowledge center. The following is her account.

A knowledge center is not just a repository of information; it is the engine that powers an organization's process improvement strategy, ensuring that the knowledge gained from each initiative is captured, shared, and applied to create a continuous cycle of improvement.

When using process improvement tools related to strategic planning and implementation, it is important to recognize that they are only as effective as the system that supports them. To maximize the impact, it's essential that the tools are systematically applied and supported by the right infrastructure. This is where a knowledge center plays a pivotal role. By integrating the tools into a centralized knowledge center – often implemented through an intranet platform or a Document Management System (DMS) – firms can ensure that these resources are accessible, up-to-date, and aligned with their strategic objectives.

There are practical considerations for integrating process improvement tools into a knowledge center:

1. *Centralization of resources.* The knowledge center, often built on an intranet platform or DMS, serves as the firm's central repository for all PI-related tools. These resources are carefully organized into intuitive categories, allowing employees to quickly access templates, process maps, and checklists as needed.
2. *User experience and accessibility.* To ensure that PI tools are readily accessible, the knowledge center should be designed with user experience in mind. This includes streamlined navigation, robust search capabilities, and tagging systems that allow users to locate resources efficiently. For instance, each tool is tagged with relevant keywords, enabling quick retrieval through a simple search query.

3. *Continuous updating and feedback integration.* A knowledge center should not be static. It should be equipped with mechanisms to capture user feedback and track tool usage, ensuring PI tools remain up-to-date and effective. This feedback should be regularly reviewed and used to refine tools, incorporating real-world insights from employees. Regular updates should then be rolled out firm-wide, ensuring that every team is working with the most current and effective resources.
4. *Training and support.* To support the consistent and effective use of PI tools, the knowledge center could be integrated with the firm's Learning Management System (LMS). This integration allows for efficient delivery of training modules, ensuring that all employees, regardless of their role, are proficient in applying these tools. The LMS tracks progress and certification, reinforcing a culture of continuous improvement across the firm.

By focusing on the practical integration of PI tools into the knowledge center, firms can ensure that these resources are not only accessible but also effectively applied, driving strategic improvements consistently across the organization.

While many firms have implemented intranet platforms primarily as vehicles for internal communication and social engagement, Levenfeld Pearlstein (LP) took a markedly different approach with its most recent intranet upgrade. Previously, the firm's intranet served a narrow function, primarily as a platform for sharing firm news, alongside lists of birthdays, anniversaries, and practice group members – a common approach among its peers. However, recognizing the shifting demands of an increasingly complex legal environment, LP reimagined its intranet as a scalable, intuitive knowledge center, purpose-built to support and evolve with the firm's PI initiatives.

The new intranet was launched with a dual focus – first, to ensure it was easy to use and intuitive by preserving familiar features like firm news and lists of birthdays, allowing team members to seamlessly transition to the new platform. Beyond maintaining comfort and usability, the intranet was also designed to serve a more strategic purpose – transforming into a centralized hub for accessing essential resources such as checklists, document automation templates, feedback forms, and financial dashboards. This centralization not only addressed immediate needs by bringing these resources together in one accessible location for the first time but also set the stage for future growth. The true innovation of the platform lay in its scalability – it was deliberately structured to integrate additional PI tools as they were developed or acquired, ensuring it could continue to support the firm's expanding needs.

As the director of knowledge management and innovation at LP, Rebecca embraced the opportunity for transformation. The previous intranet was primarily a communication tool, but the team knew it needed something more robust to support its process improvement goals. By starting with a few key tools and resources, it was able to refine the platform and ensure it was poised to handle more sophisticated process improvement tools as its needs expanded. The new intranet was designed to be an intuitive and scalable knowledge center – something that would grow with the company and continually provide value as it introduced new tools and methodologies.

The new intranet represented a significant departure from its predecessor, transitioning from a basic communication tool to a dynamic knowledge center that aligns with the firm's strategic objectives. As LP continues to integrate more sophisticated PI tools – such as process maps, risk management plans, budgeting tools, task lists, reporting tools, online training modules, and enhanced data visualization dashboards – the intranet is designed to adapt seamlessly, ensuring these resources are not only accessible but effectively utilized across the firm.

Reflecting on the impact, the shift from a simple communication tool to a knowledge center was a game-changer. By focusing on ease of use and scalability, the firm has created a platform that not only meets its current needs but is also prepared to support its future growth and process improvement efforts.

This strategic evolution underscores LP's commitment to ensuring that all team members have unimpeded access to the resources necessary to drive process improvements across the firm. By integrating these tools into the knowledge center, the firm hoped to establish a consistent, high-quality approach to delivering legal services, fostering continuous improvement, and enhancing operational efficiency.

Bryan Cave Leighton Paisner (BCLP)

In an interview with Flex Legal,[29] BCLP's global head of process improvement, Susan Whitla, highlighted how a strategic approach to process improvement can deliver value to clients directly – an approach we have seen be highly effective for law firm sales and service efforts.

Whitla said:

> *"Increasingly, clients like speaking to the legal operations roles who will be responsible for implementing new solutions, as we can bring the opportunities to life for them with previous examples. We are involved in a lot of pitches to evaluate the problems and give clients confidence in our track record and capability to optimise services and new products."*

Proclaiming it is "purposefully structured for innovation",[30] BCL states:

> *"Our solutions-based approach to innovation is based on fully understanding our clients' challenges and thinking differently about how we can help to meet them. Our track record of leading the legal industry stretches back decades and it is part of our core business strategy to deliver services in a way that meets our clients' operational and business objectives. We have a dedicated consultancy division that assists law departments with their legal operations challenges."*

Its achievements include:
- Amongst the first to use artificial intelligence in the delivery of legal advice.
- Pioneered radical pricing approaches that cut clients' costs and increased fee certainty.
- The first law firm to create a division dedicated to solving legal operations problems through a combination of process, proprietary technology, and know-how.
- The only major global law firm to have built a proprietary workflow system for in-house legal teams.
- Launched the first "managed legal service" solution from a law firm to enable cost reduction through a fixed-fee outsourcing of a client's legal function.
- Named as a Value Champion by the Association of Corporate Counsel in recognition of driving value in the delivery of legal services through our work with client Red Robin to design, build, and implement a comprehensive contract management system.

A look at Berwin Leighton Paisner's early years shows how a firm's investment in a strategic approach can pay dividends for years. BLP used a systematic approach to develop sourcing capabilities that allowed it to develop its branded Integrated Client Services Model. Its Managed Legal Services (MLS)

Chapter 12: Strategic, systematic, and structured approaches

division brokered a deal with Thames Water in 2010 to run its own in-house legal team.

The transaction was intended to give BLP greater access to Thames Water's business and more opportunities for legal instructions. MLS ran day-to-day legal matters for the company and referred work to Pannone in Manchester, south-west firm Ashfords, as well as BLP itself. Andrew MacNaughton, head of MLS, said that the business model allowed general counsels to have a more strategic role in their organization as well as making the in-house team cheaper to run.

He explained:

"In terms of your in-house legal function, we can take that burden away and achieve a reduction of up to 20 percent or more on your annual legal spend. In-house legal departments are rarely considered to be central to a company's business and could quite easily be outsourced to an organization that has the processes and technology to run these teams more effectively. Less than one percent of companies have an internal legal support and most of them still succeed without the infrastructure and support. They go for legal advice as and when they need it. They just need an agile and nimble legal function that doesn't slow them down."[31]

In March 2014, BLP announced its intention to launch a new integrated client services model. The firm indicated that legal process improvement services would be one of four key elements, along with virtual transaction teams, the use of third-party providers, and a team in a new location that allowed the firm to offer client access to a "unique range of integrated services".

BLP stated that:

"The in-house LPI team has been deploying unique processes developed by BLP that have been applied to more than 60 workflows on existing client work streams. The LPI team is now expanding to provide more consultancy services for clients helping them to improve processes and analyse which balance of the options within the Integrated Service Model best addresses their needs."[32]

The firm is the result of a 2018 merger between Bryan Cave LLP and Berwin Leighton Paisner (BLP). With over 1,275 lawyers in 31 offices across North America, Europe, the Middle East and Asia, BCLP LLP is a global law firm that combined its legal operations, consultancy, and technology resources globally to provide clients with access to market leading solutions including BCXponent, Practice Economics and Streamline.

Streamline[33] was part of BLP's branded integrated client service model and used "virtual transaction teams" to help project manage support from lawyers on demand and communicate it to clients; the use of third-party providers, such as global partners, and the BLP Manchester service delivery team. It was designed to cope with the legal challenges of big construction projects and complex or high-volume litigation and developed from BLP's existing process improvement service to help collaboration between the law firm's internal departments, their particular legal team, and other professional advisers such as architects, surveyors, and accountants.

The pilot program for Streamline[34] alone helped major clients, such as four FTSE100 firms and, both internally and externally, has been applied to over 90 projects.

Bryan Cave had a solid foundation of innovation to build upon – successes included a global rollout of an integrated suite of litigation support technologies to streamline the internal processes of its litigation practice – making it one of the few law firms to have a coherent global strategy for the use of litigation technologies.

One may argue that organizational readiness is required for a planful, systematic approach; others may rightfully claim that change management is a planned and purposeful event and that a strategy ought to be thought about in the early stages of any process improvement investment.

The key is to recognize the current state of the organization and to be thoughtful and strategic about selecting the right scope, depth, approach, and timing to achieve what should be clear goals around effectiveness and impact. Opportunistic improvements certainly deliver excellent returns on investment, however, when an organization has focused on the core processes and improved them, it results in a measurable alignment and fosters a continuous improvement culture. Moreover, it can clearly demonstrate the value and impact of connecting tactics to the organization's vision, mission, and goals.

References
1. https://medium.com/pm101/improvement-kata-a-systematic-approach-to-continuous-improvement-8bc9969ee44a
2. https://mclclaw.com/attorney-qas-c/what-is-legal-lean-sigma-and-why-is-it-important-to-me-as-a-client

3. Cynthia Karen Swank, "The Lean Service Machine": https://hbr.org/2003/10/the-lean-service-machine
4. Ibid.
5. www.webfx.com/industries/legal/lawyers/statistics/
6. https://www.lawpeopleblog.com/2009/09/convergence-and-profitability-or-bigger-is-only-bigger/
7. Thomas L. Sager Award: https://mcca.com/awards/thomas-sager-award/
8. Catherine Alman MacDonagh, Lean Six Sigma for Law Firms, 2014, Ark Publishing.
9. www.acc.com/services-initiatives/value-challenge/acc-value-champions/meet-the-champions
10. www.acc.com/2023-value-champion-enstar-group
11. Ibid.
12. www.legalleansigma.com/wp-content/uploads/2018/04/applicationofleansixsigma.pdf
13. Ibid.
14. www.morganlewis.com/services/edata
15. www.law.com/legaltechnews/2024/02/20/e-discovery-technology-and-innovation-winner-law-firm-morgan-lewis-bockius/
16. www.event.law.com/americanlawyer-industryawards/2024-honorees
17. www.seyfarth.com/delivery/seyfarthlean.html
18. Connie Crosby, *The rise of Lean and Six Sigma for improving legal service*: https://store.legal.thomsonreuters.com/law-products/news-views/corporate-counsel/rise-of-lean-and-six-sigma-improving-legal-service
19. www.abajournal.com/news/article/seyfarth_shaw_says_six_sigma_has_cut_client_fees_by_up_to_50_percent
20. www.seyfarth.com/seyfarthlean-background.
21. Damon, L. "Applying Lean Six Sigma Methods to Litigation Practice" practice note, Practical Law, January 2014: http://us.practicallaw.com/9-549-6388?q=&qp=&qo=&qe=.
22. Rohrer, Lisa, and DeHoratius, Nicole, "SeyfarthLean: Transforming Legal Service Delivery at SeyfarthShaw," Harvard Law School, The Case Studies, 19 May 2015.
23. Ibid.
24. Clifford Chance, "Applying Continuous Improvement to high-end legal services": www.cliffordchance.com/content/dam/cliffordchance/About_us/Continuous_Improvement_White_Paper.pdf.
25. Ibid.
26. Ibid.
27. Wasson, L. "An Unconventional Alliance: Lessons from a Lean Six Sigma Pilot", ILTA white paper, June 2011: https://hbfiles.blob.core.windows.net/files/fb0eea28-67b9-4119-8656-953e3e65ef81.pdf
28. www.huschblackwell.com/our-firm
29. https://flex.legal/blog/an-interview-with-susan-whitla-global-head-of-process-improvement-at-bryan-cave-leighton-paisner-llp

30 www.bclplaw.com/en-US/innovation/overview.html
31 Crow, C. "Berwin Leighton Paisner's insourcing division", The Know List report, Issue 07, March 2013.
32 *Ibid.*
33 www.legalfutures.co.uk/latest-news/blp-launches-streamline-process-improvement-service
34 www.law.com/international-edition/2002/10/02/bryan-cave-rollout-will-streamline-processes/

Chapter 13:
Case studies and success stories

Regardless of size, location, or office type, every legal practitioner or business professional in a law firm or office or department has drivers for efficiency, excellent quality of work and service, increasing the probability of successful outcomes, and predictability. Everyone everywhere has abundant opportunities to improve. The early adopters help pave the way for broader acceptance and integration of Lean Six Sigma principles in the legal industry, demonstrating the value of process improvement methodologies in enhancing legal operations and client service.

In a precedent driven industry, showcasing what others have done is not just helpful in demonstrating that the tried-and-true methodologies that come from other industries can and do work in law, it is a critical part of "making the case". The case studies and success stories in this chapter serve that purpose. They are also intended to shine a bright light and celebrate the accomplishments of advocates, catalysts, evangelists, change agents, creators, trailblazers, pathfinders, innovators, inventors, overcomers, visionaries, leaders, groundbreakers, and people who made things happen.

Early adopters of Legal Lean Sigma in the legal industry include both pioneering individuals and organizations who embraced Lean Six Sigma methodologies to improve efficiency, reduce waste, and enhance quality in legal processes. Each member of the Legal Lean Sigma Institute team is passionate and driven to help people work even better together by using these methodologies. They, and every client organization, most certainly are included in the notable figures and organizations that were among the early users of Lean Six Sigma in law.

Our work has been extensive and expansive; at this point, we have trained thousands in the law all over the world. We have had the great privilege of working with law firms, legal departments, government law offices, the United States military, the Canadian JAG Corp, academic institutions, and legal aid offices. We have seen that Lean Six Sigma works, it works for law, and is completely scalable. I hope we are known best for creatively and effectively bridging the gap between traditional legal practices and modern business process improvement methodologies, thereby fostering a culture of continuous improvement in the law.

Legal departments

Every law department leader must ensure the legal department shifts from the perceived department of NO to being the department of KNOW. That means providing quality legal advice, helping decision makers understand risks, managing resources such as outside counsel, adhering to a budget, building and constantly improving operations, and delivering value to their clients.

That is not enough, however. To effectuate the shift, they must be able to work in alignment with others and show how they are contributing to the organization's successes. One of the most impactful ways to demonstrate this is to deliver a "report card" about how they are operating to the leaders and the board of directors.

Corporate legal departments have implemented Lean Six Sigma (LSS) strategies to optimize their operations, reduce costs, and improve service delivery for years now. Perhaps that is because they are more aligned than ever with their own clients and speak the language of business. It is now routine that legal operations and procurement have a proverbial "seat at the table" and those roles, as well as more of the legal and business professionals in the law department, are filled with impressive individuals who skillfully bridge the work performed by the law department with the language and tools of business. Naturally, that includes process improvement and project management. Common applications of Lean Six Sigma in law departments include:

- *Contract management:* Streamlining the entire lifecycle, including the process of drafting, reviewing, and approving contracts, leading to reduced cycle times and improved quality of work product.
- *Litigation support:* Improving discovery processes, document review, and case management to handle litigation more efficiently.
- *Compliance:* Using Lean tools to ensure compliance with regulations and internal policies while reducing the effort and cost of compliance audits.
- *Cost control:* Implementing alternative fee arrangements (AFAs) and controlling legal spend by using data and metrics to track performance and value.
- *Internal efficiency:* Applying process mapping and workflow improvements to reduce bottlenecks in the handling of legal matters and improve responsiveness.

There are many notable, early adopter corporate law departments that have embraced Lean Six Sigma or similar process improvement techniques, some of whom are mentioned in this book.

Covered in detail in chapter 12, Dupont and Thomas Sager are inarguably pioneers in legal process improvement. DuPont was among the first to adopt Lean Six Sigma principles in its legal operations. The DuPont Legal Model was a groundbreaking initiative that focused on consolidation of resources, reducing costs, and improving efficiency by using process improvement and partnering with outside law firms. The model has been widely emulated across the legal industry.

The legal department at General Electric (GE)[1] has been a strong proponent of Lean Six Sigma for years, following the broader company's commitment to these methodologies. GE's legal team has used Lean Six Sigma tools to streamline contract management, litigation processes, and internal workflows, leading to cost reductions and greater operational efficiency.

Other examples include Allied Signal, Honeywell (which created something called "Six Sigma Plus"), 3M, Kimberly Clark, Glaxo Smith Kline, Royal Dutch Shell, Boeing, Barclays, Microsoft, ConocoPhillips, Caterpillar Legal and many other legal departments, which incorporated Lean Six Sigma to reduce inefficiencies and improve collaboration with external law firms. By applying process and continuous improvement methodologies, there are abundant case studies of law departments achieving excellent results, from reduction of overall cycle time, optimization of the management of contracts, resource and cost management, and demonstrably improved service delivery to internal business clients. In short, law departments are run like any other business unit, taking the unique characteristics of the department into account. They have improved quality of work product and service, while improving collaboration with external providers.

The legal department at Caterpillar has used Lean Six Sigma to reduce inefficiencies in contract negotiations, dispute resolution, and regulatory compliance. When a law department such as this is able to report metrics such as these, it shows that it is not just a department of NO but a department of KNOW:

> *"The [Caterpillar Law] department spent several months using Six Sigma to understand their toxic tort load. They cut the number of law firms hired for those cases from 250 to about ten and worked out a method to decide*

Chapter 13: Case studies and success stories

which cases can be resolved quickly and easily. The restructuring of this litigation "saves the company up to $250,000 a month."[2]

Legal aid

There are resources available to legal aid offices who wish to focus on improving processes. The Legal Lean Sigma Institute has supported projects in different capacities over the years and we enthusiastically applaud and are available as resources to those who are committed to improving access to justice and access to law.

An excellent and consistent source of support is the Legal Services Corporation (LSC), whose Technology Initiative Grants (TIG) support projects that improve the delivery of legal services and information to people who would otherwise have to navigate the legal system alone. These projects use technology to leverage scarce human resources and increase access to justice for low-income individuals and families facing critical legal needs such as unemployment, evictions, or domestic violence.

The impact of LSC support is impressive:

- *2019:* LSC awarded Technology Initiative Grants (TIGs) to 30 legal services organizations totaling $4,230,718. LSC's grant awards include projects that use technology to improve self-help resources, enhance internal efficiency, and improve access for vulnerable populations.
- *2020:* TIGs were awarded to 26 legal services organizations totaling $3,941,298.00. LSC's grant awards include projects that use technology to improve self-help resources, enhance internal efficiency, and improve access for vulnerable populations.
- *2021:* LSC awarded 35 TIGs to 29 legal services organizations totaling over $4 million. Among the grants awarded were several projects that will improve online self-help resources. Other projects will increase access to justice for vulnerable populations and improve internal efficiency so that grantees can serve more clients.
- *2022:* LSC awarded TIGs to 33 legal services organizations totaling $4,679,135. Grant recipients used this funding to enhance cybersecurity, build educational platforms, strengthen program capacity and support the work of pro bono attorneys. Successful TIG projects are often replicated by organizations around the country, creating wide-reaching impacts.
- *2023:* LSC awarded 33 TIGs to 29 legal services organizations totaling over $5 million. The TIG recipients are taking several innovative

approaches to leveraging technology to strengthen their organizations and expand access to legal services.[3]

More information on the most recent round (2023) of funding can be found on the Legal Services Corporation website.[4]

Anyone who has ever worked with or for a legal aid office knows that resources are always scarce, those who work in that environment are committed to the mission, and there is a relentless and overwhelming need for access to law. Lean Six Sigma offers appropriately sophisticated solutions for the complexities of this environment as well. Even a cursory review of the extraordinary applications of Lean Six Sigma by legal aid organizations show inspiring results. Access to law and better experiences all around are shown in case studies that detail improvements to areas such as intake and case assignment and management, document drafting and review, clearly communicated and timely status updates, the all-important quality time spent with clients, and better utilization of always limited resources with which legal aid works.

Law firms

There are many business drivers causing increasing interest in Lean and Six Sigma by law firms. In addition to financial, wellness, and inclusion reasons, there are significant client collaboration, financial, and marketing and business development opportunities, along with competition and award-winning ideas, programs, and innovations from other law firms that support the notion that "a rising tide lifts all boats".

Some law firms have embraced market-facing approaches, progressed further along the continuum than others, and demonstrated how to flexibly combine and scale strategic and tactical approaches. From understanding value in the eyes of the client to making value flow at the pull of the client, reducing waste and variation, aligning and empowering employees, and continuously improving, these firms serve as powerful examples of Lean Sigma methodologies and principles in action.

Fisher Matthews PLLC

Commercial real estate attorney Rebekah Fisher offers one of the best examples of a service that realized extraordinary benefits from combining process improvement and project management.

Fisher of Fisher Matthews PLLC, formerly of Waller Lansden Dortch and

Davis, Dinsmore & Shohl LLP, developed an excellent process to prepare, negotiate, and execute a great number of commercial leases each year for a large retailer client. She improved her commercial real estate practice in a way that resulted in the highest levels of client satisfaction that includes a client referring others to her and excellent profitability for her practice and firm.

To perform this work profitably using a fixed fee pricing structure for the entire portfolio of work, Fisher focused on standardizing her process, communications, forms, and leases. She also staffed the work only with very organized and efficient timekeepers. This involved assigning the lowest-cost resources capable of doing each activity to each element of the workflow. Each worker captured detailed data about the effort it takes to do and deliver this work, which allowed Fisher to continually refine her model process and very effectively manage the work and resources.

The results are impressive, and the improvements translate into notable benefits for the client as well as the firm. Fisher reports that response time was greatly improved, reducing the time it took from the receipt of the client's initial request to producing a draft of lease to either the same or the next day, so, very nearly on demand. Remarkably, they also reduced by 68 percent the overall time it took from their receipt of the client's request to the execution of a lease from 168 days to 62 days.

Fisher's fast, reliable results have allowed the client to open stores an average of eight weeks earlier than was possible based on the previous process capability. This ability to move into the space sooner is worth tens of millions of dollars in increased revenue for their client. It is an excellent example of how to use process improvement in a client-centered way to be a real business partner, contribute to the client's goals, and drive revenue. In addition to the fact that this process allows the law firm to deliver this service profitably and reliably for a predictable, fixed fee, the client's high satisfaction with the results has them singing Fisher's praises. In turn, it has resulted in new, referred business for the firm.

Ogletree Deakins

Ogletree Deakins created a Lean Sigma culture starting in 2010, when it began the process of immersing managers and employees in Lean Sigma principles and practices. With a managing partner determined to make process improvement a cornerstone of the firm's approach, processes and teams were selected to participate in their first Legal Lean Sigma Institute Yellow Belt Certification Course.

According to Sharon M. Wardrip, SPHR, SHRM-SCP, chief administrative officer:

"While working on actual firm processes, we were able to obtain Yellow Belt, Green Belt and Team Leader certifications. By using proven, disciplined approaches, tools and skills, we have increased productivity and efficiency, positively affected our bottom line, and identified and reduced costs and errors in our existing processes."

Ogletree has utilized the DMAIC approach in a range of applications to core processes like timekeeping, billing, RFP responses, record retention, lateral partner onboarding, and litigation management. Wardrip explains:

"More than a program or a catch phrase, Lean Sigma became a way of thinking differently about work processes and discovering more creative improvements and solutions. Every day our firm is faced with new challenges and opportunities to maximize efficiencies. We will continue to develop and employ strategies and tactics based on the client perspective. Lean Sigma methods have given us the tools for each of us to take our role, our departments and our firm to a new level of excellence."

Among the many projects undertaken, an improved OFCCP audit process was one championed by practice group leader Leigh Nason, whose practice includes representing federal contractors and sub-contractors in compliance evaluations and administrative enforcement actions triggered by the United States Department of Labor's Office of Federal Contract Compliance Programs (OFCCP).

The project team included lawyers, paralegals, knowledge management professionals, and data analysts. The goals of the project were to create a consistent, branded process for AAP preparation, OFCCP audit defense, and various other services such as EEO-1 reporting, compliance assessments, etc. – anything in the group's area of service that would benefit from a consistent workflow process, define the lowest cost timekeeper capable of doing a task, and ensure that appropriate work is funneled to those people, promote the new process internally (to their referrers) and externally (to new and existing clients), and ensure that all practice group members are "on board" with the new process.

Additionally, Nason wanted to train and generate awareness among other practice group members and referrers within the firm as to what the service was and how the work was performed. She knew that it was important to "ensure a basic level of competence among all attorneys and specialized knowledge of various areas (such as applicant/hire analysis, testing, etc.) among a few attorneys. The improved process had to facilitate the ability to generate a specific dollar amount (number intentionally omitted) in additional revenue and we had to be able to measure that revenue with some degree of certainty."

The project goals also included an increase in practice group services-related billings of each timekeeper (other than the top generator) by at least ten percent. Underlying this idea was the need to create such a good process that Nason, the practice group leader, could manage a "virtual" practice group of attorneys, analysts, and staff in various offices.

Following the thoughtful work in the Define phase, the team had a lot of data and insights after measuring and analyzing the process performance. With focus areas selected and root causes identified, the team used the structured "analogy" approach to brainstorming, drawing inspiration from great coaches and sports teams to develop creative improvements and solutions. Examples included developing a "playbook" with a current roster/directory, and specific "plays" (checklists, forms, etc.) for certain situations, so that quality assurance and consistency is guaranteed, regardless of the client or attorney working on the project. The team also clarified guidelines regarding credits, opening matters, and rates and ensured that the premium rates for this niche practice work were not watered down by insurance rates.

As is the case with many (even most, if not all) process improvement projects, and in keeping with the project goals, the team identified specific training and professional development needs for the group, including business analysts. An effective communication strategy and specific procedures for working with referrers that included checkpoints, exchanging client development information, and otherwise ensuring that they continued to keep referrers "in the loop" with regard to clients entrusted to them were developed and implemented.

Additionally, standardized communications were established for consistency in messaging within the practice area and the firm. This included simple but critical items such as file naming conventions across the practice area team and organizing data files in a highly specified file structure on a shared drive with standardized file names and email subjects. The new process also ensured that relevant information is stored on the firm's document management system and on a dedicated drive for practice group matters.

The team also developed new practice group codes to better identify various components of practice areas in order to measure profit, utilization, growth trends, and contractions. Another outcome of the project was an established standard operating procedure of formalizing the relationship with the client on new matters, e.g. use of specific language (on documents such as engagement letters) to clarify details and logistics.

Following the project, the practice group took additional actions based on the team's recommendations. They engaged in strategic planning, where they developed core values and a mission statement to ensure that the team had a common purpose and was going in the same direction. Later, the practice group organized and conducted a two-day "boot camp" for all practice group members (attorneys, non-attorneys, administrators, and coordinators) to increase knowledge and train on the new processes.

The project also led them to establish a practice group administrator and coordinator. The administrator worked directly with Nason as the practice group head on administrative matters, assigned analysts to prepare AAPs, monitored workflow and timeliness of AAP and audit preparation, interfaced with clients to respond to questions or triage them to attorneys, and served as final quality control. The coordinator assumed marketing and client service responsibilities that formerly were handled by the firm's client services group. This ensures that the practice group had a person with an intimate knowledge of their practice group services to staff exhibit booths and talk with clients (and potential clients) at conferences and seminars. The coordinator also sourced various seminars for speaking opportunities and was responsible for quality control for AAP preparation. Both the practice group administrator and the coordinator are also timekeepers who bill hours.

This project delivered important results. The practice group's fixed-fee AAPs are profitable and they know which fixed fee arrangements are the most and least profitable. Also, OFCCP work is now delivered even more profitably and by an expanded team. Overall, they have increased the number of new matters over previous years, increased their billings and hours, and have robust and successful marketing.

Current practice group co-chair and team member T. Scott Kelly, a shareholder who is also an active member of the American Bar Association's Section of Labor and Employment Law (where he was the employer co-chair of the Section's marketing committee), reflected on the OFCCP audit process improvement project his team delivered. He said:

"We initially sought to improve the manner in which we performed and delivered services to our clients. Our new process has increased our internal efficiencies, which we are able to pass along to our clients. These efficiencies are not confined to competitive pricing, which is a benefit, but also include precise and thoughtful client interactions."

Kelly continued:

"Additionally, the Kaizen identified specific improvements to the interactions with lawyers in our firm that referred us work. Focusing on the manner, the content, and the amount of information we communicate with them has raised the referrers' level of satisfaction with our practice group. Another plus is the standardization of this process reduces the time involved in the process. So, we are keeping our clients and internal referrers happier, providing them more value."

Kean Miller

Kean Miller was the first firm in Louisiana to incorporate Lean Sigma into its practice, starting in 2016 with certification courses and programs that have continued to be offered at the firm over the years. It quickly began to use process mapping to remove bottlenecks, improve communication, and forge further relationships with its clients. Now, the firm has a page on its site[5] dedicated to innovation and continuous improvement:

"At its core, Process Improvement and Project Management (PI&PM) helps law firms deliver greater value and better counsel. PI&PM helps develop the right approaches to carry out a certain type of legal work to produce efficiency, excellent quality, predictability, and successful outcomes. PI&PM is not just about doing more with less; it is about doing the right things and doing them right – every single time. Kean Miller has embraced PI&PM and has conducted process mapping and improvement exercises with clients and internal client teams. More than 60 of our attorneys have been trained by the Legal Lean Institute."

Kean Miller sent a clear message to the world when it began to employ Lean

Six Sigma that the firm was making changes and employing these powerful tools. Unlike other firms that refuse to expand their view of the "law as a profession" and not a business, KM built on its legacy and ensured its lawyers got white belt certification, were empowered to speak the language of business, and continued "walking the walk". In this way, the firm continued to be aligned with its clients and develop unmatched competitive advantages. By starting with training various functions in the firm and then working on key processes and workflow, the firm embraced the idea that streamlining workflows meant things could be done faster without sacrificing quality.

One of the first firms to engage in collaborative process mapping with clients as well as client teams on achieving mutual improvements and cross-functional teams focused on internal processes, Kean Miller continues to build on its foundational successes. Its goal in process improvement and project management is to find the lowest cost resource capable of doing a task, and Kean Miller has applied this thinking to its legal work and business processes.

The firm now has more than 200 attorneys in Louisiana and Texas and serves as legal counsel to the people and industries that drive the regional economy.

It has used process improvement and process mapping in its work as national coordinating counsel, leveraging resources, and managing the work and local counsel more effectively. It has also engaged in workshops onsite with clients. By mapping processes, visualizing workflow, and working collaboratively to identify areas of improvement, the firm's legal and business professionals have been able to forge bonds through a shared experience that facilitates their abilities to engage in rich, highly productive conversations, which deepen the relationships and help isolate opportunities.

From Fortune 500 companies to local and regional businesses, the firm can rightfully claim to provide efficient and effective legal services in a cost-efficient manner.[6]

Barley Snyder

Another example of a long-standing, firm-wide initiative is found at Barley Snyder, a firm with 11 main offices and four community offices in Pennsylvania and Maryland. The firm launched its Practice Excellence® program focused on quality, knowledge, and service in 2010 with a mission of creating a firm-wide and pervasive program of continuous improvement. It remains committed to the program today.

"Barley Snyder has made much progress using internal resources and knowledge, but it was time to take Practice Excellence® to the next level," said Tim Dietrich, former managing partner of the firm. Dietrich continued:

"One method that [the firm used is] Lean Six Sigma, a recognized business strategy for increasing efficiency, identifying and eliminating obstacles, lowering costs, and improving the quality of the product or service."[7]

Practice Excellence is a prominent aspect of the firm's branding efforts with a dedicated page on its site that explains it is an ongoing effort by everyone in the firm to constantly increase the capacity to provide excellent service, professional quality, and outstanding value to its clients, emphasizing continuous improvement based upon Lean processes and using Lean techniques and tools to improve legal processes.

This includes mapping processes to eliminate waste and improve responsiveness to clients, producing consistent work product, providing pricing information and estimates based on Lean processes, continuously evaluating new areas and methods to serve clients, and annual training for all firm members in Lean concepts.

The firm's Practice Excellence Champions® group is comprised of attorneys and administrative leadership across the firm dedicated to the lean process and quality improvement mission. The firm reports this initiative has been well-received by clients and has attracted national attention. While larger firms have more recently started to pay attention to process improvement, it started its program in January 2008.

The firm does not stop there, but also provides examples of Practice Excellence® applications:
- A large client with operations in multiple states needed a process to streamline and provide legal advice to mid-level managers. We analyzed the need and implemented a technology solution enabling managers to directly access lawyers who are knowledgeable of the client's business and available to provide a prompt response – allowing the client to save time and provide quick service to its customers. Upper management of the client is able to review matters to identify training needs or troubleshoot issues. The system was also designed to cut down on repeat questions by creating a searchable knowledge base for the client.
- Merger and acquisition deals require a high level of sophistication under tight time constraints. Our M&A team utilizes comprehensive

work plans, customized by transaction parameters which they use to not only organize the deal but, more importantly, to educate and help identify decision points for clients and their advisors who are considering or about to embark upon a transaction.
- Large scale contract review projects can be risky, cumbersome and expensive. We partner with clients to analyze their needs and provide customized solutions that fit their business, reduce risk and provide fee certainty. Because we have delineated the basics by process mapping, our strategic thinking lawyers are empowered to offer prompt viable solutions that satisfy both time and fee concerns.
- More than ten years ago, our Intellectual Property Practice Group became our first paperless practice area.
- Ninety-five percent of litigation cases settle. Our Litigation Practice Group analyzed the work required after a settlement decision with the goal of streamlining the process to reduce legal spend during this phase.[8]

Elliott Greenleaf

Demonstrating the scalability of these methodologies, this 50-lawyer, full-service law firm in Delaware and Pennsylvania produced *"13 Green Belts for a firm with fewer than 90 employees, or approximately 15 percent of the firm"* and is not shy to point out that *"By comparison, [another pioneering] firm has 75 Green Belts and one Black Belt among its 1,500 employees, only five percent."*

As reported by the Delaware Manufacturing Extension Partnership:

> *"'We were excited about learning the Six Sigma language and skills,' says Neil Lapinski, shareholder. 'We not only can talk the talk everywhere that business people gather, we can now walk the walk.'"*[9]

As a smaller firm, Elliott Greenleaf offers quality work at lower rates. Six Sigma training – learning how to grow even leaner – was the natural next step in the firm's evolution. Six Sigma also enables the firm to provide clients with detailed budgets, updated at milestones, a key tool in conducting a litigation risk benefit analysis. The principles are also applied to complex work, providing a clear blueprint for allocating resources. In short, the company is able to staff work with the most effective mix of higher-cost hours by senior attorneys and lower cost hours by associates and paralegals.

Faegre Baker Daniels / Faegre Drinker

One of the first firms to add a Six Sigma Black Belt from outside legal to its roster, AmLaw 100 and, later, AmLaw 50 firm Faegre Baker Daniels hired Tom Snavely, now a principal consultant in the Thomson Reuters Advisory Group, as manager of legal process improvement and project management.

At the time, the firm had approximately 750 Lawyers in 14 offices across the US, UK, and China. According to Snavely, the firm applied legal process improvement (LPI) and legal project management (LPM) to address the expanded use of alternative fee arrangements (AFAs), and the increased emphasis clients placed on efficiency and value.

Faegre Baker Daniels drew a clear distinction between LPI and LPM and employed them in that sequence, using both top-down (i.e. efficiency is strategically important to the firm) and bottom-up (i.e. efficiency is important to my client/practice) approaches to promote internal adoption. This allowed the firm to make great strides and achieve significant milestones in a short time.

In 2009, a legal process improvement/legal project management working group was formed at legacy firm Faegre & Benson. It included cross-functional operational executives. The first 30 professionals achieved Legal Lean Sigma? certification through the Legal Lean Sigma Institute, followed by additional training for more than 130 individuals.

Within one year, the firm achieved early Legal Lean Sigma successes with real estate, eminent domain, and immigration projects. It also formed a Legal Process Improvement Community. By 2011, process improvement was included as a key topic at a firm partner retreat. In 2012, the firm applied Legal Lean Sigma tools for post-combination integration work. The employment litigation and government advocacy and consulting groups also implemented project management tools. In 2013, Faegre Baker Daniels hosted efficiency-focused continuing legal education (CLE) from the firm's South Bend office. Process improvement projects were led by an even broader population from the internal LPI community.

In 2020, Faegre and Drinker merged to become Faegre Drinker. It actively applied LPI/LPM tools and methods in a variety of areas, including employment litigation (single-plaintiff claims defense), charitable solicitation registration for nonprofit organizations, various corporate filings, electronic court filings, immigration visa applications, time entry/client billing, and a joint LPI/LPM project for one of the firm's largest litigation clients.

As internal and external demand for these services continues to grow, the number of legal services and administrative functions touched by process improvement expanded. In May 2024, Faegre Drinker announced[10] it had *"launched a client-focused predictive analytics program in partnership with Orgaimi, Inc., a data-driven artificial intelligence (AI) technology company and client intelligence provider for law and accounting firms"*. Orgaimi provides real-time, predictive insights and actionable recommendations that enable attorneys to better serve and create value for clients.

Faegre Drinker has adopted the Orgaimi software platform to accelerate its next- generation analytics and firm intelligence capabilities. Orgaimi will help the firm leverage significant value and insights from existing internal data, enabling partners and client relationship professionals to objectively analyze the services being provided to firm clients and anticipate client needs.

Government

Government law offices have increasingly adopted Lean Six Sigma methodologies to improve efficiency, reduce costs, and enhance service delivery, especially given the rising demand for more transparent and accountable public services.

Lean Six Sigma projects allow government at every level to produce impressive returns on investment, including vastly improved public confidence and experience, such as:

- 14 × ROI.
- $213,374 average saved per project.
- 55 percent average reduction in downtime.
- 54 percent average reduction in processing time.
- 53 percent average defect reduction.
- 61 percent average increase in production.[11]

Research into government law offices and the processes used shows examples of shockingly inefficient systems. Too often, they produce unacceptable, serious, egregious outputs, such as over-detention of people in custody:

"While people convicted of a crime and sentenced to prison must serve their time, LDOC routinely confines people far past the dates when they are legally entitled to be released from custody. Since at least 2012, more than a quarter of the people set for release from LDOC's custody each year are instead held past their release date, in violation of the due process protec-

tions of the Constitution. These violations are severe, systemic, and are both caused and perpetuated by serious ongoing deficiencies in LDOC's policies and practices. LDOC has persisted with these unconstitutional practices despite at least a decade of notice and clear recommendations for fixing the problem. LDOC must act to end the over-detention of people in its custody."[12]

The following are just a few examples of how Lean Six Sigma has been used in government law offices.

Irish Court Services (ICS) – 5S
The ICS provides judiciary and legal services to all the counties in Ireland. Over time, many changes have taken place within the court system and the services have had to respond to such changes very rapidly with limited resources. As such, many processes have evolved and are being analyzed for improvement opportunities.

In an article titled "Creating a culture of order and cleanliness at Irish Court Services",[13] Salil Kalghatgi and Dan Bumblauskas discuss how the operations and efficiency of the Irish Court Services have been improved. The authors conclude that *"Empowering staff with Six Sigma, Lean, and statistical perspectives provides staff with the ability to methodically and continuously improve their organizational operations"*.

Serving as an application of Lean Six Sigma and 5S within the Irish Court Service's (ICS) Dublin Circuit Court office, the case study follows the deployment of the Define-Measure-Analyze-Improve-Control (DMAIC) Six Sigma project management approach. Government is an industry where time is critical to quality, and in conjunction with project and cultural restraints, it used Six Sigma as a scientific method to evidence the improvements created by Lean and 5S efficiency.

Ministry of Justice
HM Prison and Probation Service (HMPPS) in the UK, an executive agency sponsored by the Ministry of Justice, was awarded the prestigious International Lean Six Sigma Institute "Project Excellence Award" by ILSSI in June 2021. HMPPS adopted the Lean Six Sigma process improvement methodology in 2018 to assist in the analysis and improvement of its many processes used to provide services within the UK justice system. Productivity and customer satisfaction were improved by the use of Lean and Six Sigma principles and tools.

Dr Sanjay Bhasin, probation service head of continuous improvement (business strategy and change), commented:

"As a direct result of our association with the ILSSI, we are now examining our processes using Lean and Six Sigma principles and tools. Through the projects which are increasingly embracing LSS principles and tools, we are realising a reduction in waste and delivering greater value for our service users in a shorter period of time."[14]

US Patent and Trademark Office (USPTO)
The USPTO[15] has an Office of Process Improvement (OPI) that provides the methods, resources, and training to optimize United States Patent and Trademark Office business processes and strengthen the agency's strategic goals of timeliness and quality.

The OPI applied Lean Six Sigma to streamline the patent examination process, reducing the time and cost associated with patent reviews by:
- Mapping the patent review process to identify bottlenecks and delays, allowing for more streamlined communication between patent examiners and applicants.
- Reducing backlog in pending patent applications through improved workflow systems.
- Implementing a centralized review system that standardized key steps, resulting in faster decision-making and fewer errors.

California Department of Justice (Cal DOJ)
The California DOJ[16] used Lean Six Sigma principles to address inefficiencies in various legal and administrative functions. Projects included:
- Streamlining the process for responding to public records requests, which often involved multiple departments. By mapping out and improving the workflow, response times were cut significantly.
- Improving the handling of criminal investigations and litigation support, reducing the amount of time spent collecting, reviewing, and filing documents.
- Standardizing internal document management to reduce errors and delays in accessing and retrieving files.

Public defender offices
Public defender offices across the US have used Lean Six Sigma to improve

case management and client services. Lean Six Sigma has been used to redesign intake processes, ensuring that cases are assigned more quickly and efficiently to the appropriate attorneys, and to improve the way cases are prepared and handled.

In Miami-Dade County, Florida, the public defender's office applied Lean Six Sigma to reduce case preparation times and improve communication between attorneys, support staff, and investigators. This led to faster case resolutions and improved client satisfaction. This is believed to be the first office using AI for research and case preparation.

> "We're already seeing that it's meeting our expectations, just by usage and talking to lawyers that are using it. We haven't run into any complaints or any serious concerns," said Cindy Guerra, chief deputy public defender of operations.[17]

Guerra led the Palm Beach clerk's award-winning project in 2018, to implement the nation's first machine learning-based court docketing system. Audits determined the system was 98-99 percent accurate, far better than humans.

Guerra credits Miami-Dade Public Defender Carlos Martinez with recognizing AI's potential for his office.

> "He really is at the vanguard. We were one of the first to use remote depositions before the pandemic, and we were one of the first to do jail interviews remotely," Guerra says. "He is always the first to say there has to be a way to use technology..."[18]

Moreover, several progressive levels of Lean Six Sigma training are available to Miami-Dade County employees.[19]

Prosecutor's offices

Prosecutor's offices have employed Lean Six Sigma to optimize operations and reduce the time taken to handle criminal cases. In King County, Washington, for example, there is a Continuous Improvement team[20] in place whose mission is to turn King County into a Lean organization. Legal system dashboards can be viewed to see the trends and data related to King County's criminal legal system transformation. For example, the Diversion and Alternatives to Incarceration Dashboard provides an overview of trends of referrals by law enforcement into the system and filings by the prosecuting attorney's office. It also dives into each program examining the background, the intended policy outcome, the eligibility criteria of the population intended to be served, and the program's definition of completion. Available data can be interacted with using filters, hovering, and clicking on icons.

The King County prosecutor's office applied Lean Six Sigma to improve case-flow management in the criminal justice system. This initiative involved:
- Reducing the number of case continuances by ensuring that documents and evidence were prepared in advance.
- Speeding up plea agreements through better communication between prosecutors and defense attorneys.

In Cook County, Illinois, Lean Six Sigma was used to streamline the discovery process, reduce the time taken to prepare cases for trial, and speed up prosecution of criminal cases by more comprehensively storing and tracking digital evidence.[21] The new system enables prosecutors and defense attorneys to use a unified and more manageable platform for relevant evidence. Prosecutors had long struggled with the challenge of dealing with large digital files, which can cause delays in the trial preparation phase. The program aims to bring all the case's relevant evidence, including hundreds of hours of video and other large digital files, into a single and easy-to-use system. The technology allows the office to spot cases in which key evidence has yet to be submitted and spot prosecutors who are taking longer than others to gather evidence.

State and local government legal departments
State and local governments have used Lean Six Sigma in their legal departments to improve their overall operations. Common applications include:
- *Contract management improvements.* By applying Lean Six Sigma, many legal departments have been able to streamline the process of negotiating, drafting, and approving contracts, reducing time delays and legal risks.
- *Legal services for regulatory compliance.* Some state government legal offices have applied Lean Six Sigma to help manage regulatory compliance across various sectors, improving the monitoring and enforcement processes.

- *Litigation management.* Legal departments have used Lean Six Sigma to ensure that cases move through the system more efficiently, with better tracking of case milestones and outcomes.

Consider how Lean Six Sigma principles can be applied to processes performed by a government law office. The applications are endless. Litigation divisions in a large metropolis, such as the New York City Law Department, have shown reduced cycle time for responding to lawsuits and other legal claims filed against the city and improved coordination between legal staff and other city agencies, ensuring that relevant documentation and information were shared more quickly and efficiently. Government law offices involved in immigration services and courts have also employed Lean Six Sigma to improve the efficiency of legal proceedings. For example, the US Citizenship and Immigration Services (USCIS) applied Lean Six Sigma to improve the processing of applications, reducing delays in legal proceedings related to naturalization, visas, and work permits and immigration courts in some states used Lean Six Sigma to reduce case backlogs by improving the scheduling of hearings and simplifying documentation processes.

There are tremendous benefits to employing Lean Six Sigma in government law offices. Those using Lean Six Sigma have been able to eliminate unnecessary steps and reduce redundancies, leading to faster case resolutions and better service delivery. By streamlining processes and reducing the number of errors, these offices have cut down on waste and saved taxpayer money. Standardizing legal procedures through Lean Six Sigma has led to higher quality outputs, with fewer mistakes in legal filings, document management, and case tracking, all of which reduces the need for rework. Lean Six Sigma enables better allocation of legal staff and resources, ensuring that workloads are balanced and equitable, and that the office has the capacity to handle more cases or legal tasks without sacrificing quality.

Finally, and perhaps most importantly, faster and more accurate legal processes improve public perception and trust in government law offices, as these offices are seen as more efficient and effective in serving the public. Enhanced service delivery and meeting the increasing demands for efficiency, transparency, and accountability is part of government's responsibility to its citizens.

Military

Lean Six Sigma is used in military law offices to enhance efficiency, reduce waste, and improve the quality of legal services provided to military personnel and their commands. Given the unique structure and demands of military legal operations, which can range from handling criminal cases under the Uniform Code of Military Justice (UCMJ) to managing the law office and administrative legal services, the application of Lean Six Sigma offers significant benefits.

Military law offices serve many stakeholders. They include military personnel, command staff, and external partners. Lean Six Sigma can produce improved communication and service delivery by standardizing how legal advice and counsel are provided to military leaders and service members, reduced wait times for legal services, particularly for soldiers or military personnel seeking legal assistance on matters such as housing, benefits, or family law. By improving the timeliness and accuracy of legal responses and ensuring that legal offices operate efficiently, process improvements can greatly enhance the satisfaction of the military clients.

The Legal Lean Sigma Institute has had the tremendous honor of working with the US military's and the Canadian JAG Corps' chief warrant officers (CWOs). We were humbled to be selected to deliver certification courses at the JAG School and enjoy serving as informal resources to the CWOs – the experts. Warrant officers are the few technical experts in their field, making up less than three percent of the army. Enlisted soldiers who pursue becoming a warrant officer can expect to:

- Solve problems within their area of expertise;
- Serve as advisors to commanders and other leaders;
- Train enlisted soldiers and commissioned officers in a specific career field; and
- Organize and support missions.

Lean Six Sigma is used to improve training programs for military lawyers, paralegals, and support staff. As in any other environment, when everyone receives the same level of instruction, there is increased ability to "speak the same language", reduced variability in knowledge and performance, and encouragement to think and approach things from an improvement point of view.

Lean Six Sigma has many applications in military law offices. Those that are dealing with large caseloads such as courts-martial, administrative hearings, or non-judicial punishment (NJP) processes, can use Lean Six Sigma to improve case workflow by identifying bottlenecks in the system, such as delays in receiving evidence or coordinating with command staff. By optimizing the steps involved in preparing for trials, hearings, or legal reviews, case processing times can be reduced.

Standardized procedures for handling common cases reduces variability in how cases are processed and ensuring consistency across different legal offices. For example, by mapping out the court-martial process, offices can identify steps that are redundant or cause delays, such as lengthy evidence collection or delayed responses from other agencies and eliminate or improve those steps.

Like any large firm (the JAG Corps is one of the world's largest firms), military law offices often handle large volumes of legal documentation, including contracts, legal opinions, investigation reports, and trial records. Lean Six Sigma may be used to streamline document processing and filing by using tools such as process mapping and workflow optimization. This effort ensures that documents are reviewed, stored, and retrieved efficiently, reducing the time spent searching for critical information. Legal research can be improved through knowledge management efforts as well, by organizing and systematizing the process of accessing previous cases, statutes, and regulations. By reducing redundant searches and creating more efficient research protocols, Lean Six Sigma helps military lawyers work more effectively.

Lean Six Sigma is an excellent application for improving the processes associated with litigation, defense, and prosecution under the UCMJ, offering an array of tools to optimize case preparation and communication between trial defense counsel, prosecutors, and investigators. This may involve better scheduling or standardized methods for sharing evidence and information. Certainly, it is to every stakeholder's benefit to reduce cycle times in the discovery process by identifying inefficiencies in document review and witness preparation, and to have enhanced coordination between different legal departments, military branches, and external civilian legal agencies especially where complex, multi-jurisdictional issues are involved.

Military law offices are often tasked with providing legal advice on administrative law and compliance issues, such as employment law, environmental regulations, procurement, and contract disputes. Lean Six Sigma can help standardize contract review processes to ensure legal consistency and reduce the risk of errors, especially in procurement and acquisition matters.

The magnitude of this can be better appreciated in context. How was funding distributed in FY 2024 for the Department of Defense (DOD)? Each year, federal agencies receive funding from Congress, known as budgetary resources. In FY 2024, the Department of Defense (DOD) had $2.10 trillion distributed among its six sub-components. Agencies spend available budgetary resources by making financial promises called obligations. The Department of Defense alone has a reported $272.68 Billion in award obligations.[22]

Somewhat obviously, there are many compelling reasons to use Lean Six Sigma to improve compliance with legal standards. By optimizing internal workflows to ensure all necessary regulatory and legal requirements are met without delay, faster review and approval times of military contracts and acquisitions and reduced legal risks are realized.

Military law offices provide crucial support to command leadership, including handling non-judicial punishment (NJP) proceedings and advising on military justice matters. Lean Six Sigma improves these services by optimizing the NJP process to ensure that cases are handled swiftly and fairly, reducing delays in issuing and carrying out punishments. Also, legal counsels' quality of responses and abilities to command are improved, since the advice on legal issues (such as disciplinary actions or legal interpretations) is timely, accurate, and aligned with military goals.

Every organization that onboards employees benefits from training and improved processes that help them integrate quickly. Because there is so much movement in the military from one base, office, role, or area of responsibility to another, there are many opportunities to help new recruits quickly learn the military legal system and operational protocols through more efficient training processes as well as capture and transfer the significant knowledge that one gains in a two-year stint, for example. Reducing ramp up time from one soldier to the next would make a significant difference, both in efficiency and experience. All other human resources and legal staff management issues, such as personnel evaluations, assignments, and workload distribution, can be improved as well. Assignment and staffing, performance evaluations, and feedback processes are excellent areas on which to focus.

Finally, military law offices tasked with running the military justice system also use Lean Six Sigma to improve the court-martial process from scheduling, by optimizing the use of judges, legal staff, and court facilities, ensuring that cases are heard promptly to reduce administrative delays in the processing of disciplinary actions and court proceedings, from the initial investigation to the final verdict and post-trial processing.

Sometimes it takes a bright light and a bad experience to force improvements. *US v. Foster* is a well-known case that revealed a serious problem with post-trial processing delays; the initial appellate review took almost ten years to complete, the case was assigned to six different appellate judges during its pendency at the Court, and only two gave it immediate attention and review. The final reviewing judge noted the legal issues were readily identifiable with cursory review.

In looking for reasons why this occurred, the O'Toole report[23] pinpointed the root cause – the judges involved in the Foster case were:

"The product of an environment in which military justice was not viewed as a career enhancing experience. Accordingly, military justice litigation experience and judicial expertise were not primary factors in the selection of judges to the court. Indeed, few had sufficient judicial experience to recognize that 25 delays by counsel in a single case should be a matter for concern... the lead appellate judge originally entrusted with the Foster case... did not have an adequate military justice litigation background, he never attended the Military Judges Course [not mandatory until recently], [and] he was not well-suited to the appellate bench... Another issue highlighted in the Foster inquiry was the apparent lack of judicial supervision."[24]

The Senate Armed Services Committee directed the DoDIG (Department of Defense Inspector General) to review the systems, policies, and procedures for post-trial review of courts-martial in the Department of the Navy (DON) and to assess their adequacy.[25]

As with any project, the initial steps included defining the project objectives and developing clear problem statements. For example, the team identified that, *"Some post-trial processing problems resulted from non-existent or inadequate process standardization, guidelines, checklists, and responsibility assignments across the Navy and Marine Corps"* and that, *"There is no reliable database or reporting system to identify or assess either the nature or extent of the DON's post-trial processing problems, either historically or currently".*

The data showed lengthy *"delays and inadequate process/tracking at every major action point"* and *"inadequate, nonstandard processes, and procedures as the root cause for post-trial delays"*. This offered them plenty of improvement opportunities on which to focus.

The report shows that, *"Overall, the Administrative Support Division (Code*

40) now has good processes in place and there is no case backlog. Due to a Lean Six Sigma process completed in approximately 2007, the division reduced processing times to the current one- to two-day turnaround."[26]

These standout case studies are all examples of a wide range of proof that Lean Six Sigma works in every kind of legal environment. In also works for every kind of organization, regardless of focus, size, geography, culture, mission, vision, strategy, conditions, or drivers for improvement and efficiency. It is completely scalable and can be applied to virtually any process, whether business or legal and it can be used over and over again. The only way it does not work is when it is not employed.

References
1. www.6sigma.us/ge/six-sigma-case-study-general-electric/
2. www.lawdepartmentmanagementblog.com/six-figure-savi/
3. www.lsc.gov/grants/technology-initiative-grant-program/technology-initiative-grant-awards-tig-projects-funded-year
4. www.lsc.gov/press-release/legal-services-corporation-awards-51-million-technology-grants-29-legal-aid-organizations
5. www.keanmiller.com/innovation-continuous-improvement.html
6. www.businessreport.com/business/baton-rouge-kean-miller-lean-six-sigma
7. www.barley.com/practice-excellence/
8. *Ibid.*
9. Law Firm Adopts Lean Strategy, Delaware Manufacturing Extension Partnership: www.demep.org/success-stories/law-firm-adopts-lean-strategy/
10. www.faegredrinker.com/en/about/news/2024/5/faegre-drinker-partners-with-orgaimi-leveraging-ai-to-better-anticipate-client-needs-and-strengthen-firm-relationships
11. https://goleansixsigma.com/for-government/
12. Investigation of the Louisiana Department of Public Safety and Corrections: www.justice.gov/opa/press-release/file/1564036/dl
13. www.pomsmeetings.org/ConfProceedings/065/Full%20Papers/Final%20Full%20Papers/065-0264.pdf
14. www.einnews.com/pr_news/551048863/ministry-of-justice-embraces-lean-and-six-sigma-for-service-excellence
15. www.uspto.gov/about-us/organizational-offices/office-commissioner-patents/process-improvement
16. www.sixsigmadaily.com/california-county-turns-to-continuous-improvement/
17. www.floridabar.org/the-florida-bar-news/miami-dade-public-defender-is-using-artificial-intelligence-for-research-and-for-case-preparation/
18. *Ibid.*

19 www.miamidade.gov/global/management/lean-six-sigma.page
20 https://kingcounty.gov/en/dept/executive/governance-leadership/performance-strategy-budget/legal-system-transformation/dashboards
21 https://thecrimereport.org/2023/05/01/illinois-county-launches-system-to-streamline-criminal-case-prosecution/
22 www.usaspending.gov/agency/department-of-defense?fy=2024
23 https://media.defense.gov/2010/Dec/10/2001712138/-1/-1/1/NavyAppellateFinalReport_V1.pdf
24 *Ibid.*
25 www.armed-services.senate.gov/imo/media/doc/Evaluation%2007-20-11.pdf
26 *Ibid.*

Chapter 14:
Using process improvement to collaborate with clients

From DuPont Legal's pioneering approach to collaborating with outside counsel to Kean Miller's process mapping workshops with clients and Morgan Lewis' Yellow Belt Certification Courses, there are abundant opportunities to use the tools and frameworks together. It's interesting, it's valuable, it facilitates the kinds of conversations that people really want and need to have, and it can also be a lot of fun. There can be other reasons to work together, but at its core, using process improvement (PI) to collaborate is about helping people work better together.

Tom Sager and I co-authored an article entitled "Collaborative improvement: Use Lean Six Sigma to become a trusted business partner to clients"[1] in September 2014; we could have written it today as it is still just as relevant and true. The ideas were offered with law firms in mind, but this version of our ideas takes a more expansive, inclusive approach. The case for using PI to collaborate with clients is for everyone in the legal ecosystem.

Client satisfaction studies demonstrate that it is critically important for lawyers to become more than service providers and, instead, perform like partners, whether in business or some other kind of relationship. Engaging in process improvement through Lean Sigma demonstrates deep commitment on both sides to a partnership.

When law departments, firms, or offices and clients employ Lean Sigma in a collaborative fashion to identify and solve priority problems, the conversation changes to one that enables both parties to truly understand and improve key aspects of their businesses together. Those that are engaged in process improvement will have the same compelling culture and mindset of continuous improvement. This ensures they engage in activities and deliver particular types of work to a consistent, agreed upon standard – that range of acceptability where the lower and upper limits are specified, and the success in delivering within that range is measured, tracked, reported, and acted on and we have better, structured, and far more frequent communication.

By applying these tools to end-to-end processes, teams can work together to achieve greater success than either could alone. DuPont Legal has led the change in how legal departments partner with outside counsel. The DuPont Legal Model provided an integrated approach to providing services to DuPont since 1992 and is directly responsible for reduced costs, increased productivity, improved quality of internal and external legal services, easier access to new opportunities, and solidified relationships among DuPont staff members, primary law firms, and other service providers. Through this model, DuPont Legal has created a successful legal network of members with a common vision and unifying goal.

At the outset, there was little experience in the business world for Six Sigma in legal services. The drive for collaboration and bottom-line savings in the Legal Model served as an important grounding. Today, every global member of DuPont Legal and every primary law firm and primary service provider plays a part in Six Sigma. It is the way work is done at DuPont Legal and key to meeting the company's "sustainable growth" productivity goal.

Given the Legal Network members' central role in cost savings and risk management, their continued and active involvement is critical to the program's success.[2]

In "The New Reality: Turning Risk into Opportunity through the DuPont Legal Model 5th Edition",[3] the authors outline the "significant and unprecedented results for DuPont".

A few examples include:

- *Cost savings.* Total cost savings in the first three years of the program were $13.2 million, and annual savings ranged from $8-12 million. After its first 15 years, it is estimated the total savings from the program exceeded $175 million.
- *Reduced cycle time.* Cycle time (from filing to resolution) was cut in half and remains less than 22 months.
- *Better forecasting of staffing needs.* Legal staff requirements can now be forecast more accurately.
- *Leveraged purchasing power.* Purchasing power has been leveraged with both primary law firms and service providers.
- *Capacity.* The breadth and depth of the network enables DuPont Legal to effectively scale up, resource, and manage a wide range of business clients' needs.
- *Flexibility.* The Model has consistently enabled DuPont Legal to meet the requirements and needs of an ever-changing corporate environment.
- *More diverse representation.* PLFs and PSPs have employed more

women and minorities to handle and take a leading role on DuPont matters.
- *Better distribution of work.* Legal work in the vast majority of matters is performed by those at the most appropriate levels of professional responsibility, thereby better leveraging both internal and external resources.
- *Reduced case docket.* The rapid expansion of the docket was halted in 1995. As of 1999, the number of matters on DuPont Legal's docket was down nearly 70 percent compared to its peak year. In the past 13 years the docket has been very stable, and with few exceptions, total cases are less than 3,300 annually, the bulk of which are asbestos cases.

DuPont Legal has a long record of applying Six Sigma globally and in all legal competency areas to improve or design legal processes that focus on client needs, greater efficiency and savings, and enhanced risk management. PLFs and PSPs have participated in or supported this process work.

Many law firms make bold statements about their focus on "value" and being "client-centered", but not all of them actually demonstrate that they are asking or listening to what clients say is valuable to them. Corporate clients can be extremely vocal, however, about their needs, desires and expectations, so there are still plenty of opportunities for law firms to take action.

There are plenty of examples in which law firms and their clients have successfully collaborated to improve processes at both organizations. By far the most effective and impactful collaborative project we have ever experienced involved Aon's global law department and its primary outside law firms.

Success stories
One of the benefits of PI is that it provides structure for people working in teams to follow. The Legal WorkOut is a methodology developed by the Legal Lean Sigma Institute that engages cross-functional teams to "get the work out" of processes, improves the way people work and collaborate, reduces costs, develops competitive advantages, and increases efficiency – with no tradeoffs. It is designed to break down silos, smash barriers, and build bridges between people and organizations.

The Legal WorkOut is a fusion of methodologies, concepts, and tools used in process improvement, project management, and design thinking. The

Chapter 14: Using process improvement to collaborate with clients

amalgamation enables us to access knowledge and harness the power of teams quickly and effectively. In just one day of working together, we build skills, facilitate highly productive discussions, and produce specific, effective ideas that get approved and implemented – quickly.

All processes can be improved. Usually, the people performing tasks in a process or project know a lot about performance gaps and pain points. Typically, they have excellent ideas about "quick fixes", "low hanging fruit", and "no brainers" that don't require a lot of time to analyze or implement – they don't always know how, when, and where to contribute their thoughts. By engaging in highly effective, structured workshops, a cross-functional team focuses on a specific process, has open, safe discussions, and experiences revelations about how the people are doing and delivering work and tasks that produce eye opening insights. This is the reason we do this work – to help people contribute what they know and to work even better, together.

With a new and a deeper understanding of the process from the perspective of the people who operate it, we move into structured, creative problem solving. The team's focus is to develop ideas and recommendations that "get the work out" of the process – and that are easy for leadership to approve, the very same day. Next, the ideas are piloted. Our accelerated and proven approach produces measurable results in just 30-90 days that will benefit the organization, teams and individuals, and customers/clients. Then, the team regroups, shares its progress, and drafts near-term and longer-range work plans. This second workshop adds to the effectiveness of the Legal WorkOut because follow up and accountability are built into the process.

The Legal WorkOut produces compelling and sustainable results and significant returns on investment. In addition to convincing metrics that tell the success story, teams report that they have never worked better together. With the Legal WorkOut, there are no tradeoffs. Everyone wins.

Aon's global law department

This award-winning workshop approach to collaborate, also mentioned in earlier chapters, received some of the industry's highest honors, including the 2018 Process Excellence Award: Best Business Transformation Project awarded at the OPEX Week: Business Transformation World Summit; 2018 LMA Your Honor Award; Financial Times' Innovative Lawyer Shortlist 2017; and ACC Value Champion Award 2016.

The story and the results are compelling. It started with colleague feedback and ongoing budget assessments. Through these processes, Aon's law department identified a need to enhance colleague development and reduce internal and external costs, while maintaining superior service delivery. Aon's law department had 425 colleagues in 42 countries that provided legal, compliance, and government relations support to Aon globally.

Audrey Rubin, JD, former vice president and chief operating officer at Aon global law department addressed the challenges by being the first to try a new workshop style approach that focused on harnessing and then unleashing the power of teams. Twice, Rubin selected processes to improve and then asked preferred provider law firms and members of the Aon law team to collaborate.

She said:

"The Aon law department works with our preferred law firms on process improvement. In joint workshops with the stakeholders, actual processes involving both of us are mapped and simplified. It is proving to be a most valuable endeavor. Lean Six Sigma is the right approach for all law departments... the multifaceted initiative has resulted in reduced legal costs, increased budget predictability, improved legal outcomes, and greater employee satisfaction."

Overall, each team identified and implemented improvements that benefited both organizations. Working collaboratively resulted in cost savings, greater value, increased efficiency, reduced frustration, and greatly enhanced relationships.

There were logistical challenges of scheduling and gathering the individuals who comprised the cross-functional diverse project teams to work together in person at two workshops and regularly scheduled phone meetings. Rubin had to make a compelling case and convince busy people to take the time to learn and find ways to do and deliver work differently. This required leader support, communication, and a great deal of change management. As the first to pilot this novel framework, Aon's global law department is to be commended, for it is unusual for the legal profession to both try something that is somewhat untested or to work in this manner.

Perhaps the greatest challenges were to motivate people to try something new and to affect a collective shift from thinking that efficiency is about doing more with less and to take a collaborative approach where legal and business professionals worked cross-organizationally to face significant problems and seize opportunities to develop competitive advantages together.

The law department worked with LLSI to select the specific legal and business processes it executes with a particular law firm that needed significant improvement. The four processes selected were Litigation / E-Discovery, Subpoena, M&A, and Billing. For each, Rubin worked with the relationship partner of the firm to choose a cross-functional, diverse team of legal and business professionals.

To generate rapid improvements and gain alignment and buy-in, legal department and law firm staff attended Legal Lean Sigma Institute workshops together. Cross-functional, cross-organizational teams comprised of law department and law firm colleagues gathered in a room to get the "work out" of the processes, spending a day and a half in workshops.

As more organizations focus on the employee experience and the importance of teamwork, this type of workshop is an excellent vehicle. The primary stakeholders participated in workshops designed and facilitated by LLSI. Each team had the same areas of focus – faster completion time, lower cost, fewer errors, to begin building skills and cultures of collaboration and continuous improvement, and to deliver increased value for both organizations.

The workshop involved drafting project charters, drawing high level process maps, discussing pain points as well as potential future state processes that addressed areas of improvement engaging in structured brainstorming, selecting the best ideas, chartering the top three to five, and then presenting ideas that would get approved by leadership.

In this case study, participants had their initial opportunity to work together in person. Some were meeting face-to-face for the first time despite having offices in the same city and having "worked together" for years. Teams broke out of siloes, learned the fundamentals of Legal Lean Sigma® process improvement, design thinking, and project management, then applied concepts and employed tools, such as project charters and process maps, to their pre-selected processes.

With their new understanding, it became obvious that no one person had knowledge of processes as a whole before this work. For example, a senior law firm partner originally estimated a process had 12 steps. After undertaking the basic mapping, 52 steps and 17 possible handoffs were found. Respect and appreciation for individual efforts increased and relationships between the individuals and the organizations deepened dramatically. Halfway through the day, that senior partner declared the day a success already.

The new skills and vocabulary facilitated the ability to work collaboratively, empowered critical conversations, harnessed best practices and the expertise of the cross-functional, cross-organizational team. With very little "ramp up time", the structure created an inclusive, level playing field where each person's experience was valued and utilized. It also allowed everyone to understand the real effort it took to operate processes. This new way of looking at everything resulted in individuals and teams identifying many improvement opportunities.

At the end of the first day, each team presented its ideas to a steering committee comprised of decision makers from both the firm and the law department, which provided opportunities for immediate feedback and sustained momentum.

Once approval was obtained by leadership, the teams drafted a "project plan" (who / what / when) so they could start to get the "Work Out" on the next day. As such, every person left the room with go/no go decisions made and understood not only that the process was going to be improved the very next day, but how and by whom – and that every change was because of their contributions and ideas.

After a month's work and several checkpoints, the teams met again to share progress and develop additional improvements and plans for longer range work.

Overall, the projects made an airtight case for using process improvement to collaborate. The positive experience and results convinced professionals who had voiced (and were known for) some degree of skepticism! They included:

- *Subpoenas.* Improved legal outcomes decreased the average subpoena cycle time by 44 percent from 175 days to 98 days.
- *M&A.* A project management system meant deals got done faster, risk was reduced, clients (including internal business units) reported higher satisfaction, and pricing ease and accuracy improved.
- *Litigation / eDiscovery.* Aon's tech team identified an existing portal that was already being used for a different purpose with the law department's litigation team and opened it to the law firm to provide a single source of updates and status. Aon shifted responsibilities within the company for specific deliverables and tasks.

Billing process improvement metrics showed the following:
- A 43 percent decrease in the number of rejected invoices.
- A 41 percent decrease in the total dollar amount of rejected invoices.
- A 72 percent reduction in the number of invoices rejected for the incorrect set-up.

- A 56 percent reduction in the number of invoices rejected for the wrong matter ID.

The billing team's work was so successful and the team so engaged that they continued to have regular team meetings for four months after the second workshop was held. They further reported:
- A 43 percent reduction in the number of invoices rejected overall, smashing the 25 percent year 3 and 40+ percent year 4 goals.
- A 64 percent reduction in the number of line items rejected; the team set goals of 82 percent and 100 percent (error-free!) reduction in years 3 and 4.
- A 49 percent reduction in total dollar value of invoices rejected due to wrong matter identification.
- A 39 percent reduction in time of law department bill review period, exceeding the 20 percent goal.
- A 68 percent reduction in the number of timekeepers with three or more invoices rejected due to wrong matter entry.
- A total of 100 hours of employee time saved in one year alone.

This was quite the proof of concept. LLSI's amalgamation of PI methodologies and tools produced an innovative and successful structure for teams to collaboratively develop skill sets, and deliver immediate and longer-term results. It created exactly the right conditions for a collaborative experience that drove value and efficiency for every function in both organizations. No one had to give up anything. Everyone gained.

As a result of several days' total investment, Aon's alliance with a preferred law firm now includes dedicated resources and technology sharing solutions, such as a Subpoena dashboard. The law department was recognized for its work by winning coveted, meaningful awards, which improved its reputation and service to its clients. Unsurprisingly, with this kind of success, Aon planned to apply this methodology to other law firms and processes.

A culture of continuous improvement has taken root.

As a former corporate counsel, I believe in the transformative power of PI to fundamentally change the way law firms and legal departments work together. The delivery of this highly successful project and the opportunity to develop the Legal WorkOut® was a professional and personal highlight. The investment and stakes were high. I remain profoundly grateful for the trust placed in me and the chance to make a positive and lasting impact on the individuals and organizations that bravely participated in this project. Audrey Rubin is now a resident scholar and consultant with the Legal Lean Sigma Institute.

Of course, there are other examples in which Lean Sigma has been deployed effectively by law firms and clients.

Parker Poe

In 2017, Parker Poe's managing partner, Tom Griffin, welcomed a large group of clients and other legal services professionals to the firm's Charlotte headquarters.[4] Some had traveled from as far as southern Florida and eastern Pennsylvania. As he welcomed his guests, he said:

> "I know how important this is to this audience: the efficiency of how we run our businesses, how we practice law and how we do those two things together. I love the fact that we're hosting this program here because something we focus on heavily at Parker Poe is our relationships, and we pride ourselves on partnership."

Over the next two days, Parker Poe teamed up with clients to learn process improvement and project management skills geared specifically for the legal profession. The course was called a Yellow Belt Certification in Legal Lean Sigma® and Project Management. The Legal Lean Sigma Institute provided the training and certification, and enrollment was open to the public.

Parker Poe was the first law firm to host this kind of course in the Carolinas. Clients in attendance included one of the largest US banks, a leading wireless infrastructure provider, a national retailer, and a regional shipping company.

Said Peter Barr, general counsel of Rack Room Shoes:

> "I think the fact that Parker Poe was willing to do this says a lot about the firm's willingness to be innovative and to look for solutions that are win-win for both the client and the firm."

The idea of hosting the course grew out of client feedback, said Kristen Leis, Parker Poe's chief marketing and business development officer. She said:

> "Clients have made it clear that they want law firms to collaborate with them, working together to gain efficiency and predictability. This course is a chance to spend two days together focused on exactly those things."

Poyner Spruill

In 2018, managing partner Dan Cahill opened a Yellow Belt Certification course that his firm hosted for the firm's clients. Over 30 attendees from Poyner Spruill,[5] including approximately 20 percent of the firm's attorneys, the head of every administrative department, and several support staff from across practice areas completed the program. Also in attendance were were 35 client representatives, who came with specific processes in mind, from across North Carolina and neighboring states. In addition to earning a Yellow Belt, all of them went home with draft work completed and some of them created entirely new solutions through the project mapping and process improvement exercises. Said Cahill:

> "I was really pleased to hear the generous and grateful comments of clients who approached me at the event. This project management and process improvement program is a great example of the effort our firm puts into enhancing the client experience and constantly working to create a true partnership with our clients."

Legal Lean Sigma Institute's certification courses are the first and only combined process improvement and project management certification courses designed specifically for the legal profession. The two-day Yellow Belt Certification course includes lectures, exercises, simulations, videos, discussions, group and table-team work, and demonstrations covering key process improvement methodologies, tools and concepts and the stages of project management.

Said Kelsey Mayo, the employee benefits practice leader:

> "Our team is always focused on partnering with clients in a way that adds real value to the bottom line. Participating in this program alongside our clients allowed us to learn more about how and where we can help them make a significant impact."

Other examples

Foley & Lardner, an international law firm, had a long history of working with manufacturing clients. It was years before one of the firm's lawyers participated in a continuous improvement process called "kaizen" with a client. This work took place at the client site and the process was in manufacturing, not legal. The insights and relationships gained from this experience were significant and it showed the client they had a business partner in their lawyer.

At the immigration and global mobility practice at then Faegre Baker Daniels, the firm worked with a Fortune 50 client to eliminate waste from routine immigration services through process optimization and automation, document management and collation, effective delegation, and customization of cutting-edge technology. As a direct result of these collaborative efforts, the firm reduced the preparation time for various temporary and permanent visa processes for the client to just over half the average time required in other settings.

UK law firm Eversheds invested early in project management, process improvement, pricing and budget predictability to improve its services and value to clients. Its innovative billing structures for clients resulted in the firm making a 27 percent reduction in fees for its client, Tyco. The number of Tyco's litigation cases fell by 60 percent, and the amount of the firm's high-quality work for Tyco increased by over 300 percent.[6]

The collaborative approach is in no way limited to law firms; in fact, it's been successfully employed by legal and business process outsourcing providers like Integreon (see below), which worked with its client, Microsoft, to develop its contract review processes so that it delivers high quality and faster services at a lower cost.

K&L Gates, Levenfeld Perlstein, and Morgan Lewis have offered private White and Yellow Belt certification courses specifically tailored to clients. Each integrated team learns and works together, using a real process of interest for all the exercises. In this way, participants learn how to apply PI concepts, tools, and frameworks while they get draft work done. The courses are structured and facilitated to provide opportunities for the participants to identify areas where both the firm and the client could improve the process and work together. Each team develops immediate improvement ideas that work well for everyone.

By introducing clients to these transformational approaches and then employing them in a collaborative fashion, firms are more likely to have better and longer-lasting client relationships.

The increasing commoditization of legal work means there is a greater need than before for law firms to embrace lean sigma to increase both their efficiency and profit margins. Which law firm wouldn't want to use process improvement to not only improve its own business and deliver greater value to clients, but also to connect with clients in novel and more deeply satisfying ways?

Collaborating to improve processes

Everywhere in law, there are processes that range from simple to complicated, but all can be improved. Thomas L. Sager and Scott L. Winkelman[7] collaborated to offer the following recommendations:

- *Start with paper processes* – these regularly lend themselves to standardized process improvements and often yield quick victories.
- *Map the process* – mundane though it sounds, mapping often yields dramatic results by highlighting the process as it really exists.
- *Target unconscious spending* – staff often take action without even considering the costs.
- *Apply information technology* – IT fixes often bubble up early.
- *Leverage the learning* – multiply the benefits by leveraging project learning to similar processes and functions.
- *Be a forum for pent-up grievances* – pent-up pet peeves are often the stuff of superb process improvement projects.

To identify what would be a good place to start collaborating, it is useful to consider John Grant's value theory, represented by the equation:

Value = Benefit – Investment

Writing on his Legal Value Theory blog (now AgileAttorney.com),[8] Grant says:

> "The challenge is twofold: (1) How to figure out what will truly benefit the customer, and (2) How to get the customer to increase its investment in order to obtain that benefit. This is where Richard Susskind's Disruption stage comes into play. Disruptive providers will be those who figure out how to create new ways of increasing value by delivering greater customer benefit and capturing additional customer investment (fees) from the gains. And this is also where I think the true value of Lean can shine."[9]

He goes on to share his perspective on Lean by suggesting that:

> "Its core purpose is not its drive for efficiency, but its focus on understanding customer needs. Lean tools like Voice of the Customer Analysis and SIPOC charts, along with Agile tools like User Stories, can help providers understand their customer's value premise and craft solutions around those discoveries. The key is to truly understand what the customer

needs, not just what it is looking for. That is no easy task; what the customer says it wants and what it really needs are not always aligned. Digging deep to understand the customer's fundamentals is critical, and you're not done there. Next you need to consider the best possible way to deliver benefit based on those needs, and it may not be the way you, or the customer, have always done things.

"But if disruption were easy, everyone would be doing it. So my overall point is that efficiency is good, but figuring out how to change the game is much better. Fortunately, lawyers who learn how to use tool sets from Lean, Agile, and elsewhere can do both."[10]

Process improvement methodologies like Lean and Six Sigma have spread to virtually every industry in the world. A 2007 research study from trade publication *iSixSigma* magazine estimated that over half of Fortune 500 and as many as 82 percent of Fortune 100 companies have used Six Sigma methodologies to produce savings that total roughly $427 billion.[11]

In 2024, most large corporations, especially those in industries like manufacturing, healthcare, finance, technology, and logistics, have integrated continuous improvement principles into their operations. Companies like Toyota, General Electric (GE), Motorola, 3M, Honeywell, Amazon, Caterpillar, and Boeing are well-known for using Lean or Six Sigma techniques, key components of continuous improvement. It's also used in healthcare (e.g., Duke, Mayo Clinic, Cleveland Clinic) and financial institutions (Bank of America).

Every law department, firm, or office should find out whether its clients are employing process improvement methodologies; if they are, join them. If not, introduce it to them – why wait to be asked or have them demand it of you?

Take their success stories and translate them to the legal environment. Once a basic skill set has been developed, it simply takes some focus and a little experience to translate the concepts and approaches to something we can use to collaborate with them. Read this summary of Duke's *10-Year Experience Integrating Strategic Performance Improvement Initiatives: Can the Balanced Scorecard, Six Sigma®, and Team Training All Thrive in a Single Hospital?*[12] Then, see how easy it would be to follow this blueprint with legal as the focus:

- *Objective:* Duke University Hospital has taken three widely diverse quality management initiatives and melded them into a comprehensive approach to achieve strategic goals.

- *Methods:* The Balanced Scorecard (BSC) is a management system focused on developing a mission, strategic goals, and key metrics and linking these to specific operational initiatives. Six Sigma® provided a solid performance improvement framework utilizing the DMAIC approach: Define, Measure, Analyze, Improve, and Control. Team Training translated aviation's Crew Resource Management principles to a health care-specific methodology.

- *Results:* Utilization of the BSC has led to an increase in net margin of 236 percent. Six Sigma reduced the risk score in moderate sedation from 11.94 to 4.94 and event probability score from 3.31 to 1.34. Team training increased awareness of safety processes by 26 percent, communication as a team by 29 percent, and independent observations of overall teamwork by 72 percent.

- *Conclusion:* The BSC consolidates strategic initiatives; Six Sigma facilitates focused improvement within operations; and Team training improves communication across disciplines. Understanding these differences and building upon each approach's individual strengths is essential to success.

There isn't a definitive, publicly available count of how many companies worldwide use Lean Six Sigma specifically. However, Lean Six Sigma is a widely adopted process improvement methodology, and its reach is extensive due to its combination of Lean principles (focusing on waste reduction) and Six Sigma methodologies (emphasizing defect reduction and quality improvement). It isn't just for big companies either. Many small and medium-sized enterprises worldwide also apply Lean Six Sigma principles to optimize operations.

Given the scale and complexity of their operations, it's estimated that a vast majority – likely over 80 percent – of Fortune 500 companies have adopted continuous improvement methodologies to enhance performance, streamline operations, and stay competitive in the global market.

With numbers like that, it is no wonder that we are seeing questions about process improvement, continuous improvement, project management, process creation, and metrics associated with performance management in every request for proposal. Moreover, in addition to requiring responding law firms to discuss their own process improvement and project management frameworks, the RFP also requires candidate firms questions such as, "What changes could we implement in our company to make the work for us more cost-efficient?"

ALM Legal Intelligence found that:

"The concept of value is entering conversations with clients at least some of the time for 86 percent of firms. It is the beginning of an educational effort that might eventually move the industry from an hourly focus to one of value, although a change is far from certain. Legal work has such a long history of hourly billing, getting beyond the concept means changing the minds of many – never an easy task. Most seriously, the basic drives to focus on value and gain insight into profitability still have a significant road ahead. More than half of firms tell us that at least some of the time the end game of pricing work with clients usually turns into 'getting a good price' rather than understanding the cost structure of a matter."[13]

Legal departments, law firms, and service providers have not been sitting around, waiting to take action and work more closely with clients on service issues. However, a much more intense focus was brought to bear on the "value" conversation in 2008, when the Association of Corporate Counsel (ACC) introduced its Value Challenge[14] – "an initiative to reconnect the value and the cost of legal services".

The ACC stated that:

"There are many ways to improve value in the firm-client relationship. The ACC Value Challenge focuses on providing resources and training – for law firms as well as law departments – on these key value levers: Aligning Relationships, Value-based Fee Structures (i.e. not based on the "billable hour"), Staffing and Training Practices, Budgeting, Project Management, Process Improvement, Use of Technology, Data Management, Knowledge Management and Change Management."[15]

It is worth pointing out that firms that embrace process improvement and project management and perform well are also more likely to perform better in all the other dimensions.

Susan Duncan returned to her consulting practice at RainMaking Oasis (of which she is a founder) after serving as the chief strategy and development officer of Squire Sanders – a 1,300-lawyer, Global 15 law firm with 36 offices in

17 countries. Among the highlights of her work at Squire Sanders was her involvement with the integration of two mergers in 12 months; a refocus of the firm's client service and value initiative, including the introduction of client interviews and a new Covenant with Clients; and the roll out of a new planning process that resulted in 56 practice group, industry group, and regional business plans that also correlated budgeting with measurable objectives.

In an article for the ABA's *Law Practice* magazine,[16] Duncan interviewed Lisa Damon, a partner and catalyst for the Seyfarth*Lean* initiative. Damon shed insight about the firm's goal to "drive better business outcomes for clients by providing legal services in a fundamentally different way". She explained that "process improvement begins with listening. Seyfarth's approach incorporates 'voice of the client' techniques throughout the process to help establish clear goals, desired business outcomes, and benchmarks for measuring success." Seyfarth works with clients on their extensive use of process mapping, which encompasses data collection, engagement planning, work assignment, and resource management to help ensure that the legal strategy and desired outcomes support the client's objectives.

In 2011, Seyfarth Shaw established a consultancy that advises in-house departments on how to apply Lean and manage outside work. In other words, it has a separate business where it teaches its clients about process improvement and helps them become more efficient. Additionally, the lawyers in the firm are able to use process mapping and other Six Sigma approaches to identify and understand the underlying costs of providing different kinds of work. It says this allows productive two-way conversations between the firm and clients on how to achieve the best results, align costs to value, and provides a transparent pricing package. This enables clients to understand quickly what steps are involved in meeting their objectives.

Graham Richardson and Martin Hopkins of Eversheds, which has 1,200 lawyers, were also interviewed by Duncan for the article, reporting that the firm "has been pioneering new and better approaches to delivering legal services for the past decade". Duncan found that, from project management and process improvement to pricing and budget predictability, the firm continually innovates to improve its services and value to clients, using project management as:

> "*The framework for its six-year-old groundbreaking relationship with Tyco, and most recently a similar arrangement with Eni, Eversheds has applied a data-rich metric approach to delivering and managing services for these*

two companies in multiple global jurisdictions on a fixed-fee basis. For all clients, lawyers apply process-mapping approaches that align the clients' objectives with strategy and cost."[17]

Duncan also wrote about The Pfizer Legal Alliance in 2012:

"Nineteen law firms, working together to advance the value of legal counseling to benefit all Alliance partners, their clients and the legal profession... Since its inception three years ago, the Pfizer Legal Alliance, an innovative partnering strategy, continues to be highly effective both for Pfizer and for the 19 law firms currently selected as members."[18]

The article featured highlights from a roundtable hosted by Bucerius Law School's Center on the Legal Profession at the offices of Venable in New York City at which Ellen Rosenthal, chief counsel, Pfizer Legal Alliance (PLA), Jeff Chasnow, chief counsel Emerging Markets, and John Dougherty, partner at DLA Piper, shared their observations of the program's challenges and successes. These highlights covered:

- *Key features/components of the Pfizer Legal Alliance:* Fee structures, performance reviews, team composition, training and development, and a knowledge sharing platform;
- *The benefits to Pfizer:* Predictability of their annual legal budget and substantially reduced annual legal spending; and
- *Benefits to alliance law firms:* A steady flow of work, more total work/revenue, and, if efficient, matters are resolved quickly and are more profitable. Firms also use their participation "as a driver of change in pricing and measurement of value away from hours, onto efficiency and results".[19]

Duncan also interviewed a number of thought leaders for an article focused on firms looking to adapt and innovate.[20] Mike Roster, former chair of ACC, former GC, and former AmLaw 20 partner, said that:

"Whether functioning as inside or outside counsel, you've got to aim for at least one of these three targets: reduce legal cost (in-house and outside combined) by 25 percent, provide near certainty in cost, and/or significantly and measurably improve outcomes. If you're not achieving at least one of these targets, just what is it you are trying to accomplish?"

Duncan concludes with some solid advice from the late Dr John Martin, the brilliant chairman of Chadwick Martin and Bailey, and partner at South Street Strategy Group. He said that, to avoid obstacles to innovation, law firms should follow these steps:
- Establish a common definition/understanding of what innovation means for their firms as well as for their clients.
- Develop a systematic approach and framework for innovation.
- Look forward, not backward. Stop looking at the past for proof and precedents and look to the future for new ideas and solutions. Similarly, stop following and start leading.
- Identify and deal with the barriers.[21]

A collaborative approach to process improvement

Interestingly, every two years, the Process Excellence Network (PEX Network) undertakes a "State of the Industry" research project to better understand general trends in how companies are approaching operational excellence. In 2013, PEX Network conducted this survey to better understand emerging trends in process excellence, asking "What tools and methodologies are companies using in their approach process excellence? What is the outlook for budgets and resources? What are the general trends practitioners are experiencing? What are the skills and capabilities that are in demand?"

PEX reported that:

> "Only 12.1 percent of the 800+ process professionals who responded to the survey report that the legal department was one of the areas where they were applying continuous improvement. Raytheon, Tyco International, John Deere, and DuPont are a few of the companies that are widely acknowledged to have used Lean Six Sigma within their legal departments."[22]

It bears restating then – there are significant opportunities for law firms to not only use Lean Six Sigma in their own businesses but also work with the many legal departments that have not yet learned about or employed process improvement methodologies.

Correspondingly, law department office (LDO) professionals are experiencing increased opportunities to collaborate with their clients – the other departments, business units, and functions in their businesses.

LDO professionals are having substantial interactions on matters that stretch beyond the legal department. Findings from the 14th Annual Law

Department Operations survey (2021) show that, when asked how often they are involved in cross-functional objectives such as a contract management program that involves both procurement and legal, 73 percent of respondents reported frequently or very frequently, a small increase from 70 percent in 2020. And more than half of respondents – 52.5 percent – are very frequently or frequently involved in enterprise-wide strategic initiatives, defined as those outside the legal department. That represents an increase from 44 percent the previous year.[23]

These responses illustrate an LDO function that has grown beyond internal projects. Rather, these professionals are leading projects that transcend the legal department and are becoming a crucial point of contact within the legal department in relation to other functions. In fact, survey respondents were asked if they interface with the following functions at least weekly: 68 percent of respondents said they communicate with the executive suite, 98 percent with IT, 95 percent with finance, and 75 percent with HR.

These clients (or prospective clients) would be better served by lawyers, law firms, and other service providers who introduce them to these transformational approaches and then employ these in a collaborative fashion. As has been suggested repeatedly in this book, those that do so proactively are not only going to get a better process, but they are also more likely to have a much better client relationship at the end of the day.

There are many ways of using process improvement methodologies and Lean Six Sigma tools to collaborate and further relationships with clients.

As we have seen, while some in law are new to this, others have been immersed in process improvement with their clients for a significant amount of time. DuPont Legal led the change in how legal departments partner with outside counsel. In the 2001 article mentioned earlier, Thomas L. Sager and Scott L. Winkelman shared the following:

> *"Everyone (both inside and outside) focuses on the right solution for the client, in this case DuPont. That focus may mean fewer resources allocated to a given task. But we all learn from the process and become more competitive in our respective marketplaces. This focus also explains, in part, why we chose two professionals from our outside network to join our Six Sigma effort and to become Black Belts...*
>
> *"The fact that core features of Six Sigma – attention to efficiency, elimination of process defects and redundancies, and striving for process*

standardization – are countercultural for lawyers is merely one more reason to embrace Six Sigma, because attorneys often are most in need for the wake-up call that Six Sigma provides."[24]

In the article, Michelle Fujimoto of Shook Hardy & Bacon and Eric D. Brown of Eli Lilly & Company discuss the applicability of Lean and Six Sigma methodologies and tools to legal work performed by both in-house departments and in law firms:

"In contrast to in-house lawyers who operate in a business environment and are directly influenced by business thinking and methodologies that are employed in their corporations, law firms are more likely to be skeptical about the applicability of data- and predictability-driven management processes to the practice of law. Over the last few years, this difference in mindset and the strength of inertia have resulted in a gulf between how in-house lawyers and many outside counsel approach the business and the practice of law. Many would say that a culture shift is absolutely necessary for a law firm to thrive, perhaps even to survive, in the current competitive landscape that is increasingly driven by data, predictability, and cost control, in addition to the older currency of relationships and reputations."

Additionally, they report that:

"Shook Hardy & Bacon partnered with a client to utilize Lean Six Sigma tools for a patent application process. The project focused on two goals: (1) to reduce the amount of time it takes to process an application from start to finish; and (2) to reduce the time from the date of assignment to the date the application is filed with the patent office. Shook worked with the client and used various tools, including process maps and cause-and-effect diagrams, to prepare a step-by-step analysis of the entire process. Tasks or functions were then identified for modification or elimination."[25]

With so many client satisfaction studies demonstrating that it is critically important to understand a client's business and be their partner, using Lean and Six Sigma to identify and help clients solve priority problems and seize important opportunities is an excellent way to demonstrate understanding and a commitment to a business partnership. Furthermore, process improvement provides a framework for approaching and discussing business goals in ways that allow those delivering legal services to become more than a service provider and to perform more as a business partner with legal expertise.

This approach is in no way limited to law firms; in fact, it is being successfully employed by alternative providers who now compete for and perform work that used to be the bread and butter of law firms. The issue for some law firms that are not engaged in process improvement is that they do not have the same compelling culture and mindset of continuous improvement, or metrics around what it takes to do and deliver particular kinds of work, and so they are at a serious disadvantage when it comes to competing for the same clients with firms that *are* engaged in process improvement.

Integreon and Microsoft demonstrated long ago the power of combining forces to develop contract review processes that deliver high quality – and faster – services at a lower cost. In October 2013, Integreon won the International Association for Contract and Commercial Management's 2013 Innovation Award for "Outstanding Service Provider" for its contract management services and support to Microsoft Corporation.

In a press release, Lucy Bassli, then Microsoft's assistant general counsel, explained the background to the collaboration:

"Four years ago we began the search for a service provider who could go beyond mere augmentation of resources and help us re-design and improve upon our contract review processes. Through the relationship we established with Integreon, we've seen a dramatic improvement in the efficiency of our contract review process. Our in-house team has also been able to focus on higher level activities while furthering their own legal careers here at Microsoft."[26]

The press release further explains:

"Prior to engaging with Integreon, Microsoft realized that its existing paralegal resourcing model for legal contract review was not sustainable in the long term. The volume of procurement contracts flowing into Microsoft's Global Contracting Office was significant and growing rapidly. The turn-around time for legal review was averaging three days per contract and causing delays in the procurement process for needed goods and services. In response, Microsoft initiated a dual track effort to study their current contract processes and the opportunities offered by legal process

outsourcing (LPO). After a rigorous selection process, Microsoft selected Integreon as its LPO partner.

Integreon's paralegals and lawyers operating from delivery centers in Fargo, North Dakota and Bristol, UK work as an extension of the Microsoft legal department. The close collaboration and integration of the Integreon and Microsoft teams ensured that the engagement realized short term successes and laid the groundwork for expansion of the program as greater volumes and types of contracts, including foreign language contracts, were brought into scope.

Microsoft's cost for legal contract review has been significantly reduced. The Integreon teams in Fargo and Bristol handle 20,000 contracts per year in 14 languages and across 125 countries. At the same time, the average turnaround time for legal review has dropped from three days to less than one, and the percentage of contracts meeting the agreed-upon turnaround time has increased from 86 percent to 99 percent. The increased productivity and reduced costs to manage contracts were complemented by high quality output, as results consistently exceed Microsoft's 98.4 percent quality target.

"The success we've had at Microsoft and our recognition from the IACCM demonstrate that the traditional model for legal services delivery can be changed for the better. Integreon has the legal process re-engineering expertise, industry knowledge, and global delivery platform that allow us to provide our clients with substantial legal process improvement in tandem with cost reduction," said Brent Larlee, global head, Legal Services at Integreon. "Ours is not simply a cost arbitrage approach. It is about aligning the right resources with the right tasks to deliver the right outcomes while still reducing cost."[27]

More law firms are providing consulting services in addition to their legal practice, providing expertise in areas like legal operations, regulatory compliance, risk management, and business strategy. These services often overlap with traditional consulting firms but leverage the law firm's specialized legal expertise.

- Eversheds has several consultancies and different staffing models to help the firm and its clients streamline procedures and control costs. One of the consultancies, Eversheds Consulting, was designed to help in-house legal teams address the challenges of running their departments efficiently, to use new technologies in order to facilitate process

improvement, and to help the legal department provide better value to their businesses in areas such as legal operations, governance, regulatory compliance, risk management, and financial services. This separate consulting arm assists clients with non-legal strategic needs, particularly for organizations in heavily regulated industries.
- Clifford Chance (Clifford Chance Applied Solutions) provides consulting services focused on legal technology, legal operations, and compliance through its specialized tech solutions and helps clients adopt legal tech tools, streamline operations, and manage regulatory requirements effectively.
- K&L Gates Consulting focuses on public policy, regulatory consulting, government relations, and global trade consulting. K&L Gates provides consulting in areas like government advocacy, legislative strategy, and regulatory compliance, often blending legal advice with consulting solutions for public affairs.
- Baker McKenzie provides global consulting services in compliance, supply chain management, cross-border transactions, and corporate governance. The firm is known for offering comprehensive consulting services to multinational companies needing help with global operations and regulatory challenges.
- Reed Smith Consulting specializes in risk management, regulatory consulting, compliance, and process improvement. Reed Smith provides clients with consulting services focused on improving operational efficiency, particularly in regulated industries like healthcare and finance.
- Dentons (Nextlaw) labs provides consulting on legal innovation, technology adoption, and legal operations. Dentons offers legal process improvement consulting and assists clients with innovative solutions to enhance operational efficiency.
- The accounting firms are finding ways to add value as well. Deloitte Legal offers legal and consulting services in regulatory compliance, data privacy, technology consulting, mergers and acquisitions, and legal risk management. Deloitte's legal division works alongside its broader consulting practices to help clients manage legal risks while enhancing business performance. EY Law (Ernst & Young) provides integrated legal and consulting services on corporate governance, regulatory compliance, employment law, and cross-border transactions. As part of the EY group, EY Law combines its legal expertise with consulting to help businesses manage legal risks while improving

operations. PwC Legal (PwC Law) is part of PricewaterhouseCoopers, providing both legal and consulting services in areas such as corporate governance, regulatory compliance, risk management, and cybersecurity. PwC's legal services work closely with its consulting branch to offer integrated solutions that combine legal, tax, and operational strategies.

Using process improvement to collaborate with clients effectively can be approached with training, workshops, and project work using an array of process improvement methodologies and tools. At its core, employing Lean Sigma with a cross functional, cross-organizational team produces extraordinary results. Regardless, by working together, teams can tackle streamlining workflows, increasing transparency, enhancing communication, and focusing on delivering consistent value together and creating a more efficient, client-focused experience.

Starting with Lean Sigma principle number one – specify value in the eyes of the client – begin with discussions about the client's business goals, pain points, and expectations. This will help tailor process improvement initiatives to directly address what matters most to the client. Use VOC (Voice of the Client) tools to gather detailed insights through surveys, interviews, and/or feedback sessions. Understand what they value in the collaboration, such as faster turnaround, clarity in communication, or cost predictability.

Consider "low hanging fruit" opportunities to work together:
- *Review the criteria for selecting a process improvement project* – this should give you plenty of opportunities for collaboration.
- *Contract lifecycle management* – streamline the approval process for client contracts by using automation tools and standardizing contract templates to reduce turnaround time.
- *Intake and client onboarding* – implement a lean intake or onboarding process with clear steps, defined roles, and automated notifications to minimize delays and confusion.
- *Feedback* – set up continuous feedback loops using surveys after major milestones, then applying that feedback to improve the next project phase or future engagements.

Process mapping of all kinds is an excellent starting point. Kean Miller, Krieg Devault, and Levenfeld Pearlstein have all spent a day with clients mapping a process together. The conversations are rich. The map that is produced generates profound respect and appreciation for all the stakeholders and workers. Identifying all the steps, pain points, and bottlenecks allows us to see inefficiencies like delays, redundant steps, or miscommunication and reduce or remove waste, especially focusing on those that impact key performance metrics, including the client experience. Other visual tools that are fit for purpose – like Kanban boards, shared calendars, or dashboards – can be developed to give leaders and clients visibility into each project's progress, milestones, and timelines.

Finally, roles, responsibilities, budgets, and timelines can be clarified, and feedback loops put in place at the beginning of projects to avoid misunderstandings and keep both the internal team and clients on the same page. This proactive approach to detect inefficiencies or address client concerns strengthens the relationship by showing not just responsiveness but anticipation.

This is how we all know what we are doing, who is doing it, when things are getting done, how to do those things and how we're doing – because we have a process for all that and a way to manage it. Tracking and measuring the KPIs, such as project timelines, response times, or client satisfaction scores ensures we stay in lockstep with each other. Then planning, doing, checking, acting, and getting better all the time give us ongoing and endless opportunities to collaborate.

Collaborating and co-designing solutions is a bonding, energizing, and motivating activity. Working with clients on continuous improvement initiatives where there is brainstorming, uncovering best practices, catching people doing things right, alleviating stress, tackling pain points, and finding better ways to work together and develop innovative solutions to challenges – this is the best work a team can do together. For those who are in it for the LTR, a long-term relationship and partnership means being able to flexibly adapt processes to each client's unique needs and focus on outcomes that add measurable value to the client's business. Whether it's cost reduction, time savings, or strategic insights, we want to deliver results that directly align with their goals.

References
1. https://legalleansigma.com/wp-content/uploads/2018/04/Collaborative-improvement-by-C.-MacDonagh-and-T.-Sager.pdf
2. www.dupontlegalmodel.com.
3. www.cba.org/cba/cle/PDF/10PM_Schmitt_Dupontchapt1-2.pdf
4. https://parkerpoe.azurewebsites.net/news/2017/08/parker-poe-teams-up-with-clients-to-increase

5   www.poynerspruill.com/2018/07/27/poyner-spruill-redefines-attorney-client-collaboration-and-raises-the-bar-with-recent-client-service-initiatives/
6   MacDonagh C.A. and Sager T.L., "Collaborative improvement: Use Lean Six Sigma to become a trusted business partner to clients." https://legalleansigma.com/wp-content/uploads/2018/04/Collaborative-improvement-by-C.-MacDonagh-and-T.-Sager.pdf
7   Sager T.L., and Winkelman, S.L. "Six Sigma: Positioning for Competitive Advantage", ACCA Docket 19, No. 1, 2001.
8   www.agileattorney.com
9   *Ibid.*
10 *Ibid.*
11 "Six Sigma Saves a Fortune", *iSixSigma magazine*, January/February 2007.
12 10-Year Experience Integrating Strategic Performance Improvement Initiatives: Can the Balanced Scorecard, Six Sigma®, and Team Training All Thrive in a Single Hospital? https://pubmed.ncbi.nlm.nih.gov/21249921/
13 ALM Legal Intelligence, "Pricing Professionals – Essential to Law Firms, An Ally to Clients" (white paper), 2014.
14 www.acc.com/services-initiatives/value-challenge/resources
15 *Ibid.*
16 Duncan, S. S., "5 Firms Take Bold Approaches", *ABA Law Practice magazine*, volume 38, No. 6, November/December 2012.
17 *Ibid.*
18 Duncan, S. S., "The Progressive Model for Law Firm/Client Partnering", *ABA Law Practice magazine*, vol. 38, No. 6, November/December 2012.
19 *Ibid.*
20 "Eight Tips for Innovative Client Service", *ABA Law Practice Magazine*, vol. 38, No. 6, November/December 2012. www.americanbar.org/publications/law_practice_magazine/2012/november-december/8-tips-for-innovative-client-service.html.8.
21 *Ibid.*
22 Davis, D. "Lawyers jump into process improvement", 28 March 2014, Process Excellent Network. www.processexcellencenetwork.com/lean-six-sigma-business-transformation/articles/lawyers-jump-into-process-improvement.
23 www2.deloitte.com/content/dam/Deloitte/us/Documents/Tax/us-tax-key-findings-from-the-14th-annual-law-department-operations-survey.pdf
24 Sager T.L., and Winkelman, S.L. "Six Sigma: Positioning for Competitive Advantage", ACCA Docket 19, No. 1, 2001.
25 *Ibid.*
26 www.prnewswire.co.uk/news-releases/integreon-wins-iaccm-2013-innovation-award-for-outstanding-contract-management-services-and-support-to-microsoft-corporation-228760121.html
27 *Ibid.*

Chapter 15:
Creating a culture of continuous improvement

"It is not necessary to change. Survival is not mandatory."
W. Edwards Deming

By now, readers won't be surprised to arrive at the final chapter to learn that there's a process for creating a culture of continuous improvement. That is because continuous improvement is a series of repeatable, describable steps that generates outcomes.

A continuous improvement (CI) culture is where people believe there is always room for improvement and that each is not just empowered but expected and encouraged to take an active role in identifying issues or opportunities and then works on them. It means being comfortable with being uncomfortable, for it involves challenging the status quo, suggesting ideas, and surfacing improvement needs. It is part of daily activities, not something that only happens when we gather for workshops.

To have a culture of CI, evolving into a learning organization is fundamental. It means that development is valued and that things that are less than perfect or even outright failures are viewed as growth opportunities. At its core, the relentless pursuit of doing things better is integral to the organization's DNA – it is baked into every single thing that every person does every day. The elements are known, but building a culture is not easy – it requires commitment, solid management practices, leaders and followers.

Building the culture is a collective journey that involves changing mindsets, leadership that sets an example, designing the architecture and building the program, implementing structure and processes that fuel innovation. This takes a lot of focused attention, communication, employee engagement, positive reinforcement, education and incentives, purpose, and mission – they are all ingredients for success. Progress along the continuum does not happen automatically; leaders must deliberately choose to build organizational capability and accrue permanent benefits. The best programs are part carrot and part stick. Celebrating success is important, and so is compliance.

The first thing to keep in mind is that every team and each organization is unique. As with everything else in this book, the idea is to use the frameworks, concepts, and tools with the right balance of rigor and discipline on the one hand, and flexibility and adroit artistry on the other. Be willing to try things and try saying, "How fascinating!" (a nod to Benjamin Zander, conductor of the Boston Philharmonic and co-author of the book, *The Art of Possibility*) when the unexpected happens.

From the outset and at every turn, we must recall that improvement work necessarily affects all the other Ps in the P+ EcoSystem. In particular, the organizational development, strategy, and structure must align with continuous improvement objectives.

The "Ps" in business refer to key components or strategies on which businesses focus to achieve success. Traditionally, the "Four Ps" of marketing were introduced by E. Jerome McCarthy, which later evolved into broader frameworks as the business environment became more complex. The first is Product, meaning the work product and service that is offered to meet the needs of clients, with design, quality, features, branding, packaging, and lifecycle included. The second is Price – the amount of money paid. This requires us to think about pricing strategies and value, both real and perceived. The third is Place – the locations and mechanisms where the product is distributed and made available to clients. Fourth is Promotion – the methods used to communicate with and persuade potential clients about the product, which includes ads, business development, public relations, and marketing.

Additional Ps are People, Process, Physical evidence (meaning the tangible and intangible proof that exists in the product or service, such as the company's office, branding, online presence, reputation, reviews and referrals, etc.), Packaging, Positioning, and Performance.

All the Ps help organizations structure their strategies and continuously improve to meet client and market demands, optimize operations, and achieve long-term success.

To combine accountability for goals and a positive culture of growth, consider the following four Cs of continuous improvement:
1. Continuous operator training and education.
2. Clear and frequent communication about upcoming changes.
3. Chances for employees to ask questions or offer ideas.
4. Consistent positive attention to successful improvements.[1]

The four Cs contribute to accountability by fostering value in existing team members rather than whittling down the workforce as a shortcut to savings.

In the long run, no upgrades to machinery or production method adjustments can replace the value of a team committed to continuous improvement manufacturing.

Since our sequence is always People, Process, Platform, it makes sense to focus there first. For those who think machines will replace lawyers entirely, take heart, keep calm, and focus on the people.

Why being a human in the workplace is hard
An inquiry into what makes people do what they do is a good place to start to understand how to build a culture of CI. Legal Lean Sigma Institute scholars in residence, Jessica McBride and Jerry Rosenthal, are at the forefront of exploring the intersection of behavioral economics and process improvement. They were the first to publish on this fascinating area and their work on connecting important concepts related to the irrationality of humans and how to design for them is instructive.

The following is by them, reproduced with permission.

It is far easier to continue using our Automatic system to work a process that we are so used to using, it has become habit; rather than engaging our Reflective system to learn something new and feel uncomfortable and vulnerable. And that is what the authors love most about the space of process improvement. It's not just the tools of Lean, Six Sigma, Theory of Constraints, and the like. It is the lifelong process of learning new ideas across the wide spectrum of disciplines and determining if they apply to our work in meaningful ways.

Behavioral economics might be that new set of ideas and tools to take our processes to another level.

Neoclassical economics is a broad theory that focuses on supply and demand as the driving forces behind the production, pricing, and consumption of goods and services. Neoclassical economics tells us that people will behave in ways that are in their best interest; individuals maximize utility and firms maximize profit.

Behavioral economics studies the effects of psychological, cognitive, emotional, cultural, and social factors on the decisions of individuals and institutions. Some examples of behavioral economics include recency bias, confirmation bias, and loss aversion.

Humans are biased by recent information and do not look at the total amount of information available to them or even consider asking for more relevant data to support or disprove their position. This is called recency bias. This then leads to confirmation bias or looking for those data points that only support one's position. Humans are loss averse, which means that losses are avoided more than equivalent gains are sought. People fall in love with things they already have, placing higher value on them than what the actual value and market price might be. Humans are affected by bounded willpower, which is the idea that even given an understanding of the optimal choice, humans will often still choose whatever brings the most short-term benefit.

Lean practitioners will never be able to fully debias anyone. Yet we can become more aware that perspectives exist which may not have been arrived at through rational means. Using tools already within the Lean toolbox such as the 5-Whys, Fishbones, and Iceberg to engage in structured problem solving and understanding root cause yields beneficial results. No doubt, behavioral economics in one form or another has played a role in arriving at the current state of any process and will have a stronghold on it as the team seeks to create an enhanced future state.

Never underestimate the power of emotions and why being a human in the workplace is hard. Most often, we assume people will see the problem from the same perspective that we do (False consensus effect.) As leaders of change (and let's face it, process improvement *is* change), we must seek to understand the other's perspective to find that lever to pull to move that person to the perspective we want them to see. We want to help them move to the right solution.

One great thing about these concepts is that we don't need to add more tools or frameworks to our toolbox. We can use Lean tools we are already familiar with, such as structured problem solving and root cause analysis to learn. We all navigate through our own biases and blind spots. For example, the aptly named "blind spot bias" is where we fail to see our own cognitive biases. "Sure, other people might be irrational, but I'm not!" Yes, you are. We all are. How can we combat her own innate biases while also guiding others through change? We suggest Awareness. Make yourself aware of the change and the need for it. Then you can start to build desire for the change.

In addition to stakeholder awareness, there is also the important concept of self-awareness. Physicist Richard Feynman (Nobel Prize winner in Physics in 1965) had some guiding principles. The first principle is that you must not fool yourself, and you are the easiest person to fool. One way we fool ourselves is by imagining that we know more than we do; we think we are experts. Yet, there are many ways in which we fool ourselves simply by a lack of self-awareness. How many of us are really aware of what we think, why we hold a certain perspective, and why we are resistant to change our view in light of new information?

We are all guilty of clouded judgement due to confirmation bias and availability bias. Confirmation bias is the tendency to interpret new evidence as confirmation of one's existing beliefs and theories. Availability bias is the tendency to rely on information that comes readily to mind when evaluating situations and making decisions. Being a human in the workplace is hard and change is one of, if not the hardest aspect of one's professional journey. To further complicate, there is no one magic answer for this scenario, or other similar scenarios you've likely encountered during your career. We suggest starting with Awareness (both self and situational) and consider all biases to be what we call a "lens" – a way of looking at a situation through specific criteria. It takes some practice, yet what it will do is allow you, and anyone else involved, to consider and ask better questions to gain a deeper understanding of both the human and the situation (people and process.)

Bringing people along for the ride is more easily said than done. There is a direct financial impact which is about getting from A to B in the most efficient way possible. Yet there is a human cost when there is resistance, lack of clarity, and various biases at play. And people are operating in both an existing way and transitioning to a new way simultaneously. Speed is important and moving things too quickly or too slowly has consequences.

Behavioral economics is a key tool in understanding the financial and human costs concurrently. We offer select biases for the reader to consider, selected based on our own experience and utility. Consider using these as a starting point for your journey.

- *More labor bias:* How often do our leaders default to a position of the need to hire more people as the path to solve process delays? What are the consequences of adding more labor without full comprehension of current state and root causes? Using the Lens of "more labor bias" and thinking through what has happened in the past and what could happen in the future is a good starting point.
- *The calculus of value:* Humans overvalue (overestimate) what we have, what we know, and what we believe. And we undervalue (underestimate) the opposite. For example, Dan Ariely has stated that managers overvalue proactive participation in group settings

and undervalue quiet people. Many of us can relate to this type of experience almost daily. How can we be more aware of this when leading groups, and give opportunities for less extroverted employees to add value comfortably?
- *Magic bullet bias:* Technology will fix everything. Technology can fix a lot, but if your process is garbage, it will likely not fix what is broken. People and process is nearly always the place to start.[2]

Creating a culture of continuous improvement requires finding ways of reducing resistance to facilitate transformation for serving both internal and external customers wherever possible. Planning for change and managing it well is going to be key.

One of the principles of Lean Sigma is to align and empower employees. This is a key idea for developing and sustaining a culture of continuous improvement and, obviously, there are many ways to accomplish this. One soap box item relates to website listings. If the only "people" who work at a firm are lawyers, then it's fine to limit the list to them. But that's not the case. I propose either call the list "lawyers" or include the "people" at the firm! We do understand that not every law firm is quite ready to become the type of environment where the term "non-lawyer" that is so offensive to some is not used to describe the "people". However, surely there is recognition that exclusive behavior does not support an inclusive culture and that it is more challenging to create a culture of continuous improvement if the only "people" engaged in the effort are the lawyers.

It is instructive to consider how law can employ Toyota's "Pull the Cord"[3] system, also known as Andon (which means "lantern" in Japanese). This is a critical component of Toyota's Toyota Production System (TPS) and reflects its commitment to quality control, continuous improvement, and empowering workers. The Andon system allows any worker on the production line to immediately stop the production process if they notice a problem, defect, or issue that could affect product quality or safety.

When the cord is pulled, it triggers an Andon board (a visual display system), which lights up or sounds an alarm to signal that a problem has been identified in a particular station or area of the production line. The team leader or supervisor is alerted and comes over to assess the issue. They either help resolve it on the spot or, if the problem cannot be quickly fixed, the production line is stopped. The goal is to catch defects or issues as early as possible in the production process, preventing faulty products from moving further down the line. This helps avoid expensive rework and ensures high-quality products.

It also empowers workers since they have the authority and responsibility to stop production. This creates a culture of ownership and continuous improvement where every worker is actively involved in maintaining quality. By stopping the production line when an issue arises, problems are addressed in real-time, preventing them from recurring and improving overall operational efficiency. The "Pull the Cord" practice also ties into Just-in-Time (JIT) production, another pillar of Lean manufacturing, by ensuring that each step of the process only proceeds if the previous step has been completed without defects.

This approach fosters continuous improvement. When problems are identified, it creates an opportunity for teams to improve processes, equipment, or training to prevent the issue from occurring again. Workers are more engaged because they play an active role in maintaining quality and improving processes, and their contributions are valued by the company

This focus on respect for people is a key part of Toyota's corporate culture and the Toyota Way. Instead of punishing mistakes, Toyota encourages workers to raise issues. This fosters a problem-solving culture where errors are seen as opportunities to improve the system rather than failures.

How might law embrace this people-centered philosophy, where we eliminate fear of reprisal? There is no one right answer, but the "People, Process, Platform" approach, combined with the foundational principles of Lean Sigma, is always going to be a winning formula. Lean Sigma and Change Management models are processes with philosophies, art, and science that help us manage, innovate, and reimagine the way we do and deliver our work. If we strive to be learning organizations rather than places where perfection is the singular goal, we create a culture where people are encouraged – even expected – to experiment and innovate.

Pick the right methodology and the right tools to help build a culture of continuous improvement and isolate the drivers of change that are most relevant to your organization. For law, there are significant business drivers that give us plenty of reasons to continuously improve. One of those is the truth that more legal professionals have been forced to accept – many legal services are commodities.

The International Bar Association's 2016 report, "Times are a-changin': disruptive innovation and the legal profession":

"Seeks to investigate Professor Christensen's 'disruptive innovation' theory as applicable to the legal profession. It provides a brief analysis of various changes occurring within the legal market, their potential consequences for both buyers and sellers of legal services, and the drivers and barriers to innovation. Of particular interest is the evolution of legal services from the purely bespoke to the commoditized.

"There are three main drivers of such a change. First, the 'more-for-less' challenge, which refers to the growing number of clients demanding more efficient legal services for less money. Secondly, the gradual liberalization of the profession, referring to the alternative business structures model. Thirdly, the vast improvements in information technology and, in particular, 'big data' and artificial intelligence, which offer significant efficiencies for the profession.

"Other drivers include growing competition from the 'big four' accounting firms and the spread of legal service providers using alternatives to the traditional law firm business model. Innovations – particularly those transforming legal services into standardized or packaged services – are likely to yield significant benefits for consumers in terms of cost, quality and access to justice. They also offer substantial opportunities for those firms who are able to deliver real value to consumers."[4]

Approaches to process improvement in law

The Legal Lean Sigma Institute conducted a study on how law was approaching PI and evolving into a CI culture and the results were published in a white paper entitled "Law Firm Approaches to Process Improvement".[5]

Many questions were asked about the different approaches that respondents were taking with regard to employing process improvement. The years of working with clients around the world validates the responses we got some time ago. Law approaches process improvement in the following three primary ways:
1. Strategically, including organizational design and development.
2. Education and skill building.
3. Demonstration projects.

It is more typical now for a CEO, CLO, COO, general counsel, commanding officer, managing partner, or director with a CI mindset and a background in process improvement to join an organization. Overnight, continuous improvement becomes a "pillar" or a "cornerstone" of the strategy and all initiatives must be aligned and supportive of it. As such, we do see that an increasing number of organizations are taking a strategic approach and are doing organizational development and structuring work at a firm, department, or practice group level. Some have made a strategic decision to bring process improvement into their firm because of a strong belief that there will be competitive advantages to building a culture, a structure, and deep process improvement disciplines and skills into the organization.

The objectives of such a program are to comprehensively redesign the processes of a business, to make them as capable and efficient as possible and transform the performance of the business and build the capacity and infrastructure for ongoing change. Some of the elements to support a systematic change program may be naturally present. To create the others, the program must include activities to build them.

The key elements to support a strategic approach to process improvement are:

- Process perspective – performance targets and measurements related to process performance.
- A method for surfacing, selecting, prioritizing and resourcing process improvement work.
- Clear needs and goals for change that are documented and communicated as a "compelling business case" and that include problem/opportunity statements that articulate the worst-case scenario for doing nothing.
- Assessment and decision-making process to create changes in plans and scope.
- Change skills and tools such as leadership training, change agent training, and awareness training for the general employee population, mentoring and coaching to supplement skills.
- Improvement culture including ownership, areas of responsibility, program champions and sponsors, support for change agents/teams.
- Knowledge-building – mechanisms to share learning, such as events, intranets, programs, courses, and, of course, a knowledge management system.
- Benefits capture – measurement systems to monitor results that allow translation of improvements into benefits.
- Change infrastructure – steering committees, extensive communication, goals linked to employee objectives, performance management, and reward systems.

Another strategy, as we reviewed in the last chapter, is to take direct part in a client's own process improvement activities. This helps to instill a culture of continuous improvement quickly, where it offers significant and unique opportunities for relationship and client development along with opportunities to truly demonstrate alignment with the business and being a "good partner".

Naturally, for law departments in manufacturing companies and firms with manufacturing clients, there are immediate, ongoing, and endless opportunities for delivering excellent client service using PI and building a CI culture.

MassMutual

MassMutual started with a company-wide focus on the principles of lean manufacturing. Within two years, the philosophy made its way to the law department. One of the initial undertakings was to map out the law department's value stream, documenting everything it takes to get to a finished product, examining how each step flows (or doesn't) to the next, and analyzing that process. It also ended up being an opportunity to increase collaboration, as the team hunkered down in a room together to work through it, step-by-step.

That diagnosis laid the groundwork for where the department needed to go, what to pay attention to, and how to approach problems. As a result, MassMutual overhauled its legal operations function. Building that foundation, essentially from scratch, was an opportunity to streamline the work, which is a key principle – ensuring that the most appropriate personnel are handling each task. It became clear that lawyers were wasting too much time chasing invoices and negotiating with outside counsel, and that each attorney had their own approach.

The ops team took on the opportunity to tackle these inefficiencies and created positions for legal intake and workflow coordinators, a completely new concept for the law department. From there, the team standardized and streamlined the engagement process with outside law firms. Before the changes, invoices would sit for 300 days on average. The average turnaround time changed to 60 days – an 80 percent reduction, freeing up several million dollars of accruals, enabling more predictable financial forecasting and improved relationships with the company's firms.

Today, it is not unusual to hear a senior leader in MassMutual's law department say, "We really need a standard process for that". The shift in thinking and overwhelming buy-in have been remarkable over a short time period, especially considering that some lawyers were resistant to the lean approach at first.[6]

Foley & Lardner

Foley & Lardner launched its Legal Innovation Hub[7] in 2013 for NextGen manufacturers, a firm-wide business development and marketing program devoted to next-generation manufacturing. With an approach reminiscent of the Dupont Legal Model, the hub is comprised of a dedicated network of departments, industry teams, and practice groups and helps manufacturing clients engage in dialogues and tackle the transformational issues associated with next-generation manufacturing.

At the time, Foley had been serving US manufacturers for nearly 175 years, so the firm knew the industry well. As a result of this program, Foley strengthened its reputation as the "go-to firm" for next-gen manufacturers, helping them collaborate on the legal and business challenges presented by the convergence of technology and manufacturing.

Legal Lean Sigma training for continuous improvement – methods and qualifications

A planned approach is required for building and sustaining a culture of CI. It involves strategic thinking, goal setting, and preparation. It involves discussions and decisions about roles and responsibilities related to both process improvement and project management. It also requires developing and enhancing skills, so training, mentorship, and project experience with a thoughtful cadence of work is essential. Finally, the structure itself must be designed, built, tested, and rolled out. This includes developing a project selection and prioritization method that works for the enterprise and then teaching people how it is used.

Typically, then, members of the management, executive, and steering committee teams will receive some level of training. Several key constituencies will need specific skills in order to support and drive change.

- Leaders: must be capable of communicating the need for change and the vision of the future, steering change teams, eliminating roadblocks, and modeling new behaviors.
- Facilitators/change agents (internal) will need skills in specific Lean Six Sigma tools, change agency, team leadership, and project management.

- Team leader training for the people who will lead projects, which focuses on facilitation, project management, change agency, and project communication skills.
- Staff in general will need some facility with Lean Sigma tools, as well as possess process knowledge and interest in improving their processes.

Many organizations prefer to begin with education and skill development. This is always suggested as it becomes challenging to think about a program without a basic understanding of concepts, possibilities, and terms.

Whether they are introductory workshops or a deeper dive, for law, learning about PI in context is so helpful. It greatly reduces the amount of time they would need to spend (and do not have) bridging concepts from other industries (like manufacturing or software development). With certification courses, legal and business professionals participate in programs together as cross-functional, diverse teams. One objective is to begin generating interest in and developing knowledge about Lean and Six Sigma as they specifically relate to the law. As soon as we introduce the concepts and tools of process improvement, we also begin using the client's perspective and a data-based approach to identify potential projects to use in tailoring our certification courses.

In our open enrollment courses, participants take a survey to indicate a process of interest to use during the exercise components of the courses. In privately delivered programs, we usually identify a portfolio of potential/high-impact projects and then carefully select cross-functional teams and team leaders who might carry out each project if the client decides to improve that process following the course. This may involve clients, vendors and/or suppliers as well.

With this approach, the participants successfully complete the course and are able to take part in the first project; we accomplish this by providing the teams with an opportunity to begin applying the concepts they are learning in our courses. They draft elements of their process improvement projects, such as project charters and rough process maps in the class together. They also earn a White or Yellow Belt Certification in process improvement and project management. Additionally, we work with our clients in their applications for continuing legal education credits – and, interestingly, we have always been approved. As such, we accomplish multiple objectives with this approach.

Because the exercises in these tailored courses will deal with projects under consideration, it becomes easier to assess them. Outputs of the course include excellent teamwork, discussions, thinking, engagement, and work product in the form of draft business cases, problem/opportunity statements, and process maps. All artifacts can be used in making the determination as to whether and which projects will be selected.

Speaking about the structure of our training programs, Amy Hrehovcik of Ailey Advisors observes:

> *"While fear of failure is universal, the less accustomed a person is to failing, the larger this fear becomes. By creating a safe environment where the firm or department engages each other – and their clients – in process conversations, they begin to develop muscles that have been dormant. They realize that employees and clients are craving these dialogues. The structure of the Legal Lean Sigma courses and project give a voice and a platform to all members of the team in a way that levels the playing field. Emotion is removed from decisions, frustration is reduced, and firms demonstrate respect for their workers and clients by not pretending to understand their wishes better than they do."*

Clients are using their training and certifications as a competitive advantage. For example, Monaco Cooper Lamme & Carr PLLC boasts:

> *"Our Firm Administrator practices Legal Lean Sigma® and Project Management and she trains our staff with those best practices. That means MCLC operates efficiently and consequently so do your cases."*[8]

Typically, developing foundational knowledge allows leaders to identify and assess opportunities and the people who will contribute to the development of the continuous improvement mindset and culture. It is significantly easier to think and talk about, plan, and do this when a common language and understanding is established.

Process improvement is transformative within the legal industry, and how those that embrace it can create an upward spiral of efficiency, cost savings, and client satisfaction. Yet, those in the law may be risk averse or unwilling to depart from traditional ways of working, even when those ways may not be working well.

According to Fred Esposito,[9] COO of the regional law firm Rivkin Radler, process improvement changes this thought process. He says:

"Process improvement methodologies and tools are invaluable for understanding ways to improve how legal work is currently produced. Once data shows the magnitude of the problems and opportunities, those risk-averse lawyers realize very quickly that it is less risky to change than it is to continue to operate in the way they always have. They are also getting more attuned to the importance of creating a continuous improvement (dare we say innovative!) culture that focuses on the employee experience and develops new competitive advantages in a marketplace where the war for talent is real.

"There are also many case studies, so we have plenty of precedent and good responses to the age-old question, 'Who else is doing that?' Despite traditional resistance to innovation, many law firms are recognizing the benefits of training their people and their clients about process improvement and project management methodologies. This kind of "speaking the same language" facilitates all sorts of productive and positive discussions, including how law firms can increasingly assist clients with their own strategic initiatives, which contributes greatly providing added value and being a good business partner."

Another approach that law firms are taking is to engage in project work to experience what Lean Sigma can do and consider how it might work best in their organization more broadly. Initially some of our clients are unsure as to whether process improvement is advantageous enough to provide a good return on investment. They might be unwilling to make a significant training investment at the outset. Some just want to begin right away. Clients in these categories often prefer to start with minimal training followed by a demonstration project with Just in Time training and coaching to assess the methodologies, the results, and the fit of Lean Sigma with the firm's culture.

If a firm elects to proceed in this manner, without the support of the classroom training to provide context and frameworks and begin developing skills internally, we are always obligated to suggest that the projects will rely in largest measure on expert facilitation from experienced external consultants to lead the projects and deliver the results (whether it is us or someone else). In this case, our expectations should be limited to providing a robust demonstration of the power of the Lean Sigma methodology, with results that provide a good return on investment.

Conventionally, we will work only on engagements that we believe have an excellent chance of succeeding, especially as we begin and there is less tolerance for anything but a "slam dunk". So, selecting the right project with the right scope and getting the right people and structure in place is important – it becomes the blueprint immediately. We know we won't have a second chance to get it right the first time and we will not let our clients fail on their first attempt.

The standard DMAIC process is carried out, during and after which the organization evaluates both the success of the project and the ability of process improvement to deliver benefits. At this time, many choose to discuss a more in-depth approach that will not only provide project results but will also transfer skills and knowledge so that the organization starts on the path toward self-sufficiency in process improvement and project management skills.

Because the tools of process improvement and project management are so linear and sequential, they work well – extremely well – and are a natural fit in a law environment. The DMAIC structure is effective for many reasons – it is logical and rigorous, requiring us to exercise great discipline, and it simultaneously encourages us to be our most creative within a failsafe framework. This translates to good experiences right away with working on operational excellence and innovation.

The treatment that we have found particularly useful in the law is the Kaizen methodology. This approach allows a tightly scoped project to be delivered in a compressed time period. Because lawyer leaders usually prefer to start and finish things quickly once they have decided to move forward, we have found that the shorter duration and more incremental improvement approach of Kaizen is appealing to our clients.

Regardless, to get started and structure for success, it is important to consider existing culture, drivers, and any misconceptions that exist, including the idea that, "In order to win professionally, someone else must lose, that creativity and innovation are bi-products of speed and uninhibited and unstructured, workflows," as Hrehovcik says. "Others include the beliefs that there is no process, that talented people can overcome a broken process and that what we're doing is working."

In the words of Jim Collins:

"The great task, rarely achieved, is to blend creative intensity with relentless discipline so as to amplify the creativity rather than destroy it. When you marry operating excellence with innovation, you multiply the value of your creativity."[10]

While some firms, departments, offices, and service providers have made their work visible, others are engaged in efforts well under the radar. Nonetheless, evidence exists to suggest that all approaches produce successes and certainly position firms that employ PI and PM to great competitive advantage.

Leadership

One key to success, regardless of approach, is leadership. In the executive summary to its 2020 special report, "Law Firms in Transition", Altman Weil says the following:

"We are not suggesting a total overhaul of law firm structure, systems and culture. We know that won't happen. In the history of law firms, we have never really seen rapid, radical change, and we don't expect to see it now. However, firm leaders should be trying to push through four persistent barriers to change:

1. *Partners resist most change efforts. Of course they do. Your firm's most powerful and influential partners – the ones who control client relationships, decide work assignments, and enjoy the highest incomes – have the most to lose from any potential disruption to their relationships and workflows. Therefore, you might need to conduct experiments with adjacent partners and practices, develop proof of concept and work your way in.*

2. *Clients aren't asking for it. Many clients never did ask for significant changes from outside counsel, and some never will, but they have undeniably voted with their feet. Nearly seven in ten law firms have seen their corporate clients pull work in-house and most of the remaining firms said they see it coming. If you wait for clients to ask how you can serve them better, you'll have waited too long. Clients want and expect to have conversations with your partners about pricing, budgets, project staffing, matter management efficiency and value.*

3. *Firms are not feeling enough economic pain to motivate change. Some years are better than others, high earners can live on less, and partnerships know how to tighten the belt when necessary, as they have demonstrated over the past few months. It might provide some comfort to know that through the last recession, partnership cohesion was found to have been sustained or even strengthened in most law firms. It takes a lot to kill a law firm, but still, it is going to be necessary to keep your most important partners happy (which is to*

say, well paid) and not let other firms entice them away with enough incremental compensation to overcome their loyalty, comfort and inertia. Improving your firm's margins, profitability and incomes will help you retain and attract key talent.

4. *Most partners are unaware of what they might do differently. Curiously, we have observed that the class of intellectuals known as law firm partners are not a hugely curious lot when it comes to changing their ways. You'll have to work selectively and collaboratively with those who will work with you to identify new pricing and delivery models and try them out. If it's still true, year after year, that partners don't know what they might do differently, we see that as a failure of leadership. Firm management should be facilitating and requiring discussions along these lines to generate ideas, commitments and buy-in and to accelerate learning.*

"Law firm leaders do not have to develop their own ideas of what might work – we have years of data to answer those questions. Get the information into the hands of your management committee members, practice leaders, industry team leaders and key administrators. Challenge them to test new approaches with urgency and purpose. Hold them accountable."[11]

In an article on culture change through Lean Sigma, the Measure by Measure consulting firm asked, "As Lean Six Sigma practitioners, why should we care about culture?"[12] They answered that, based on their experience:

"We believe that top management understands the importance of values and cultures but prioritizes cultural change efforts low because of the perceived resistance, disparate consulting approaches, length of the effort, and correspondingly low probability of success...

"Lean Six Sigma consultants are uniquely positioned to approach cultural change from a fresh perspective. Our experience and follow-up research taught us that culture change is path dependent and that high trust / high cooperation cultures desired by so many senior management teams require the foundational discipline and support that is embodied in the Lean Six Sigma principles. The new Lean Six Sigma professionals can assist senior management in designing and implementing the systems, measurements, processes, and controls that will provide the foundational support for the high trust / high cooperation cultures required in the 21st century."

In a 2020 article on how law firms can overcome "innovation fatigue", Amol V. Bargaje, global chief innovation officer at Mayer Brown LLP, said:

> "Understanding and overcoming the barriers to adoption is both an art and a science. It is specific to each organization's culture, but there are some time-tested techniques with higher success rates. These include visible support from top leadership within the organization (firm leadership is visible, engaged and active on our innovation team); clear communication tailored to key audiences; adequate training in convenient formats (an online knowledge base and videos vs manuals); and an experienced support team. Innovation is a marathon, not a sprint. Just as a marathon requires preparation on many fronts, the successful pursuit of innovation requires a holistic strategy."[13]

In a 2023 KPMG survey of transformation leaders, 82 percent of respondents said the pace of transformation is accelerating.[14] The survey also found that organizations are typically running multiple change programs simultaneously and 60 percent of respondents said transformations have essentially become continuous.

> "Successfully managing continuous transformation requires four capabilities:
> - Tracking value – throughout the program, not just at the end.
> - Building roadmaps to turn a clear vision into quick, measurable outcomes.
> - Orchestrating multiple initiatives to take into account interconnections; it is no longer possible to manage projects independently or sequentially.
> - Managing the people experience. Transformation burnout is a risk and getting buy-in and adoption of new ways of working remain key to transformation success.
>
> "These capabilities will bring clarity and capacity to support continuous transformation. They deal with different aspects of the challenge, but they have a common theme: this work calls for more collaboration, innovation, and partnership across the organization. To truly succeed, you will need a cultural shift to encourage collaboration and adopt new ways of working."[15]

Knowledge management

I think of knowledge management as one of those "binding ingredients" that helps pull all of this together. To achieve greater collaboration, innovation, and partnership, we must develop mechanisms for documenting what we plan, what actually happened, and how we responded in ways that allow us to save and then access the information when we need it and in the formats that are most helpful.

A KM team or professional helps find and develop ways to capture, organize, find, and share knowledge across organizations, both internally and externally by creating systems and processes. They also use knowledge to improve and innovate. For any organization that has decided to create a culture of continuous improvement, KM is a must – and again, this is not one size fits all. Each organization will implement KM differently, according to its needs.

In a 2020 article titled "Knowledge Management as an Innovation Imperative" published in Legaltech News,[16] Jordan Galvin and Philip Bryce of Mayer Brown wrote:

> "Much has been written about the legal industry's efforts to provide greater value to clients at a lower cost. But the special challenges that large, global law firms face when implementing this innovation mandate are often overlooked. Increasingly, savvy clients want their firms to leverage meaningful data, streamline their workflows, and provide greater clarity and reliability on pricing. Doing so requires outside counsel to properly collect and store data, standardize work product to the extent practical, automate where possible, and develop holistic solutions that meet the aforementioned goals and promote client collaboration.
>
> "Knowledge management (KM) teams are essential to meet firms' innovation goals… KM serves as the bridge between practicing attorneys, business services teams and IT. Because many KM professionals are lawyers themselves, they have a level of subject matter expertise that allows them to relate to practicing lawyers, anticipate their needs, and communicate the value of products and initiatives. KM professionals also share an understanding of, and adaptability to, new technology, and can help the firm make wise investments by advising which tools will serve real business needs. As a liaison, a KM team solves several innovation struggles within large law firms."

The challenges in Big Law are, of course, different than other organizations. Management ought to respond thoughtfully and methodically (hint: that does not mean slowly!) by ensuring the firm has appropriate resources that are focused on and allocated to continuous improvement. An organization's adoption of continuous improvement techniques will pay for itself many times over. This investment will produce more efficient legal processes, which creates the capacity and capability to handle complex legal matters more quickly and with the right resources. By focusing on process improvement and project management, a firm or department can offer better service and more predictable outcomes, which contributes to higher satisfaction and stronger relationships with clients.

Looking to the future

Being a "forward-thinking" team that continually adapts to changes in the legal landscape is what clients want. Transforming culture and the way the entire organization carries out its work starts with the belief that improvement is required (i.e. there is a compelling case for change) as well as what improvements are needed and why. Awareness and desire to continually improve are conditions precedent to change.

We already know that most of our processes are falling far short of their potential and that improving them will benefit all concerned. We also know that changes in the business environment are constant. In fact, they are taking place at an ever-increasing rate. Clients keep saying they want their lawyers to speak their language, be their business partner, anticipate their needs, and provide greater predictability. Literally, they say it over and over and over.

There are many excellent examples in law of those that are providing excellent responses to those needs – but recent data suggest a gap has formed. BTI Consulting[17] outlines the following:

> *"Every year, we ask more than 300 corporate counsel about the law firms they recommend to a peer – no name, prompts, or suggestions provided. It's all organic. The results:*
> - *Only 35 percent recommend their primary law firms to a peer – down from 69.1 percent a mere four years ago. This rivals an 18-year low.*
>
> *One big contributor to the drop in client service is corporate counsel's new expectations. Law firms targeting yesterday's expectations are at a clear disadvantage. These new expectations include:*

- *Including clients early in strategy and approach.*
- *Being trusted enough to be relied on for cost control.*
- *Higher client service standards for their primary law firms.*
- *Being easy to work with.*
- *Fielding the absolute best team.*

All these new components make clients' lives easier and get them to their goals... But, that's not all.

Our research shows corporate counsel point to seven reasons for not recommending their primary law firm:

1. *Little interest in understanding corporate counsel's goals. Almost all the new goals are focused on advising management on transforming their business – and using it as a career booster.*
2. *Hard to work with. The legal prowess may be there, but the administrative obstacles are enough to ruin the most elegant of strategies. Clients point to:*
   - *Time and effort to start a new matter.*
   - *Renegotiating rates for every matter.*
   - *Negotiating conflict waivers.*
   - *Delays between conflict clearance mobilization.*
3. *Getting the B Team. Clients don't know who is performing the work, some see a flurry of names on the bills. These experiences make clients think there is little thought into who is doing the work.*
4. *Reluctance to provide an early assessment in litigation.*
5. *Learning new deal strategies and structures their primary firm used from a third party.*
6. *Ghosted when their relationship partners leave the firm.*
7. *Don't share ideas and strategies about current issues and problems.*

Corporate counsel are busy managing their own journey while relying more on outside counsel than at any other point in the last 23 years. BTI research reveals that 67 percent of corporate counsel are busy helping pave their company's path for transformational change. They want advice and advanced thinking – and excellent client service depends on law firms meeting today's and tomorrow's expectations."[18]

The fast-paced changes in the business environment and increasing client demands create ever-greater requirements for even-higher process capabilities and process efficiencies. Once we make things better, requirements and changes will drive us to improve again. This explains why the cycle of improvement is continuous, like waves. They keep coming.

This is why continuous improvement must eventually become part of the culture. Shift happens. Change is constant. By embracing Lean Sigma, organizations both avoid performance gaps and create opportunities for innovation and competitive edge.

Writing in *The Financial Post* in 2014, Denise Deveau suggests that achieving an internal culture change is something that requires patience and a consistent commitment from the top down. Laura Croucher, partner with KPMG Management Consulting, tells Denise that "Management tools and processes play a key role in driving cultural change, including performance management and measurement, training, and hiring for fit".[19]

Amy Hrehovcik says:

"Changing a culture is especially difficult in the legal space. Talent is razor sharp and seems to dissect improvement efforts for sport. Plus, governing bodies view 'non-lawyer' expertise as subpar, and partners continue to be slow to adapt. The 2014 Law Firm in Transition survey reported that only seven percent of firm leaders think their partners are highly aware that the industry is even changing. For those who are at all competitive, this is a statistic that should create serious drive."

She reminds us that, *"A practical approach trumps a theoretical one; this is why the Yellow Belt Certification Courses are the way to go. They are even better when they include clients."* All our clients tell us that, like most things, building momentum requires maximum effort at the beginning. By involving clients, there appears to be lighter lifting in terms of driving cultural change. As one client reported, *"Legal Lean Sigma's collaborative Yellow Belt is the perfect opportunity to differentiate the firm in the eyes of the client and serve as the primary catalyst to change the firm culture as it creates an environment where people change themselves."*

We know that culture beats strategy – but we can create a strategy to develop a culture of continuous improvement. By developing an enterprise-wide approach to employing the methodologies and tools of Lean Six Sigma, we can more easily reach consensus and clarity around the selection and prioritization of our projects and project teams. By first evaluating our processes and prioritizing by determining which processes (and then which aspects of them) most need attention, we are able to begin to develop our plans, messaging, approaches, leaders, champions, stakeholders, skills, and teams that span the firm.

Plus, by working together as high-functioning, cross-departmental, diverse teams, we improve by employing the DMAIC framework and Lean and Six Sigma tools to bring the process to the required performance and efficiency levels.

Many teams report that working on a project in this fashion is one of the best work experiences they have had. Those who become educated and experienced in Lean Six Sigma never see the firm (or the world) in the same way again. For one thing, they see that *everything* can be improved. They are encouraged and empowered to not just think, but to ask "why" and "what if" more often. They are not as quick to accept, "That's the way we have always done it" as the reason for continuing to perform in a particular way. They are also less likely to treat comments that begin with, "Anecdotally..." as evidence for what is or is not working in a process.

Because Lean Six Sigma thinking is grounded first in learning what a client finds valuable about a process, it is inherently supportive of a "client-focused" or "client-centered" culture, which nearly every firm boasts in its marketing materials. At this point, clients are less impressed with talk – they want specificity with regard to the behaviors in which the firm engages that demonstrate a commitment to that promise.

Making process changes doesn't necessarily translate into improvements in the desired metrics or the bottom line. Often managers get involved to translate a process improvement into financial and other benefits. Determining return on investment requires us to consider the tangible returns, such as increased client satisfaction with process and outcomes leading to repeat business and referrals, more efficient process (we can handle more business with the same number of employees), and fewer out-of-pocket costs for a process. There are also intangible returns, such as increased client satisfaction and goodwill, increased employee satisfaction and morale, and increased reputation for professionalism and results.

These data points are used to tell the story and help ensure that the benefits achieved by process improvement can – and should – be sustained.

After improving processes, we do not rest on our laurels – we repeat so that we can apply our learnings and get better for the benefit of our clients and our organization.

Thompson Hine LLP, a full-service business law firm with approximately

400 lawyers in nine offices, aligned with the needs that clients said were most vital to them early on. The firm's "Client Service Pledge"[19] was a first in the industry and is a commitment by the law firm to deliver exceptional service to its clients by adhering to specific principles focused on efficiency, transparency, and client satisfaction. The firm set itself apart by making this pledge a formal part of its client relationships and service approach, reflecting the firm's dedication to continuous improvement and innovation.

Thompson Hine's then managing partner, Deborah Read, led by example with the philosophy "client needs – firm heeds". This cultural imperative has driven structure and purpose in the firm according to what is most valued by clients – and has continued to adapt that alignment over time as client needs change.

Why have some waited for the clients to drive these changes? Why would any organization decide not to make things better until their collective back is up against a wall? Even if only driven by self-interest – which is something I have never observed, as the thousands of lawyers and business professionals I have worked with have all cared deeply about clients – the evidence is abundant that delivering better value to clients results in many benefits, including increased profitability.

Some in law, while talking the talk and making bold statements about their focus on "value" and being "client centered" still are not adequately demonstrating that they are actively listening or responding to what clients say is valuable to them. After many years of corporate and other clients being extremely vocal about their needs, desires, and expectations, there are still plenty of opportunities to demonstrate that legal teams are listening and taking action.

For every legal team that is not doing a good job with "voice of the client", there is a provider, or five, or ten that is dialed in – and these providers are actively pursuing that same team's clients for business. It is only a matter of time before those clients turn elsewhere. No firm or legal team can afford to rest on its laurels or take any client for granted – this is why having an enterprise-wide culture of continuous improvement is so important.

Whatever approach is taken, do not delay. The rate of change is not slowing down. For every organization mentioned in this book, there are many others who are quietly employing Lean Six Sigma. It is likely we may learn about them in the very near future, as the use of key process improvement methodologies is moving closer to mainstream every day.

Particularly in a continuous improvement culture, Lean Six Sigma offers infinite opportunities to be an architect and design the way that legal work and business processes are performed – over and over again, as we learn and adapt. Plan, do, check, act. Continuously improve.

What could be better than helping people work even better together in ways that deliver ever more value and improved experiences to everyone in the process?

This is the promise of Lean Sigma for law – and it delivers.

References

1. https://info.panelshop.com/blog/the-4-cs-of-continuous-improvement-manufacturing
2. https://img1.wsimg.com/blobby/go/d5e19b58-7124-421d-9db6-ad5d13591bc1/downloads/WhyBeingAHumanintheWorkplaceisHardPart2.pdf?ver=1687962021537
3. https://mag.toyota.co.uk/andon-toyota-production-system/
4. International Bar Association, 2016, *"Times are a-changin': disruptive innovation and the legal profession."* www.ibanet.org/MediaHandler?id=2C42BEFA-DDC4-4EF5-BDD5-41FA502B987B
5. https://legalleansigma.com/wp-content/uploads/2018/04/3approaches.pdf
6. https://docket.acc.com/print/pdf/node/1432
7. www.foley.com/insights/publications/2013/06/foley-lardner-llp-launches-legal-innovation-hub-f/
8. https://mclclaw.com/attorney-qas-c/what-is-legal-lean-sigma-and-why-is-it-important-to-me-as-a-client/
9. www.thomsonreuters.com/en-us/posts/legal/leveraging-process-improvement-future-transformation/
10. www.jimcollins.com/
11. www.altmanweil.com/wp-content/uploads/2022/05/Law-Firms-in-Transition-2020-An-Executive-Summary-.pdf
12. Measure by Measure Consulting LLC, "Why Culture Change May Be Lean Six Sigma's Greatest Value: One Award Winning Company Discovered the True Value of Lean Six Sigma", 15 February 2010.
13. "How Law Firms Can Overcome 'Innovation Fatigue'", Legaltech News, 14 May 2020. www.law.com/legaltechnews/2020/05/14/how-a-law-firm-can-overcome-innovation-fatigue
14. https://kpmg.com/kpmg-us/content/dam/kpmg/pdf/2025/art-continuous-transformation.pdf
15. *Ibid.*
16. www.law.com/legaltechnews/2020/06/29/knowledge-management-as-an-innovation-imperative/

17 Michael Rynowecer, President at The BTi Consulting Group, https://bticonsulting.com/themadclientist/law-firm-client-service-plunges-7-reasons-why
18 *Ibid.*
19 Deveau, D. "How to convince workers you actually care about what they think", *Financial Post*, 28 May 2014. https://financialpost.com/executive/management-hr/how-to-convince-workers-you-actually-care-about-what-they-think?
20 www.thompsonhine.com/about/overview/

About Globe Law and Business

Globe Law and Business was established in 2005. From the very beginning, we set out to create legal books that are sufficiently high level to be of real use to the experienced professional, yet still accessible and easy to navigate. Most of our authors are drawn from Magic Circle and other top commercial firms, both in the United Kingdom and internationally.

Our titles are carefully produced, with the utmost attention paid to editorial, design and production processes. We hope this results in high-quality publications that are easy to read and a pleasure to own.

In 2021, we were very pleased to announce the start of a new chapter for Globe Law and Business following the acquisition of law books under the imprint Ark Publishing. Our law firm management list is now significantly expanded with many well-known and loved Ark Publishing titles.

We are also pleased to announce the launch of our online content platform, Globe Law Online, which allows for easy access across firms. Details of all titles included can be found at www.globelawonline.com. Email glo@globelawandbusiness.com for further details and to arrange a free trial for you or your firm.

We'd very much like to hear from you with your thoughts and ideas for improving what we offer. Please do feel free to email me on sian@globelawandbusiness.com. Happy reading and thank you for your time.

Sian O'Neill
Managing director
Globe Law and Business
www.globelawandbusiness.com